Carol Ann Tomlinson

ne Cunningham Eidson

Differentiation in Practice

A RESOURCE GUIDE FOR DIFFERENTIATING CURRICULUM

Grades 5–9

Association for Supervision and Curriculum Development
Alexandria, Virginia USA

Association for Supervision and Curriculum Development
1703 N. Beauregard St. • Alexandria, VA 22311-1714 USA
Telephone: 800-933-2723 or 703-578-9600 • Fax: 703-575-5400
Web site: http://www.ascd.org • E-mail: member@ascd.org

All Web links in this book are correct as of the publication date below but may have become inactive or otherwise modified since that time. If you notice a deactivated or changed link, please e-mail books@ascd.org with the words "Link Update" in the subject line. In your message, please specify the Web link, the book title, and the page number on which the link appears.

Printed in the United States of America.

s2/2003

ASCD product no.: 102293
ASCD member price: $24.95   nonmember price: $29.95

Library of Congress Cataloging-in-Publication Data
Tomlinson, Carol A.
    Differentiation in practice : a resource guide for differentiating curriculum, grades 5-9 / Carol Ann Tomlinson, Caroline Cunningham Eidson.
        p.   cm.
Includes bibliographical references and index.
    ISBN 0-87120-655-2 (alk. paper)
  1. Middle school education—United States—Curricula. 2. Ability grouping in education—United States. I. Eidson, Caroline Cunningham, 1968- II. Title.
LB1623.5 .T66 2003
373.19—dc21

                                 2002151115

12   11   10   09   08   07   06   05   04   03   10   9   8   7   6   5   4   3   2   1

*For the teachers
whose interest has given life to our work
on differentiated instruction*

✳

*For the students
who daily inspire that interest*

✳

*For the colleagues
whose partnership fuels that interest*

✳

*For the administrators
who value and support that interest*

✳

*And for those outside of school
who care about us so that we may find
the energy to care about others.*

Differentiation in Practice

A Resource Guide for Differentiating Curriculum, Grades 5–9

Acknowledgments

In a conversation with young learners in her hometown of Stamps, Arkansas, Maya Angelou tells the students that she would like to be an encouragement to them. That simple phrase lingers. It is a powerful wish. Perhaps there is little we can do for one another that's more important than to give encouragement along the journey we call life. Encouragement is a testament to the belief that each of us can become more than we could have envisioned alone. This book is a product of encouragement and the belief it reflects in the human capacity to keep "becoming."

The motivation for this book comes from teachers throughout the world who continue to work to make classrooms a better fit for students, who simply are not a matched set. These teachers' encouragement to "keep the ideas coming" inspired us to extend our thinking and return to the keyboard. Those teachers themselves receive daily encouragement to differentiate instruction, thanks to students who continue to flourish in the context of academically responsive classrooms.

As authors, we have been encouraged by the partnership of the teachers whose differentiated units provide the substance of this book. In the midst of lives that often seem too busy, and in the face of demands that often seem too many, they not only found it within themselves to share what they teach and how they teach it, but they also seemed to enjoy the opportunity to be part of a professional exchange.

This book has been long in the making. As it has evolved, the conversation and partnership of three colleagues have been especially valuable. Catherine Brighton contributed significantly to early decisions about what the book should become. Holly Hertberg worked extensively with formatting and with decisions about content. Cindy Strickland played the role of "critical friend," providing a keen mind, a sharp eye, and hours of editing as we neared the end of the process. The contributions of time and insight from these three educators have been an encouragement that made both the book and the authors stronger.

Publishing with ASCD is always an encouragement. Their work stems from a belief in high-quality teaching for a full range of learners and a belief in the will of teachers to become stronger professionals throughout their teaching lives. ASCD staff exemplify the principle of partnership for success. In this particular endeavor, the encouragement of John O'Neil, Anne Meek, Leslie Kiernan, and Sally Chapman has been indispensable.

Finally, for all of us who have worked on this publication, the encouragement of friends and family provides the daily fuel to think and write and think some more and rewrite. That encouragement inevitably comes at a cost to them. We appreciate their willingness to support our growth.

Differentiation is like jazz. It is continual improvisation, based on solid themes and shared experiences. As authors, we are keenly aware that we are part of a larger jazz ensemble, that we could not play so richly alone, and that we are improved as music makers by the encouragement and partnership of other connoisseurs.

Introduction

This book is part of a series of ASCD publications on differentiating instruction. Each is designed to play a particular role in helping educators think about and develop classrooms that attend to learner needs as they guide learners through a curricular sequence.

How to Differentiate Instruction in Mixed-Ability Classrooms (Tomlinson, 2001) explains the basic framework of differentiation. Such a framework allows teachers to plan in consistent and coherent ways. *The Differentiated Classroom: Responding to the Needs of All Learners* (Tomlinson, 1999a) elaborates on the framework and describes classroom scenarios in which differentiation is taking place. A third book, *Leadership for Differentiating Schools and Classrooms* (Tomlinson & Allan, 2000), discusses how to link what we know about school change with the goals of differentiation and seeks to provide guidance for educational leaders who want to be a part of promoting and supporting responsive instruction. In addition to these books, an ASCD Professional Inquiry Kit called *Differentiating Instruction for Mixed-Ability Classrooms* (Tomlinson, 1996) guides educators, in an inductive manner, to explore and apply key principles of differentiation.

Three video programs, all produced by Leslie Kiernan and ASCD, give progressively expansive images of how differentiation actually looks in the classroom. *Differentiating Instruction* (1997) shows brief applications of differentiating content, process, and products according to student readiness, interest, and learning profile in primary, elementary, middle, and high school classrooms. It also illustrates a number of instructional strategies used for purposes of differentiating or modifying instruction. *At Work in the Differentiated Classroom* (2001) shows excerpts from a month-long unit in a middle school classroom as means of exploring essential principles of differentiation, examines management in differentiated settings from primary grades through high school, and probes the role of the teacher in a differentiated classroom. *A Visit to a Differentiated Classroom* (2001) takes viewers through a single day in a multi-age, differentiated elementary classroom. Each of these materials attempts to help educators think about the nature of classrooms that are defensibly differentiated and move toward development of such classrooms. Each of the publications plays a different role in the process of reflection, definition, and translation.

This book uses yet another lens to examine differentiation and support its implementation in classrooms. It presents a series of actual curricular units developed by teachers who work hard to differentiate instruction in their classrooms. The book thus moves from defining and describing differentiation to providing the actual curriculum used to differentiate instruction.

Differentiation and the Middle Grades

It can be argued that the middle-grade years constitute the greatest learner variability of any segment in school. Dissimilar rates of growth are a defining element of middle school. Students of the same age vary tremendously in intellectual development, as they do in physical, emotional, and moral development. Schools that aspire to be successful in educating young adolescents must vigorously attend to their varying needs, interests, and readiness levels (National Middle School Association, 1995). Such schools will begin where learners are, understanding and addressing their individual needs, interests, and modes of learning.

> Given the developmental diversity in any middle-level classroom, gearing curriculum to students' levels of understanding is a daunting task. In addition to different rates of development and learning styles, varying cultural backgrounds and prior experience must be taken into account. Efforts to reduce tracking and to include students with special needs in regular classes increase the diversity even further. . . . Both content and methods must

be individualized. (National Middle School Association, 1995, pp. 21–22)

Ironically, the prospect of teaching with the inevitable diversity that typifies middle school is one of the factors that makes it easy for teachers to "slip into a teaching mode in which all students in a class are expected to be doing or learning the same things at the same time according to a single mode of instruction" (Stevenson, 1992, p. 20). Nonetheless, middle school experts caution that reliance upon such instruction is ill-suited to the population middle schools exist to serve.

> In order for all students to experience successes that matter to them, schoolwork must accommodate individual differences of talent and development. Students are developmentally unequal. Therefore, educators must ensure that for a substantial portion of their school lives, students will be able to see their success along a variety of paths. Teachers' expectations must reflect an understanding of differences. Some portions of curriculum must accommodate individual choices. Ways of presenting knowledge must complement disparities in youngsters' talents or dispositions for revealing their knowledge. (Stevenson, 1992, p. 122)

Turning Points, 2000 (Jackson & Davis, 2000), a 10-year update on the original *Turning Points* document that defined the key principles and practices of effective middle level schools, presents seven recommendations essential to ensuring success for each middle schooler in a new century. The document's explanation of one of those principles notes, in part, that "classes should include students of diverse needs, achievement levels, interests, and learning styles, and instruction should be differentiated to take advantage of the diversity, not ignore it" (Jackson & Davis, 2000, p. 23). This same landmark report calls for concept-based teaching that helps adolescent learners structure what they learn in effective and memorable ways and for classrooms procedures and processes designed to help young adolescents become more self-sufficient and confident learners.

It is difficult to imagine a setting with greater potential to realize the joy that should be implicit in learning than a middle school classroom, with learners bringing to school a spectrum of dreams for the future and a full supply of energy. Each of these students has one foot in the world of childhood and one on the brink of adulthood, combining the fullness of creativity and the infinite possibilities ahead. It is difficult to imagine a setting more pained and unnatural than a middle school classroom with a one-size-fits-all demeanor and mode of operation housing those same students.

Nonetheless, it's far easier to find examples of the latter than the former. The reasons classrooms downplay or even ignore diversity are legion, and many of the reasons are understandable. One is the absence of images of what solid, standards-based curriculum might look like in settings that both embrace and attend to learner diversity. This book provides one such image—an image we hope will help educators craft middle-level classrooms well suited to the learning needs of the students who inhabit and enliven them.

What the Book Is (and Isn't) Intended to Be

As we prepared to write this book, we had numerous conversations between ourselves, with editors, and with many colleagues in education. Each conversation helped us chart our eventual course. Our primary goal was to provide models of differentiated units of study. We wanted to move beyond necessarily episodic descriptions of differentiation to show how a differentiated classroom might flow through an entire unit. We also wanted to present units at a range of grade levels and in a variety of subjects. Providing units for grades K–12 in a single volume seemed too much, so we began by working with units that span grades 5–9, a configuration otherwise known as "the middle grades." In some districts, this grade-span includes at least a portion of upper elementary or a portion of high school. Subsequent books of differentiated units for grades K–5 and 9–12 are in the works.

Even after narrowing the range of grade-levels, we realized there were so many subjects to consider that we had to refine our focus further. Ultimately, we elected to include differentiated units in five subject areas: math, science, social studies (two units), language arts, and world/foreign language. We have developed the book, however, with the intent that it be useful to a broader range of teachers than the grade levels and subjects it specifically represents. This is a book designed to teach anyone who wants to learn about differentiating curriculum how to do so—or how to do so more effectively.

To that end, each of the units is intended to be more representative than restrictive. That is, an 11th grade social studies teacher should be able to look at a 6th grade social studies unit, see how it works, and use similar principles and formats to develop a differentiated social studies unit for high school juniors. An art teacher should be able to study several of the units in the book and synthesize the principles and procedures therein to guide the development of a differentiated art unit. In sum, we intend this book to be a vehicle for professional development.

What this book is *not* intended to be is off-the-shelf curriculum for any classroom. It is impossible to create the "correct" unit, for example, on how to teach French verbs. Teachers in one classroom will conceive that process differently than will teachers in other classrooms—or teachers in a different part of the country, in a different type of school, or responsible for a different set of academic standards. In the end, then, we are presenting educators with a learning tool, not a teaching tool. If teachers (and other educators) can read this book and say, "There's something I can learn here," then we will have succeeded.

How the Book Is Designed

Because we want the book to be a learning tool for a maximum number of teachers, we have made key decisions about its presentation. First, we decided to begin the book with Part I's primer on differentiation—an essential piece for readers new to the topic and a helpful refresher for those already familiar with it. We also opted to include an extended glossary (page 233), which explains terms and strategies that might not be familiar to all readers. Collecting this information in the back of the book, we thought, was preferable to interrupting the units themselves with "sidebar" explanations.

Part II, the body of the book, is devoted to instructional units. We think it will be helpful to share some of our thinking about the layout and contents of the units, each of which is presented in four parts.

• **Unit Introduction.** The first component of every unit is the introduction, which includes a prose overview of the unit; a list of standards addressed in the unit; the key concepts and generalizations that help with teacher and student focus; a delineation of what students should know, understand, and be able to do as a result of the unit; and a list of the key instructional strategies used in the unit. Some of the units also make links across units and disciplines and promote connections with students' lives and experiences.

• **Unit Overview Chart.** The second component is an overview chart, designed with three goals in mind: 1) to provide orientation in the form of a "big picture" snapshot of the unit's steps or events; 2) to provide an estimate of the amount of time each step or event requires; and 3) to clarify which portions of the unit apply to the class as a whole and which are differentiated.

• **Unit Description.** The third component is the unit description itself. It appears in the left-hand column of each unit page and gives a step-by-step explanation of what takes place in the classroom during the unit. Asterisks in the margins highlight differentiated components. All referenced supporting materials (samples such as worksheets, product assignments, rubrics, and homework handouts) appear at the end of the unit.

• **Teacher Commentary.** The fourth component is an explanation, in the voice of the teacher who created the unit, of what she was thinking as she planned and presented instruction. For our purposes, this is a particularly valuable element. To listen to the teacher who developed the unit is to move well beyond what happens in the classroom and to begin to analyze why teachers make decisions as they do. At one point in the writing and editing process, we thought we should reduce the teacher commentary sections to the fewest possible words; we quickly discovered that when we did so, we lost the magic the book has to offer. We hope you enjoy listening to the teachers as much as we have.

We tried to balance two needs in our editing of the units. First, we wanted to maintain the integrity of each teacher's unit. Second, we wanted to be sure to have both consistency (of terminology, of format, of essential philosophy) and variety (in instructional strategies, use of groups, assessment methods, etc.). The teachers who created the units have approved the changes we made or have helped us see how to make necessary modifications more appropriately.

Also, please note that we have opted to make the units somewhat more generic than specific. As teachers, we sometimes have the habit of looking for exact matches for our classroom needs and jettisoning whatever doesn't match. As authors, we can't eliminate the habit, but we wanted to make it a little harder to exercise. For example, although we have taken great care to list state standards reflected in a unit, we have intentionally not listed the name of the state from which the standards came. (It's amazing how similar standards on the same topic are across states.) We're hopeful of making the point that good differentiation is attentive to standards and other curricular requirements, but we want to help readers avoid the inclination to say, "Oh, these aren't *my* standards, so this wouldn't work in my classroom."

Finally, we decided to include solid units rather than "showcase" ones. What's here is more roast beef than Beef Wellington. We wanted to include units that demonstrate coherence, focused instruction, thoughtful engagement of students, and flexibility; we *did not* want to include units that dazzle the imagination. After all, although it may be fascinating to watch someone tap dance on the ceiling, few of us are inclined to try it ourselves. Hopefully, the units in this book are familiar enough to be approachable, but venture far enough into the unfamiliar to provide challenge for future growth. In fact, in this regard, our aim for readers is similar to what we recommend for students: pushing them a little beyond their comfort zones. If all readers feel totally at ease with the units, we've lowered the bar. If we send all readers running, we've set the bar too high. (In the latter instance, some judicious rereading over a period of professional growth just might be worthwhile.)

It may well be that the greatest pleasure of teaching comes from learning. It is our hope that the book as a whole will serve as one catalyst for helping teachers become the very best professionals they can be.

PART I

A Brief Primer
on Differentiation

The Students

Marqui is four and very smart. He really likes stories, and he's teaching himself to read. Trouble is, there aren't any books for him to read in his house, and it's difficult for his mom to get him to the library, which is two busses away from their house.

Yu-chu likes math, but no one in school knows that. She can't understand the teacher and the teacher can't understand her. Yu-chu goes to a special class to help her with English, but math doesn't come up there. In her regular classroom, she feels invisible. Her math problems look neat on the page, but she doesn't get called on, and she's afraid to raise her hand.

Repp is bright—or at least he used to be. He has a learning disability and nearly everyone works with him on what he can't do very well. Now, in middle school, he's forgotten what it was he used to be good at.

Adam just seems to march to a different beat. He works really slowly and often doesn't catch the directions the first time they're given. Explanations are slippery, too.

Darryl is consumed with rhythms and music. They live in his head, and he sometimes can't make them move over so there's room for schoolwork. But in school, there seems to be almost no room for his music.

Michelle is one of a small population of black students at a primarily white school. Her parents value school and encourage her to learn. Nonetheless, Michelle's school feels like a pair of shoes that's the wrong shape and size. To go there is to leave the world in which she belongs and to enter one where she's at best a stranger and at worst an unwelcome stranger. Language, habits, the ways of working, textbook content, the push and pull of peers, the lack of eye contact from the teacher, and a hundred other elements send Michelle coded messages that she doesn't really belong. Anyhow, what is she supposed to *do* with what she learns in school? No one from the world where she does belong seems to use this stuff.

Philip wrestles with both physical and cognitive challenges. He likes the other kids. He wishes he could be more a part of their work and games and conversations.

Donna is 13—at least chronologically. Her conversations and writing sound more like she's a college student, or perhaps even older than that. She's also tall for her age and physically mature. She's good at fitting in with her agemates, but she's often hungry for more probing conversations. Donna wants to pursue her interest in astronomy, but schoolwork takes so much time (even though it's mostly busywork for her). Astronomy has not been a topic in science class during the last four years, and she fears it's not likely to come up again until college.

Ben likes school well enough. He's okay with reading, is impatient with writing, thinks science is fun when there are labs, and dreads math. He stays afloat with math when there's time to ask questions and have more demonstrations. Lately, everyone seems to be in a huge hurry to get through the textbook. Ben's feeling more lost than he used to.

The Teachers

Mr. Walters teaches a class in which there is a seven-year span of reading levels. He teaches students with Individual Educational Plans (IEPs) and students identified as gifted, and yet, he has just one language arts text for all his students. He also has class sets of novels that go along with the 5th grade history themes. Trouble is, each set is roughly at grade level, and he loses much of his class when they read the novels.

Ms. Grant's math class has 21 students, representing 6 different languages. She speaks English and Spanish, but that leaves her uncertain about how to communicate with the nine students who speak the other four languages. Some of Ms. Grant's English language learners are proficient readers in their native languages. Some aren't.

Ms. Mastrangelo has taught for 15 years. She's grown both comfortable and proficient with teacher-directed, whole-class instruction. Over time, however, her students have become much more diverse, both culturally and academically. She sees that her classroom is somehow less inviting to her students than it used to be . . . and less inviting than she'd *like* it to be.

Mr. Herrera's Spanish I class includes students who speak Spanish as a first language, but don't know its grammar; students who know English grammar well and those who don't; students who are great memorizers of patterns, but are afraid of the risk of oral production; students with a great ear for language and no patience for homework; and students who somehow seem to be learning to speak the language faster than he's teaching it.

Nearly all of these teachers feel escalating pressure to prepare their students for a high-stakes test. The test reveals no concern for students who struggle with school or for students eager to learn at a more challenging pace or in greater depth. Even as classrooms become incrementally more heterogeneous, the message from the test-makers seems to be one of mandated homogenization. The dilemma is clear: How do teachers provide instruction that honors the uniqueness of each individual in a classroom that is likely to be overpopulated, undersupplied, and perpetually short of time?

There is no add-water-and-stir solution to the dilemma, of course. Complex challenges like this never have simple solutions. But those of us involved with writing this book hold tight to two beliefs. First, we believe that every teacher is a learner, and as such, every teacher can become better and better at the effective instruction of academically diverse student populations. Second, because all indications are that classrooms will continue to diversify, we believe there is no choice but to learn to teach well the students who trust us—voluntarily or involuntarily—to prepare them for the future. Based on these two beliefs, we find that the best response to the complex challenges today's schools present is differentiated instruction.

What Is Differentiated Instruction?

As we use the term in this book, *differentiated instruction* refers to a systematic approach to planning curriculum and instruction for academically diverse learners. It is a way of thinking about the classroom with the dual goals of honoring each student's learning needs and maximizing each student's learning capacity.

This approach to effective instruction of heterogeneous student populations (and in truth, all student populations are heterogeneous) suggests that teachers concentrate on two classroom factors: the nature of the student and the essential meaning of the curriculum. If, as teachers, we increase our understanding of *who* we teach and *what* we teach, we are much more likely to be able to be flexible in *how* we teach.

There are five classroom elements that teachers can differentiate, or modify, to increase the likelihood that each student will learn as much as possible, as efficiently as possible:

- **Content**—What we teach and how we give students access to the information and ideas that matter.
- **Process**—How students come to understand and "own" the knowledge, understanding, and skills essential to a topic.
- **Products**—How a student demonstrates what he or she has come to know, understand, and be able to do as a result of a segment of study.

- **Affect**—How students link thought and feeling in the classroom.
- **Learning environment**—The way the classroom feels and functions.

In addition, there are three student characteristics that teachers can respond to as they craft curriculum and instruction:

- **Readiness**—The current knowledge, understanding, and skill level a student has related to a particular sequence of learning. Readiness is not a synonym for ability; rather, it reflects what a student knows, understands, and can do today in light of what the teacher is planning to teach today. It is very difficult to maximize the capacity of learners like Repp and Yu-chu if we are unaware of their learning gaps, or if we are impervious to the fact that Donna has already learned the material we are planning to teach for the next week. The goal of readiness differentiation is first to make the work a little too difficult for students at a given point in their growth—and then to provide the support they need to succeed at the new level of challenge.
- **Interest**—What a student enjoys learning about, thinking about, and doing. Interest is a great motivator. A wise teacher links required content to student interests in order to hook the learner. The goal of interest differentiation is to help students connect with new information, understanding, and skills by revealing connections with things they already find appealing, intriguing, relevant, and worthwhile.
- **Learning profile**—A student's preferred mode of learning. Individual learning profile is influenced by learning style, intelligence preference (see Gardner, 1993, 1997; Sternberg, 1988, 1997), gender, and culture. There is neither economy nor efficiency in teaching in ways that are awkward for

learners when we can teach in ways that make learning more natural. The goal of learning profile differentiation is to help students learn in the ways they learn best—and to extend the ways in which they can learn effectively.

It is not the purpose of this book to teach the key elements of differentiation. That has been done in other places. Nonetheless, a quick review of what it means to differentiate the five classroom elements in response to the three student characteristics should facilitate a common understanding among our readers.

Differentiating Content

Content is what students should know, understand, and be able to do as a result of a segment of study. It's the "stuff" we want students to learn, and therefore, it's the "stuff" we teach. Content is typically derived from a combination of sources. Certainly national, state, and local standards provide guidance about what we should teach. That said, a set of standards is unlikely to provide complete and coherent content. Some standards documents emphasize knowledge and skill and largely omit the concepts and principles that lead students to genuine understanding of subject matter. Some standards documents are so general in nature that they omit the specific knowledge necessary to illustrate the principles identified.

Content is further defined by local curriculum guides and by textbooks. However, one of the most critical factors in determining content is the teacher's knowledge of both the subject and her students. The teacher is the source of synthesis for standards, texts, and guides. It's the teacher who must ask questions such as, "What matters most here?" "What is this subject really about?" "What

will be of enduring value to my students?" "What must I share with them to help them truly understand the magic of this subject in their lives?"

When the teacher answers these questions, she is ready to specify what students should know, understand, and be able to do in a particular subject as a result of instruction presented over a day, a lesson, a unit, and a year. The teacher's overarching goal is to hold the essential knowledge, understanding, and skills steady for most learners. In other words, if the intention this week is to help students learn to solve simple equations, that will be the goal for all learners. Some may need to work (at the process stage) with more complex formats and more independence; others may need to work with greater scaffolding from teacher and peers. In general, however, the knowledge, understanding, and skills related to solving simple equations belong to everyone.

There are exceptions to this guideline, of course. If a student already knows how to solve both simple equations and more complex ones, it makes no sense to continue teaching that student to solve simple equations. Likewise, if a student has serious gaps in number sense and basic operations, the solutions to simple equations are likely to be out of reach until the student can build the necessary foundation of knowledge, understanding, and skill.

Once the essential knowledge, understanding, and skills of a unit or topic are clear, the teacher also begins thinking about the second facet of content—how she will ensure student access to that essential knowledge, understanding, and skill set.

Students access content in many ways. Teacher talk is one. There are also textbooks, supplementary materials, technology, demonstrations, field trips, audiotape recordings, and so on. A wise teacher asks, "What are *all* the ways I might help my students gain access to new knowledge, understanding, and skills as we move through this topic or unit?"

Because students vary in readiness, interest, and learning profile, it is important to vary or differentiate content in response to those student traits. Figure 1 (see page 6) illustrates just a few ways in which teachers can differentiate content in response to student readiness, interest, and learning profile.

Differentiating Process

The line between process and content is a blurred one, but for purposes of discussion, we'll think of process as beginning when the teacher asks the student to stop listening or reading and to begin making personal sense out of information, ideas, and skills they've accessed. Under this definition, process begins when the student stops becoming the consumer and starts making meaning in earnest.

Process is often used as a synonym for "activities." Not all activities are created equal, however. A worthwhile activity is one that asks students to use specific information and skills to come to understand an important idea or principle. Furthermore, a worthwhile activity is unambiguously focused on essential learning goals. It calls on students to work directly with a subset of the key knowledge, understanding, and skills specified as content goals. It requires students to think about ideas, grapple with problems, and use information. It moves beyond "giving back information" to seeing how things work and why they work as they do. Finally, a worthwhile activity is one that snags student interest so that they persist at it, even when the task is difficult.

Figure 2 (see page 7) illustrates just a few

ways in which teachers can differentiate process in response to student readiness, interest, and learning profile.

Differentiating Products

A product is a means by which students demonstrate what they have come to know, understand, and be able to do. In this book, we use the term *product* to refer to a major or culminating demonstration of student learning—that is, one that comes at the end of a long period of learning, such as a unit or a marking period, rather than a demonstration of learning at the end of a class period or a two-day lesson, for example.

As with activities, effective product assignments are likely to have certain hallmarks. Product assignments, too, should focus on the essential knowledge, understanding, and skills specified as content goals. They should call on students to use what they have learned—preferably working as much as possible as a professional would work. They should have clear, challenging, and specified criteria for success, based both on grade-level expectations and individual student needs. They should endeavor to capture student interest. Finally, high-quality product assignments are written and guided in ways that support student success in both the process of working on the product and the product itself.

Products can take many forms. In fact, it is the flexibility of products that make them so potentially powerful in classrooms sensitive to learner variance. If, as a student, I can show the teacher that I have come to know, understand, and do the non-negotiables of the unit, *how* I do so may be open. Thus, a student with a learning disability that makes writing laborious (if not impossible) may do a better job of showing what he has learned in

---

FIGURE 1

STRATEGIES FOR DIFFERENTIATING CONTENT

Student Characteristic	Strategy
Readiness	• Provide texts at varied reading levels. • Provide supplementary materials at varied reading levels. • Reteach for students having difficulty. • Offer extended teaching groups for advanced students. • Demonstrate ideas or skills in addition to talking about them. • Provide audiotaped materials. • Use videotapes to supplement and support explanations and lectures. • Use texts with key portions highlighted. • Use reading buddies or reading partners to work on text or supplementary materials. • Provide organizers to guide note-taking. • Provide key vocabulary lists for reference during note-taking.
Interest	• Provide interest centers to encourage further exploration of topics. • Provide a wide range of materials on a wide range of related student interests. • Use student questions and topics to guide lectures and materials selection. • Use examples and illustrations based on student interests.
Learning Profile	• Present in visual, auditory, and kinesthetic modes. • Use applications, examples, and illustrations from a wide range of intelligences (based on Gardner and Sternberg models). • Use applications, examples, and illustrations from both genders and a range of cultures/communities. • Teach with whole-to-part and part-to-whole approaches. • Use wait time to allow for student reflection.

FIGURE 2

STRATEGIES FOR DIFFERENTIATING PROCESS

Student Characteristic	Strategy
Readiness	• Use tiered activities (activities at different levels of difficulty, but focused on the same key learning goals). ✓ • Make task directions more detailed and specific for some learners and more open or "fuzzy" for others. ✓ • Provide resource materials at varied levels of readability and sophistication. • Provide teacher-led mini-workshops on varied skills at varied levels of complexity to support student work. • Use both like-readiness and mixed-readiness work groups. ✓ • Use a variety of criteria for success, based on whole-class requirements as well as individual student readiness needs. ✓ • Provide materials in the primary language of second language learners. • Provide readiness-based homework assignments. • Vary the pacing of student work. ✓
Interest	• Use interest-based work groups and discussion groups. • Use both like-interest and mixed-interest work groups. • Use the Jigsaw cooperative strategy to allow students to specialize in aspects of a topic that they find interesting. ✓ • Design tasks that require multiple interests for successful completion. • Encourage students to design or participate in the design of some tasks.
Learning Profile	• Allow multiple options for how students express learning. • Encourage students to work together or independently. ✓ • Balance competitive, collegial, and independent work arrangements. ✓ • Develop activities that seek multiple perspectives on topics and issues. ✓

science by creating a high-quality museum exhibit, complete with tape-recorded narration, than with an essay. A student who is skilled in music may develop a musical interpretation of the rights and responsibilities of a U.S. citizen under the Constitution with more engagement and commitment than she would have demonstrated had her assignment been to make a poster.

Tests are certainly one form of product. In today's schools, all students need guidance in how to take tests effectively. Nonetheless, when tests are the only form of student product, many students find that their ability to show what they know is restricted. With tests, it's important to remember that the goal should not be regurgitation of information, but rather, demonstration of the capacity to use knowledge and skills appropriately. It's also important to remember that tests should *enable* rather than impede a student's ability to show how much he or she has learned. Thus, some students may need to tape-record answers to tests. Some may need to hear test questions read aloud. Some may need additional time to write their answers. When the goal is to see what a student has learned, those adaptations are "fair" for students with learning difficulties just as using Braille is "fair" for students who cannot see.

Figure 3 illustrates just a few ways in which teachers can differentiate products in response to student readiness, interest, and learning profile.

Differentiating Affect

Students, because they are human beings, come to school with common affective needs. They need to feel safe and secure, both physically and emotionally. They need to feel that they belong to the group and are important to it. They need to feel a sense of kinship with the group, a sense that they share common ground with their peers. They need to feel affirmed—to be assured that they are valuable just as they are. They need to feel challenged and to know that they can succeed at a high level of expectation (helping them to develop a sense of self-efficacy). Humans have these needs in common. Nonetheless, our particular circumstances cause us to experience these needs in different ways.

For example, a child with mental retardation has a need to belong to the group—to feel important to the "wholeness" of the group. That need may go unmet if he finds himself always on the outskirts of class activities, conversations, and plans. If the teacher sees this student as a "fringe" member of the class, it is likely that other students will see him that way as well. To help this learner achieve a sense of belonging, the teacher must understand the child's need to be a part of the daily fabric of the class, and must consciously weave that fabric with the legitimate participation of this student in mind.

A highly able child also needs to feel a sense of belonging and importance to the group. This learner may already be a part of the social fabric of the group and may be recognized as an achiever. However, if the highly able child feels uneasy asking questions important to him because the teacher is impatient with or threatened by them, he, too, feels uncertain about his status in the group. He may elect to act out a role that maintains the status quo, feeling that he is not free to be himself in the classroom. In a case like this, the teacher may not have to plan activities in ways that integrate this learner, but in order to address his need to belong, the teacher must make the class a place where legitimate questions are sought, valued, and celebrated.

A child whose first language is not English cannot feel integral to the group when she can never

---

STRATEGIES FOR DIFFERENTIATING PRODUCTS

Student Characteristic	Strategy
Readiness	• Use tiered product assignments. • Provide bookmarked Internet sites at different levels of complexity for research sources. • Lead optional, in-class mini-workshops on various facets of product development (e.g., asking good research questions, using the Internet to find information, conducting interviews, proofreading). • Use similar-readiness critique groups during product development (especially for advanced learners). • Use mixed-readiness critique groups or teacher-led critique groups during product development (particularly for students who need extra support and guidance). • Develop rubrics or other benchmarks for success based on both grade-level expectations and individual student learning needs.
Interest	• Encourage students to demonstrate key knowledge, understanding, and skills in related topics of special interest. • Help students find mentors to guide product development or choice of products. • Allow students to use a range of media or formats to express their knowledge, understanding, and skill. • Provide opportunities for students to develop independent inquiries with appropriate teacher or mentor guidance.
Learning Profile	• Encourage students to work independently or with partner(s) on product development. • Teach students how to use a wide range of product formats. • Provide visual, auditory, and kinesthetic product options. • Provide analytic, creative, and practical product options. • Ensure connections between product assignments and a range of student cultures/communities.

read the text, understand directions, or make a real contribution to the work of groups to which she is assigned. The teacher in this instance must see the link between communication and belonging and ensure that this learner has a voice in the class.

A student from a minority culture feels anything but central to the operation of the group when all of his cultural peers are consistently placed in low-achieving groups and are assigned work that looks dull. Belonging is not a reality when the teacher is more likely to call on, chat more affably with, and make eye contact with students from cultures other than your own. Your importance diminishes when the teacher shows she expects less of you by settling for incomplete work, overlooking missed assignments, or failing to coach you on how to enhance the quality of a product.

These are just a few examples to make the point that every learner in a class needs the teacher to help him or her grow in affective competence, just as every learner needs the teacher to help him or her grow in cognitive competence. (In fact, the two are inextricably linked.) It is essential to remember that although our affective mileposts are similar, our journeys toward them may take many different routes. In a differentiated classroom, the teacher is continually attuned to student feelings, just as she is to student knowledge, understanding, and skills. She repeatedly asks herself, "What can I do to ensure that students of all readiness levels feel safe, integrated, affirmed, valued, challenged, and supported here?" "What can I do to ensure that students know their interests and strengths are important to me as a person, important to their peers, and important to our success as a class?" "How can I increase the likelihood that each student comes to a better understanding of his or her particular learning

patterns, finds opportunity to work in ways that are comfortable and effective, and respects the learning needs of others?"

A wise teacher takes a number of measures to support the affective climate of the classroom. These might include

- Modeling respect.
- Teaching about and for respect.
- Helping students develop an escalating awareness of and appreciation for the commonalities and differences among their classmates.
- Helping students see themselves and their peers in the important ideas and issues they study.
- Helping students examine multiple perspectives on important issues.
- Helping students learn to listen to one another so that they hear not only the words, but also the intentions behind the words and the implications beyond them.
- Helping students to develop empathy for each member of the class.
- Ensuring consistently equitable participation of every student.
- Providing structures that promote and support student success.
- Seeking and responding to legitimate opportunities to affirm each student.
- Establishing shared and individual benchmarks for success at the appropriate levels.
- Coaching students to work for their personal best.
- Celebrating growth.
- Helping students to be more reflective and effective in peer relationships.
- Helping students to be more reflective and effective in decision making.
- Helping students to become effective problem solvers, both personally and interpersonally.

• Building positive memories for all individuals in the group and for the group as a whole, and revisiting those memories to help students develop a sense of shared experience.

In the case of affect, the teacher differentiates both proactively (in ways that are planned) and reactively (on-the-spot). She does both based on her understanding of the shared affective needs of all humans, the reality that we experience those needs in both similar and dissimilar ways, and her continued reflection on how each student's readiness levels, interests, learning style, intelligence preference, culture, gender, economic status, home experiences, and general development shape his or her affective needs.

Affect is, in large measure, shaped by learning environment—the weather in the classroom. Its lights and shadows, sun and storms profoundly influence everything else that happens for a learner in that classroom. The teacher's role is often that of "weather-maker." At the very least, it is the teacher's job to help students learn more effectively as a result of the classroom weather.

Differentiating Learning Environment

It's helpful to think about learning environment in terms of both visible and invisible classroom structures that enable the teacher and the students to work in ways that benefit both individuals and the class as a whole. A *flexible* learning environment is a hallmark of a differentiated classroom. The teacher's guiding question for a differentiated learning environment is, "What can I do to allow students of varying readiness levels, interests, and modes of learning to grow most fully in this place?"

One way of thinking about a differentiated

learning environment is to examine how space, time, and materials can be used flexibly. It's also critical to understand the rules and procedures that must govern a flexible learning environment. Although it is the teacher's responsibility to engineer a flexible classroom, a wise teacher involves students in decisions about how to make the environment work. Not only does this give students a sense of ownership of their classroom, but students are often able to see what needs to be done more quickly and creatively than the teacher (who may be bogged down with other responsibilities and pressures).

Decisions About Space

The goal of flexible space is to enable the teacher and the students to work in a variety of configurations and to do so smoothly and efficiently. To that end, teacher and students might ask questions such as

• What are the various ways we can rearrange the furniture to allow for individual, small-group, and whole-group work?

• How can we rearrange ourselves when we don't want to or cannot move the furniture?

• How can we arrange space for conversation and movement as well as space for quiet concentration?

• How can we display student work and other important artifacts and still have places in the room that are not visually distracting?

• When we need to move furniture, who will do it? At what speed? At what noise level?

• How will we know the appropriate placement for furniture when we move it?

• What is the appropriate way to deal with student materials and supplies when we move furniture?

• Who may move around the classroom?

For what purposes? When? At what noise level?

• What signal will we receive when it's time to move from one place or task to another?

• What will happen if someone's movement in the classroom is disruptive to others?

Decisions About Materials

Goals related to flexible materials in a differentiated classroom include making sure students have both what they need to pursue their own learning goals in preferred ways and what they need to work together toward class goals. To make decisions related to classroom materials, teachers and students might ask questions such as

• What materials and supplies should always be available in the classroom?

• What materials and supplies will be needed only from time to time?

• How can we rotate and store materials and supplies?

• Which materials and supplies should students have ready access to and which should be accessible only to the teacher?

• How will students know which materials and supplies are appropriate for their tasks at a given time?

• Who may retrieve materials and supplies? When? At what speed and noise level? How and when will we put them away?

• What guidelines will we use to share materials and supplies when there aren't enough to go around?

• What constitutes appropriate care for materials and supplies?

• What will happen if someone uses materials or supplies in ways that are inappropriate or disruptive to others?

Decisions About Time

Time is perhaps the most valuable classroom commodity. It enables or inhibits learning at every turn. And there is never enough of it. Because time is always nipping at our heels, it's easy to assume the most efficient way to use it is to carve it into chunks distributed to everyone in an equal manner. When there is academic diversity in a classroom, however, that is seldom the judicious choice. Some students will need additional instruction from the teacher in order to move ahead. Some will finish work more rapidly than others (even when the work is appropriately challenging). Some will need longer on a few tasks. Some will need longer on most tasks. It often makes sense for the teacher to teach a small group while other students are working alone or in small groups. In fully differentiated classrooms, in fact, the teacher may be working with a small group or an individual while some students work solo and others work in pairs or triads. Everyone knows what to do, how to do it, and everything works (at least most of the time—but that's true of classroom functioning in general). To enable flexible use of time, teacher and students might ask questions such as

• When will it be best for us to work as a unit?

• When will it be helpful to work in smaller groups or independently?

• How will we know where to be in the classroom and at what times?

• How will we manage ourselves when we work without direct teacher supervision?

• What rules and procedures will govern our work at various places in the room and for various tasks?

• How will we get help when we need it and the teacher is busy?

- How will we let the teacher know we need her help?
- What do we do if we finish a task before others (even though the task was challenging and we worked at a high level of quality)?
- What do we do if we need additional time for a task (even though we have worked steadily on the task)?
- Where do each of us turn in our work when we are finished?
- When is it appropriate to move around the room and when is it not appropriate?
- How will we know which tasks to work on and which part of the room to work in at a given time?
- How can I tell if I'm succeeding on my work at a high level of quality?
- How do I keep track of my goals, work, and accomplishments?

There are, of course, many other questions related to flexible learning environments beyond those about space, materials, and time that we've listed. The reality is that students of any age can work both flexibly and successfully as long as they know what's expected and are held to high standards of performance. Ironically, we're most likely to see smoothly operating, flexible classrooms in kindergarten. Beyond that point, we teachers often convince ourselves that *our* students aren't capable of independent and flexible work. (If that were the case, it would be one of the few demonstrations of learners becoming *less* able to accomplish complex tasks as they get older!) Besides, if we expect young people to become competent, self-guided adults, evidence that they are not moving in that direction should only serve as an impetus to ensure that they do.

Essential Principles of Differentiation

There are a number of key principles that typify a defensibly differentiated classroom. The principles have been described in detail in other places. Still, it's important at the outset of this book to review a few of them. These principles should be at the forefront of teacher planning and should serve as measures of the effectiveness of differentiation for teachers and administrative leaders alike.

Principle 1: Good Curriculum Comes First

There is no such thing as effective differentiation devoid of high-quality curriculum. Multiple versions of ambiguity will net only ambiguity. Multiple avenues to boredom will only lead more students to an undesirable place. Multiple routes to trivia and irrelevance will never enhance learning in the long run! The teacher's first job is always to ensure that curriculum is coherent, important, inviting, and thoughtful. Then and only then does it make sense to differentiate that curriculum.

Principle 2: All Tasks Should Be Respectful of Each Learner

Let's be frank: Dull drills *do* have an occasional place in the classroom. They are the adult equivalent of balancing a checkbook or filling out tax forms. The vast majority of the time, however, student work should be appealing, inviting, thought provoking, and invigorating. And it should be all these things for *all* students. Every student deserves work that is focused on the essential knowledge, understanding, and skills targeted for the lesson. Every student should be required to think at a high level (and should receive support when doing so). Every student should find his or her work interesting and powerful. Differentiation won't work (and shouldn't work) when some students are assigned tasks that look "privileged" while others are assigned tasks that merit avoidance.

Principle 3: When in Doubt, Teach Up!

The best tasks are those that students find a little too difficult to complete comfortably. Good instruction stretches learners. Differentiation should never be used as a way to mollycoddle or "protect" learners. If a student wants to tackle something you think may be too demanding, it might be wise to let him give it a try (with the understanding that once begun, the task must be finished). The student may have something important to show you. At worst, next time, you and the student will both know a little more about what represents an appropriate challenge. Certainly when the teacher assigns tasks, it's critical to ensure that the tasks are tiered to provide meaningful challenge. Likewise, rubrics or other indicators of student success should push the individual student beyond his or her comfort zone. Be sure there's a support system in place to facilitate the student's success at a level he or she doubted was attainable.

Principle 4: Use Flexible Grouping

Before beginning a unit, a teacher needs to think about when it will be important for the class to work as a whole, when students will need to work and to demonstrate competence alone, and when it makes most sense for students to work with small groups of peers. There must be time for the teacher to instruct small groups and time for conversations between the teacher and individual students.

Think about the ebb and flow of students in a classroom. Plan times for similar readiness groups

to work together—and times when mixed-readiness groups can work on tasks, with each individual making a meaningful contribution to the work of the group. Plan times for groups of students with similar interests to work together—but also times when students with varied interests can meld those into a common task. Likewise, plan for both similar and mixed learning profile groups. The former allows students comfort when working; the latter is one means of extending student awareness of working modes. Also, use randomly assigned groups. Finally, be sure to provide both teacher-choice and student-choice groups.

There is little doubt that each of those configurations will benefit many students in the class in a variety of ways. Most certainly, using only one or two types of groups causes students to see themselves and one another in more limited ways, keeps the teacher from "auditioning" students in varied contexts, and limits potentially rich exchanges in the classroom.

Principle 5: Become an Assessment Junkie

Everything a student says and does is a potential source of assessment data. Teachers are surrounded by assessment options. Trouble is, we often think of assessment narrowly—as something we do *after* learning ends so that we will have numbers to put in the grade book. Far better to think of assessment as an ongoing process, conducted in flexible but distinct stages. First, there is pre-assessment, which is essential to a differentiated classroom. Whether a formal quiz, a journal entry, an exit card, or any of a dozen other means of determining student knowledge, understanding, and skill set related to an upcoming unit or lesson, it's critical for the teacher in a differentiated classroom to have a sense of student starting points. Throughout the unit, take notes in class discussions, as you check home-work, and as you walk around the room to moni-tor student work and coach for quality. Again, use quizzes, journal prompts, exit cards, concept maps—whatever you like to use—to figure out stu-dents' level of knowledge, understanding, and skill at key points in a unit. Then differentiate instruc-tion based on what you find out. When it's time for final assessments, plan to use more than one assessment format—for example, a product *and* a test. Think about ways you can modify even the final assessments to maximize the likelihood that each student opens for you the widest possible window on his or her learning.

Principle 6: Grade for Growth

A portion of a teacher's grading may, of necessity, reflect a student's standing related to grade-level benchmarks. A portion of grades, however, should reflect a student's *growth.* A very bright learner who gets consistent *As* and never has to stretch or strive will become a damaged learner. A struggling student who persists and progresses will likely give up the fight if grade-level benchmarks remain out of reach and growth in that direction "doesn't seem to count." The most we can ask of any person—and the least we ought to ask—is that they be accountable for being and becoming their best. It is the job of the teacher to guide and support the learner in this endeavor.

*   *   *

We hope this primer on differentiation provides you with tools for reflecting on the units of differenti-ated instruction in Part II of this book—and on practices within your own classroom! Additional clarification on terms and strategies is available in the Glossary, beginning on page 233. To learn more about any of the topics discussed here, please con-sult the Resources on Differentiation and Related Topics, beginning on page 241.

Differentiated Units
of Study

Readers read as they wish, of course, and there's great merit in that. We take away from a source what we are ready to take away, and we gather what we can find in accordance with how we learn best. We do not want to deny our readers this freedom. Nonetheless, we offer a few suggestions and questions to guide your learning from the units that follow:

• See if you can find colleagues to read, analyze, and discuss the units with you.

• Read all of the units—or at least several of them—not just ones from your grade level or subject area. Look for similarities and differences. Record what you see. What seem to be the non-negotiables in these units?

• Think about how the unit developers have included and yet moved beyond mandated standards. What's the difference between "covering the standards" and the ways these teachers are *using* standards?

• After you read and study a unit, go back to the list of standards reflected in the unit and the teacher's listing of what students should know,

understand, and be able to do as a result of the unit. Check off those standards and goals you feel the unit addresses effectively. Develop ways to intensify the focus on any goals or standards you feel have not been addressed adequately.

• Look for the links between the learning goals (the standards as well as what students should know, understand, and be able to do) and the individual lessons in the unit. In what ways have these teachers used the learning goals to design the specific steps in the units?

• What benefits for students are likely to occur when a teacher organizes a unit by concepts rather than teaching a list of goals without one or more organizing concepts?

• Think about students you teach. Name them in your head or on paper. Jot down ways in which these specific students might benefit from the differentiated units versus nondifferentiated versions of the same units. Think about students with a range of learning needs, including students who could be described as "typical."

• For which students in your class or classes would you need to make additional adaptations in order to facilitate optimal learning? How might you make those adaptations if you were to revise one of the units? Would it be easier to make the additional modifications in these differentiated units or in nondifferentiated ones?

• How effective do you feel the various units are at

— Beginning with sound curriculum prior to differentiating?

— Making assessment a pervasive and useful element in instruction?

— Providing respectful tasks for all learners?

— "Teaching up"?

— Using flexible grouping?

• How did the teachers who developed these units seem to have decided when to use whole-class instruction and activities and when to differentiate instruction and activities?

• Where in each unit might you incorporate additional ways to differentiate content for particular students in your class or classes? What about additional ways to differentiate process? Products? Which instructional strategies that your students currently enjoy using would you want to integrate into these units?

• Where in each unit might you incorporate additional ways to address student readiness? Interest? Learning profile?

• In what ways do these units call for flexible use of space? Of materials? Of time?

• What classroom guidelines would you want to establish to ensure effective and efficient work in one or more of these units? How would you begin the process of developing a flexible but orderly learning environment in one of these classrooms? How might you enable your students to be your partners in establishing a flexible and differentiated classroom?

• Think about connections between student affect and differentiation as it's reflected in these units. In what ways is the general classroom tone likely to impact student affect? Why? In what ways is the differentiation likely to impact student affect? Why? What connections do you see between student affect and student learning?

• How does the role of the teacher shift in these differentiated classrooms compared with classrooms in which whole-class instruction predominates? What opportunities do teachers enjoy with flexible teaching that may not be so readily available in more traditional classrooms?

• What portions of your own curriculum do you recognize in these units? In what ways can you build on what you already do in order to address the learning needs of your full range of students?

• Which elements of these units do you particularly like? Which do you question? Talk with colleagues about what you see as positive in the units and what is less positive for you. In each instance, be sure to explore why you feel as you do.

• Try adding your voice to a unit you have on paper, explaining why you have crafted the unit as you have—or why you might now think about modifying the unit in some way.

• Be sure to apply in your classroom what you learn from the units. It's wise to move at a pace and in a sequence that seems manageable to you— but it's important to grow as a teacher!

*   *   *

Our great hope, of course, is that you will be "stretched" by the time you spend with these six units. As educators, we invest our professional lives in the belief that learning is both dignifying and humanizing. We hope this will be your experience in the pages to come.

1

Weather's A System

A Science Unit on Understanding and Predicting Weather

Unit Developer: Laura C. Massey

Introduction

This four- to five-week study of weather allows students to observe and analyze both global and local weather trends. Its primary focus is what causes the weather that we see around us. Although the main concepts highlighted during this unit are **cause and effect** and **patterns,** other concepts, such as cycles, and systems are also investigated. Throughout, students examine the relationship between cause and effect and explore how understanding cause and effect can help us to better understand weather.

The unit moves through each of the components of weather (including properties of air, air masses and fronts, the water cycle, and types of clouds and storms), and students add to and synthesize their understanding of these components so that they can see the "big picture" of weather. Throughout the unit, they maintain a weather journal that includes their observations of and reactions to the weather around them. This journal allows students to draw conclusions regarding **cause and effect** and to make predictions on their own. At the end of the unit, the students apply the information they've learned to analyze global and local weather patterns.

The students come to understand the concepts and ideas presented during this unit through a variety of instructional strategies, including group investigations and experiments, observation, and reading for information. Readings come from a variety of sources, and students gather daily weather information from a variety of media.

Teacher Reflection on Designing the Unit

When I set out to plan this unit, I gave a lot of thought to what I wanted the students to know upon its completion. At first I thought it would nice for them to know the meteorological term "front," to be able to name some types of clouds, and to understand what it means when a meteorologist reports that barometer readings have dropped. And it's true—it would be *nice* for my students to know these things, but I didn't think that was enough. I pictured students leaving the unit saying, "So what if a front comes through?" or "Who cares if that's a cumulus cloud?" I began planning with this in mind.

Gathering resources and searching for information I wanted to highlight provided me with a needed refresher course on weather. I found myself amused by and interested in concepts I had forgotten or hadn't fully understood before. My excitement did not come from suddenly remembering that a barometer measures air pressure; rather, it came from finally understanding that drops in air pressure mean a storm is approaching. I was reminded that simply observing clouds could help me to interpret and predict coming weather. I quickly became more interested in the "whys" of weather occurrences than in the "whats." At that point, I knew that I wanted to share this "aha" with my students. I wanted them to understand what causes weather and to use that understanding to predict and analyze the effects. In science, students must be critical thinkers and intuitive observers.

Because my class was diverse in terms of readiness level, learning style, and interests, I knew that I would need to differentiate many of the unit activities and products while focusing on the same understandings and information with the whole group. But first, I knew I needed to begin with solid curriculum.

Using my state course of study as a guide, I chose the main topics that we would explore. It seemed logical to begin by studying the properties and movement of air and moisture and then apply this information to reading weather maps, forecasting daily weather, and predicting storms. I wanted my students to get in the habit of obtaining weather data on their own and through the media, so I decided to require students to keep a weather journal of their observations and thoughts. Ultimately, I wanted them to observe global patterns and pull together the ideas the unit presented to draw conclusions about weather and climate in their own lives. I hoped that students would leave with an understanding of the **causes and effects** that surround them daily and that they would be able to apply this understanding beyond this unit and beyond the topic of weather.

Science and Information Skills Standards Addressed

- Build an understanding of weather and climate.
- Analyze the water cycle: evaporation, condensation, precipitation, ground water.
- Analyze the formation of clouds and their relation to weather systems.
- Relate global atmospheric movement patterns to local weather.
- Compile weather data to establish climate trends.
- Evaluate oceans' effects on weather and climate.

- Select and use independently, both within and outside the school, a variety of resources (print, nonprint, electronic) and formats (print, graphical, audio, video, multimedia) to extend content of resources used.
- Recognize that ideas are produced in a variety of formats (print, graphical, audio, video, multimedia, Web-based).
- Explore primary and secondary sources.
- Recognize diversity of ideas and thoughts by exploring a variety of resources (print, nonprint, electronic) and formats (print, graphical, audio, video, multimedia, Web-based).
- Determine the usefulness of information resources.
- Develop a search strategy, which includes the continuous evaluation of the research process and the information gathered.

Unit Concepts and Generalizations

Cause and Effect, Patterns (main concepts), Systems, Cycles, Order, Change, Influence
- A cause can have multiple effects.
- An effect can have multiple causes.
- We can examine causes to predict effects.
- We can examine effects to hypothesize about causes.
- By changing a cause, we can impact effect.
- There are some cause-and-effect relationships that we can only witness and not control.
- Patterns repeat.
- We can make predictions based on patterns.
- Patterns give order to our world.

Unit Objectives

As a result of this unit, the students will *know*
- Names of common weather instruments and how to use them.
- Famous examples of extreme weather, such as Hurricane Andrew (1992), Hurricane Fran (1996), Hurricane Hugo (1989), Hurricane Hazel (1954), The Tornado Outbreak of April 1974 (148 twisters), The Northeastern States' Blizzard of 1996, "The Storm of the Century" (1993), The Dust Bowl Drought (1933–1940), The Drought of 1988, and the Los Angeles Dust Storm (December 1988).
- Properties of air.
- Steps in the water (hydrologic) cycle.
- Types of clouds.
- Weather symbols used on maps.
- Weather-related vocabulary, including *air pressure, air mass, front (warm* and

cold), water vapor precipitation, condensation, evaporation, transpiration, molecule, hurricane, tornado, typhoon, blizzard, drought, satellite, radar, and *meteorologist.*

As a result of this unit, the students will *understand that*
- There are patterns in global and local weather that enable us to predict weather occurrences with some accuracy.
- Understanding cause-and-effect relationships helps us to make more accurate weather predictions.
- Even though we may understand cause-and-effect relationships, we cannot always control them.
- We can control to some degree how weather impacts us as individuals and as societies.

As a result of this unit, the students will *be able to*
- Make observations.
- Make predictions based on observations.
- Use weather instruments accurately and appropriately.
- Read weather maps.
- Explain the steps in the water cycle.
- Explain cloud formation.
- Relate global weather trends to local weather conditions.
- Demonstrate appreciation for the forces of weather.
- Justify people's interest in the weather.
- Read for information.
- Apply the scientific method.

Instructional Strategies Used

- Brainstorming
- Informal pre-assessment
- Jigsaw
- Tiered assessment
- Graphic organizers
- Interest and learning profile self-inventory
- Small-group research
- Tiered assignments

Sample Supporting Materials Provided

Unit Overview

LESSON	WHOLE-CLASS COMPONENTS	DIFFERENTIATED COMPONENTS
LESSON 1 **Introduction** *1–2 class periods*	Brainstorming and synthesis of weather knowledge in heterogeneous groups *50–75 minutes*	
	Introduction of **cause and effect** *20 minutes*	
		Homework assignment, self-selected according to learning profile *15–30 minutes*
LESSON 2 **More Introduction** *1 class period*	Sharing of homework and large-group discussion of **cause and effect**	
	Completion of class graphic organizer *10–15 minutes*	
	Informal pre-assessment (in pairs) *10 minutes*	
	Individual self-assessment of subject matter interests and learning styles *30 minutes*	

LESSON	WHOLE-CLASS COMPONENTS	DIFFERENTIATED COMPONENTS
	Discussion of generalizations and homework assignment *5–10 minutes*	
LESSON 3 **Air Experiments** *1–2 class periods*	Explanation of daily weather reports and journal entries *5–10 minutes*	
		Journal entries based on interest *5 minutes*
	Introduction to upcoming experiments and related procedures *10–15 minutes*	
		Small-group experiments based on readiness and interest *40 minutes*
		Independent reading anchor activity *10–20 minutes*
	Jigsaw of experiment results *30 minutes*	
	Synthesis of results *10 minutes*	
LESSON 4 **Investigating Air Pressure** *2 class periods*	Demonstration and discussion of air pressure *50 minutes*	
	Mixed-ability pair work on predicting weather **patterns** *15–20 minutes*	
	Discussion of predictions and related strategies *10 minutes*	
		Individual homework assignment based on readiness and learning profile *10 minutes*

LESSON	WHOLE-CLASS COMPONENTS	DIFFERENTIATED COMPONENTS
LESSON 5 **Air Masses and Fronts** *1–2 class periods*	Discussion of reading *10–15 minutes* Sharing of results *10–15 minutes*	Reading selection based on readiness *20–30 minutes* Small-group experiments based on readiness *30–40 minutes*
LESSON 6 **The Water Cycle** *2 class periods*	Discussion of the water cycle, guided by students' prior knowledge *15–20 minutes* Sharing of products and discussion of unit concepts *30–40 minutes*	Self-selected related activities, based on learning profile and work style *40–50 minutes*
LESSON 7 **Clouds** *1 class period*	Observation, sketching, and discussion of cloud types *15 minutes* Grouping of cloud types in small groups (random) *15 minutes* Presentation and discussion of "official" cloud groupings *15 minutes* Assignment/explanation of written homework assignment on storms *5 minutes*	
LESSON 8 **Storms** *3–5 class periods*		Research activity in small groups based on interest, subject matter knowledge, and research skills *2–3 class periods*

LESSON	WHOLE-CLASS COMPONENTS	DIFFERENTIATED COMPONENTS
	Storm presentations and note-taking with follow-up discussions correlating to unit concepts *2–3 class periods*	Note-taking template offered to those who need it
LESSON 9 **Global Patterns** *2 class periods*	Introduction to weather maps *15–20 minutes*	
		Small-group work interpreting weather maps and looking for patterns, grouped homogenously by interest and heterogeneously by readiness *40–50 minutes*
	Sharing and discussion of results *30–40 minutes*	
LESSON 10 **Unit Review** *2 class periods*		Independent review, differentiated according to need for structure *10 minutes*
		Self-selected small-group preparation for review game *40 minutes*
	Class game for review *50 minutes*	
LESSON 11 **Journal Entry** *1 class period*	Individual synthesis and self-evaluation *50 minutes*	
LESSON 12 **Final Assessment** *1 class period*	Part I: Objective test	Part II: Tiered essay question, based on readiness

Unit Description and Teacher Commentary

LESSON 1	Introduction	*(1–2 class periods)*
LESSON SEQUENCE AND DESCRIPTION		TEACHER COMMENTARY
Note: Before beginning the unit, give each student a folder to keep unit materials in.		I also recommend that you set aside time periodically for students to "clean up" their weather folders.
Brainstorming and synthesis of weather knowledge in heterogeneous groups. Begin the unit by grouping students in small, heterogeneous groups of three or four and asking them to brainstorm terms associated with weather. To encourage as many ideas as possible, provide the groups with pictures of a variety of different types of weather.		I encouraged students to list anything related to weather that came to their minds, and I provided prompts (the pictures) to get some students started. I chose to conduct this activity in heterogeneous groups for a wider variety of background information.
After five minutes of brainstorming, tell the groups that they are going to create group weather webs. When they look at their lists of weather words and terms, what categories do they see? Explain that they will be sharing their webs with the rest of the groups so they should be able to defend their choice categories.		Creating webs allowed students to synthesize, organize, and arrange information and to begin considering the major components of weather.
Students should create rough drafts of their webs and then transfer their webs to chart paper.		
When all the groups have completed their webs, they should present their work to the rest of the class. Groups that finish early may want to create illustrations to accompany the terms on their webs. Post the weather webs in the classroom for the duration of the unit.		When presenting their webs, students were forced to describe and rationalize their thinking (working on metacognition here). We posted the webs so students could see how they were building on prior knowledge as we moved through the unit.
Introduction of the concept of cause and effect. Open by asking students to characterize the relationship between the terms *cause* and *effect*. What are some examples of cause and effect in students' lives? Allow students to share their ideas, but be ready to provide examples if they struggle to do so. For example, a cause might be not studying for a test, and the effect might be not doing well on the test.		My goal here was to get students to think about **cause and effect** in all aspects of their lives, not just with regard to the weather.
✳ **Homework assignment, self-selected according to learning profile.** The students' assignment is to tell about a time in their own lives when they experienced or witnessed a cause-and-effect relationship. They are to choose one of the following formats: short story, poem, song or rap, cartoon, collage, or detailed drawing.		The homework assignment required all students to think about the impact of **cause and effect** in their own lives, but allowed them to choose *how* they would show this impact, thus differentiating by learning profile or interest.

✳ = Differentiated Component

LESSON 2	**More Introduction**	*(1 class period)*

LESSON SEQUENCE AND DESCRIPTION	TEACHER COMMENTARY
Sharing of homework and large-group discussion of cause and effect. Encourage willing students to share their homework products with the class. On the overhead, display a blank **cause and effect graphic organizer** (see Sample 1.1, page 43). Ask students to contribute examples from their homework assignments to create a class listing of causes and their effects. Discuss their ideas as you go.	During this activity, I posed questions such as • What is another effect of this cause? • What could be another cause in this example? • Could you see this effect coming? Why or why not? • Does this effect always follow this cause? My goal was to lead students to some big ideas about **cause and effect** and to hear their thinking about this concept.
Completion of class graphic organizer. When the class has generated a variety of examples, discuss the relationship between the two sides of the organizer. Guide the students toward forming "big statements" (generalizations) about **cause and effect**. List these statements on chart paper and display them in the classroom.	
Informal pre-assessment (in pairs). Have paired students generate examples of **cause and effect** with regard to weather, using the same graphic organizer as before. As with the previous class period's brainstorming activity, students should write down anything that comes to their minds. As they work, observe and record individual students' contributions and levels of participation to get an idea of their prior knowledge about weather.	During this part of the lesson, I circulated throughout the classroom, clipboard in hand, taking notes about students' conversations. I later used these notes to create student groupings and determine assignments.
Individual self-assessment of subject matter interests and learning styles. As pairs complete their organizers, collect them and distribute the **Unit Self-Assessment** (see Sample 1.2, page 44). Explain to the students that this is their chance to tell you about their strengths and weaknesses, learning styles, and interest levels in science and weather.	I combined the information from this assessment with the information from the previous activity and with my existing knowledge about each of the students to ensure that the activities in this unit would address different abilities, learning preferences, and interests.

LESSON SEQUENCE AND DESCRIPTION	TEACHER COMMENTARY
Discussion of generalizations and homework assignment. Wrap up the lesson by referring back to the "big statements" about weather, and ask the students if they have any ideas to add to the list. Tell them that in their next lesson, they will be investigating air.	
For homework, each student should bring in a weather journal (for example, a small journal book, a spiral notebook, or stapled pieces of paper) to write in throughout the unit.	Students kept all of their work for this unit in this notebook. I had them staple completed worksheets into these notebooks for later reference and reflection.

LESSON 3   Air Experiments   *(1–2 class periods)*

LESSON SEQUENCE AND DESCRIPTION	TEACHER COMMENTARY
Note: In preparation for this lesson, laminate the experiment sheets for each of the seven **Differentiated Air Experiments** (collected in Sample 1.3, beginning on page 45) and choose an area in the classroom (a "station") for each experiment. Collect all necessary materials and store them in a box at the back of the classroom.	Preparation is key in a differentiated classroom!
Explanation of daily weather reports and journal entries. Explain that everyone in the class will be keeping a daily weather journal as an ongoing activity. At the beginning of each class period, while the other students are getting settled, one or two students will be responsible for gathering information about local weather conditions and reporting this information to the class. Sources may include print (e.g., a newspaper) or alternative media (e.g., the Internet, radio).	On this first day, I provided the necessary information to model what would be expected, then assigned students to the weather reporter role alphabetically. This activity provided students with opportunity to practice information gathering and recording skills.
Journal entries based on interest. When the designated student presents the weather report, the rest of the students should record the data in their journals and then write a short response to it.	I read students' weather journals frequently (examining only a few each day), and I treated them as an informal assessment of students' understanding of the concepts we were examining as well as their skill in obtaining and recording weather data.
Keep a list of journal writing prompts posted in the room for students who may have a hard time deciding what to write. For example: • How has the weather changed? • What does the current weather remind you of? • How does today's weather make you feel? • What are some pluses and minuses about the weather right now? • What do you think tomorrow's weather will be like? Why?	These prompts were one way I encouraged students to do more than just minimal writing during the five minutes I allotted to this activity each day. I wanted them to begin to use their observations to make predictions and to examine their personal reactions to the weather.

LESSON SEQUENCE AND DESCRIPTION	TEACHER COMMENTARY
Introduction to upcoming experiments and related procedures. Before beginning the air experiments, distribute and discuss the **Experiment Steps to Success** (see Sample 1.4, page 52).	Going over the guidelines in the Experiment Steps to Success established the expectations for the day and helped structure the lesson.
Distribute the **Air Experiment Conclusions and Applications** handout (see Sample 1.5, page 53) to all students and discuss the steps in completing experiments. Explain that upon completion of their experiments, all students must answer all questions on the worksheet.	This worksheet used a series of questions to take students through the steps in the scientific process. My goal here was to get students thinking about what might happen during the experiments and then, afterward, about *why* things had happened as they did.
Small-group experiments based on readiness and interest. Divide students into groups of three or four and give each group the instructions for its assigned experiment (see Sample 1.3). There are seven experiments in all, designed at varying levels of complexity and listed here from most complex to least complex: • Experiment A: How Can We Determine Relative Humidity? (version 1) • Experiment B: How Can We Determine Relative Humidity? (version 2) • Experiment C: How Can We Determine the Direction of the Wind? • Experiment D: How Does Air Move? • Experiment E: Does Air Have Weight? • Experiment F: Does Air Take Up Space? • Experiment G: Does Air Have Movement? Each group should carry out its experiment, record all of the required information on the worksheet provided, and create a plan for sharing their work with the rest of the class.	For this activity, I based my grouping decisions on the unit pre-assessment. I supplemented my knowledge of the students' interest level in science, ability to conduct experiments, and ability to draw conclusions with the students' own rankings of their interest and abilities in these areas. I also considered students' personalities and work styles and created groups I thought would be compatible. Diagrams or pictures may help some students follow the directions more easily.
Independent reading anchor activity. After students complete their work and clean up their materials and work stations, have them read a selection from *Focus on Science* (published by Steck Vaughn Co.) about the layers of the atmosphere and, as a group, answer the questions that follow. A similar text can be substituted.	This served as an anchor activity for students who finished their work more quickly than others. Students were not required to know about the layers of the atmosphere, but it served as an appropriate extension for the current lesson.
Jigsaw of experiment results. When all groups have completed their experiments, put students in jigsaw groups to share their conclusions with one another. You should have three or four groups, with a representative from each of the seven experiments in each group.	Because each of the experiments demonstrated a different aspect of air, this was a great way for students to be able to learn from one another.

LESSON SEQUENCE AND DESCRIPTION	TEACHER COMMENTARY
Synthesis of results. At the end of the lesson, review experiment conclusions with the whole class. Record the students' contributions on the board. Discuss the relationship of these experiments to the unit concept of **cause and effect.** Explain to students that they will next apply their new understanding of the properties of air as they begin examining the movement of air in the atmosphere. Allow students who read the anchor activity piece about the layers of the atmosphere to share what they learned with the rest of the class.	I wanted to give students a chance to restate (and thus, solidify) their understanding of the characteristics of air.

LESSON 4   **Investigating Air Pressure**   *(2 class periods)*

LESSON SEQUENCE AND DESCRIPTION	TEACHER COMMENTARY
Note: For this lesson, you will need several weeks' worth of weather maps published in newspapers. Gather maps that show a variety of weather conditions in different seasons.	I found that large maps showing the U.S. and weather symbols in color were the best choice. It's a good idea to laminate these maps for future use.
Demonstration and discussion of air pressure. Introduce the lesson by asking the students what they already know about air. Record their statements on the board. Then, write "air pressure" on the board and ask students to try to define this term. What does it mean? Where have students heard the term before? Lead students to the definition of air pressure: *It is the pressure air exerts on the earth's surface.* Write this definition on the board. Explain that air pressure is measured using a barometer. To demonstrate air pressure, blow up a balloon and pinch the end closed. Explain that the air inside the balloon is exerting pressure on the balloon. Ask students: Where do you think the air pressure is greater: Inside or outside the balloon? Why? When the students understand that the pressure is greater inside the balloon, tell them to take out a piece of paper and get ready to make detailed observations. Then let go of the balloon. The students should write down exactly what they see. After they've done so, call on students to share their observations. Ask them what this tells us about air pressure.	This was another chance for students to think and ask questions about the characteristics of air before we moved on to a more complex topic. Here, I focused on asking students to provide detailed observations and to explain why what they saw happened. I varied my questions for individual students based on their different starting points with regard to making observations and drawing conclusions. Simply asking "Why?" enabled most of my students to take their thinking a step further.

LESSON SEQUENCE AND DESCRIPTION	TEACHER COMMENTARY
Make sure that the students understand that the air from the high-pressure area (inside the balloon) moved to the lower-pressure area (outside the balloon). Ask the students what they now know about air pressure. Continue by asking students to think about the following scenario: Imagine that all students our school were packed into our classroom. Would our classroom be an area of high or low pressure? What would the students want to do? Where would they want to go? Why? Students should see that they would behave in the same way as the air in the balloon—they would want to go out of the high-pressure area and into the low-pressure area. Point out to students that this is how air behaves. It moves from areas of high pressure to areas of low pressure. Ask students how their observations and thinking relate to the concept of **cause and effect.** Pass out the **Thinking About Air Pressure Worksheet** (see Sample 1.6, page 54). On the overhead, display the following four statements about air pressure: • Air exerts pressure on the earth's surface. • Cool air has higher pressure. • Drops in pressure indicate stormy weather. • Air tends to move from areas of high pressure to areas of low pressure. Have the students copy these four statements onto their worksheets. Briefly discuss each of the statements to ensure that the students understand them. It may be necessary to draw diagrams to show that cool air molecules have greater density and that molecules move and expand as air warms.	
Mixed-ability pair work on predicting weather patterns. Group students into pairs and pass out weather maps. Tell the students to look at the symbols on the maps and use their understanding of air pressure to make predictions about the weather in several different places. Students should record their predictions on their worksheets. They should also complete the last part of the worksheet that requires them to consider the importance of understanding air pressure.	Here, I created mixed-ability pairs because I knew that applying the four statements about air pressure would be difficult for some of my students. I wanted my higher-readiness students to work through the challenge of applying these ideas—and to help their partners do the same.
Discussion of predictions and related strategies. End the lesson by allowing students to share their maps and predictions with the rest of the class or in small groups. Make sure that they explain why their predictions are valid.	Again, I hoped that students would learn from one another.

LESSON SEQUENCE AND DESCRIPTION	TEACHER COMMENTARY
Individual homework assignment based on readiness and learning profile. Provide the appropriate reading selection and have students complete one of two assignments. For Assignment 1, students read a discussion of air pressure excerpted from *Focus on Science* (published by Steck Vaughn Co.). For Assignment 2, they read a discussion of barometer reading excerpted from *Weather and Climate* (published by Carson-Delloa Publishing Co.). Other readings on similar topics may be substituted. *Assignment 1: What Is Air Pressure?* Read the selection on air pressure and choose one of the following activities to show your understanding of the topic: • Create a diagram that shows the movement of cool and warm air to someone who cannot read. Be sure that the relationship between this movement and our unit concept of **cause and effect** is clear. • Take the key information from the reading and create a quiz. Include questions related to our unit concept of **cause and effect.** Be sure that you include an answer key on a separate page. *Assignment 2: Using a Barometer* Read the selection on barometers and choose one of the following activities to show your understanding of the topic: • You are a barometer. Write a letter to a thermometer explaining why you are the better of the two. Point out any **cause-and-effect** relationships you perceive. Be sure to make a strong case for yourself! • Create an illustration or diagram that explains how barometers work and what they measure. Be sure to make clear any **cause-and-effect** relationships you perceive. Your diagram must clearly explain the process to someone who cannot read.	I gave the first assignment to those students who needed additional work with air pressure. The second assignment was designed for those students who "got" air pressure and were ready to extend their understanding. Both assignments allowed students to <u>choose between a verbal and a spatial</u> <u>activity to show their understanding,</u> and thus, was a <u>learning profile</u> <u>option as well.</u> I asked students to complete these assignments in their weather journals.

LESSON 5 **Air Masses and Fronts** *(1–2 class periods)*

LESSON SEQUENCE AND DESCRIPTION	TEACHER COMMENTARY
Note: In preparation for this lesson, laminate the experiment sheets for each of the **Differentiated Air Masses and Fronts Experiments** (collected in Sample 1.7, beginning on page 55) and put the materials for each experiment at designated stations in the classroom.	

LESSON SEQUENCE AND DESCRIPTION	TEACHER COMMENTARY
Reading selection based on readiness. Explain to the students that they will be learning about air masses and fronts. They will first read about and discuss the topic and then apply their understanding to one of several different experiments.	
Provide reading material on two different levels to accommodate different reading abilities. I assigned a section about air masses from the student text (*Science Horizons*, published by Silver Burdett Ginn) to my less advanced readers and a handout from *Focus on Science* (published by Steck Vaughn Co.) to my more advanced readers.	The readings I chose differed in both vocabulary and complexity. The selection for less advanced readers focused on terminology related to air masses and fronts; the selection for more advanced readers introduced the global movement of air masses and the causes of such **patterns.**
Discussion of reading. When all students have completed their reading, lead a whole-class discussion of what they learned about air masses. Be sure to call on students from both reading groups.	
Small-group experiments based on readiness. Before beginning the experiments, review **Experiment Steps to Success** (see Sample 1.4) with the class. Then place students in experiment work groups of three or four for the **Differentiated Air Masses and Fronts Experiments** (see Sample 1.7). There are three experiments in all, designed at varying levels of complexity and listed here from most abstract to least abstract: • Experiment A: What Happens When a Cold Air Mass Meets a Warm Air Mass? • Experiment B: What Happens When Two Air Masses Meet? • Experiment C: How Do Fronts Form? Assign two groups to work on each experiment. Give groups time to go over their particular instructions, and then move among the groups to make sure that they understand what they need to do. Explain that they should answer the questions on their experiment sheets when they have completed their experiments.	I designed three air mass experiments focusing on similar content but varying in difficulty. I based grouping for these experiments on both my observations and students' responses to the **Unit Self-Assessment** (see Sample 1.2) where they rated their own ability to work in groups, follow directions, and carry out experiments.
Sharing of results. Conclude the lesson by allowing students to share their experimental findings with one another. What do they now understand about air masses and fronts and the ways they move and interact? How does this relate to **cause and effect?**	

| LESSON 6 | The Water Cycle | *(2 class periods)* |

LESSON SEQUENCE AND DESCRIPTION	TEACHER COMMENTARY
Discussion of the water cycle, guided by students' prior knowledge. Begin by providing each student with a copy of the **Hydrologic Cycle Note-Taking Sheet** (see Sample 1.8, page 58).	Earlier in the week, I gave students I thought would have a difficult time contributing to this lesson's discussions a reading selection about the water cycle. Students read the selection during their anchor activity time or at home. I wanted them to get as much out of the discussion as possible and to be able to contribute to it, as well. Likewise, I often give more advanced readers complex readings on the topic for use during anchor activity time or at home.
Ask the students to guess what *hydrologic* means. Tell them that it is another name for the water cycle. Explain that the class will discuss the hydrologic cycle and that each student will be responsible for taking notes throughout the discussion. These notes should include key vocabulary as well as the steps in the hydrologic cycle. Tell students that they will need to use their notes later in the lesson.	
Begin the discussion by asking students to explain what they already know about the hydrologic cycle. Write their responses on the board. Use their prior knowledge to guide your explanation and to fill in gaps in their understanding (you may want to draw the cycle on the board).	Here, I wanted to avoid giving students information that they already had. My job was to correct errors in thinking and to fill in the missing pieces of the water cycle.
Once the cycle is clear to students and they understand the vocabulary related to it, invite them to the front of the room to act out or pantomime parts of the cycle. For example: • When does condensation occur? • What does the process of nucleation look like? • How are water droplets formed from water vapor and nuclei? Be sure to highlight key terms as students move through the steps. Address any student questions and give them a few minutes to add to the notes in their weather journals before moving on to the next part of the lesson.	Allowing students to act out or pantomime parts of the water cycle helped to solidify their understanding by getting them physically involved with the information. Such activities particularly appeal to kinesthetic learners.
Self-selected related activities, based on learning profile and work style. Put the following list of activities on the overhead, and allow students to choose one to complete. *Option 1: Group Work* Role-play the life of a tiny water droplet. Include narration and props as appropriate. Speak clearly, loudly, and stay in character as you act.	I had differentiated by readiness in earlier activities, and I wanted students to have the opportunity to work with a variety of other students. Students chose not only how they would show their understanding (verbally, spatially, kinesthetically, creatively), but also with whom they would work and in what type of group configuration.

LESSON SEQUENCE AND DESCRIPTION	TEACHER COMMENTARY
Option 2: Individual Work Write about the life of a tiny water droplet. Include details and vivid descriptions so that your readers will understand what it might feel like to be the droplet. *Option 3: Individual Work* Make a detailed diagram of the life of a tiny water droplet. Your diagram must be extremely neat and clear and must help your viewers understand the steps in the hydrologic cycle. *Option 4: Individual or Group Work* Use materials in the classroom to create an experiment that demonstrates a part of the hydrologic cycle. You must write down the materials you use, the procedures you follow, and your observations. Give students the remainder of the class period to finish their products.	
Sharing of products and discussion of unit concepts. Students present their water cycle products before the rest of the class. Afterward, review the statements about **cause and effect** and **patterns.** Have the students share what they have learned about these statements thus far in the unit.	Presenting to their classmates gave students another opportunity to learn from one another. At this point, I felt it was time to look back to our overarching concepts and examine what we had learned about them so far.

LESSON 7   **Clouds**   *(1 class period)*

LESSON SEQUENCE AND DESCRIPTION	TEACHER COMMENTARY
Observation, sketching, and discussion of cloud types. To introduce this lesson, take students outside to observe the clouds (you might have to be somewhat flexible with the timing of this lesson). Give them the opportunity to draw the clouds they see. Depending on the amount or types of clouds in the sky, you may want to discuss the similarities and differences between them.	This "hook" activity gave students a chance to begin examining the characteristics of clouds. It also appealed to both visual and tactile learners.
Grouping of cloud types in small groups (random). Place students in randomly assigned groups of three or four. Provide each group with pictures from magazines that show different types of clouds. Tell groups to sort their pictures into cloud groups. They can form as many cloud groups as needed and can base their groupings on any characteristic that they choose. Tell the groups to choose names for their cloud groups. (Students who already know the names of different types of clouds may use those names.)	This activity allowed students to generate their own ideas and to discover for themselves differences between clouds.

LESSON SEQUENCE AND DESCRIPTION	TEACHER COMMENTARY
As groups complete their cloud categories, provide them with a cloud identification chart that will allow them to compare their cloud groups to the official classifications of cloud types. Questions to ask include the following: • How are your groupings the same or different? • On what characteristics did you base your groups? • How are clouds actually classified?	Here, I encouraged students to evaluate their thinking based on the standard classification system for clouds. My goal was to enhance their learning by helping them come to understand cloud classification rather than just writing down a classification system someone else had created. This is an example of a concept attainment lesson.
Presentation and discussion of "official" cloud groupings. Allow groups to share some of their cloud pictures with the rest of the class. What kinds of clouds do the pictures show? Also, have groups share how closely their own cloud groups matched the standard cloud classifications. What does each type of cloud tells us about the weather? Is there evidence of **cause and effect** with regard to clouds? Why or why not? Post a chart showing cloud types and corresponding weather conditions so that students can use the chart to make weather observations and predictions.	Before providing students with information about how clouds can be used to predict weather, I gave them the chance to come up with their own ideas. This was yet another opportunity to reexamine our unit concepts.
Assignment/explanation of written homework assignment on storms. Tell students that the next topic of study will be storms. Invite them to begin thinking about some of the severe weather conditions that they have experienced and to consider some of the **causes and effects** of storms and the kinds of **patterns** they might observe in various types of storms. Then announce the homework assignment: Students will write a short narrative about a time that they experienced extreme weather. Extreme weather might include hurricanes, snowstorms, thunderstorms, or other storms.	I like to personalize activities whenever possible to enhance student interest.

LESSON 8	**Storms**	*(3–5 class periods)*

LESSON SEQUENCE AND DESCRIPTION	TEACHER COMMENTARY
Note: In preparation for this lesson, collect information about the different types of storms you plan to study from a variety of sources and at a variety of reading levels.	Because of the generally high interest level in this particular topic, I thought this would be a good opportunity for students to work on their research skills.

LESSON SEQUENCE AND DESCRIPTION	TEACHER COMMENTARY
Research activity in small groups based on interest, subject matter knowledge, and research skills. Place students in groups of three or four. Each group should chose one of the following storm types as their research topic: • Rain and hailstorms • Thunder and lightning • Snowstorms • Storms at sea • Hurricanes, typhoons, and cyclones • Sand and dust storms • Tornadoes Students should find a famous example of their type of storm (see the list included in the Unit Objectives on page 21) and learn all they can about that storm's **causes and effects.** No two groups should study the same storm, but try to get at least one group working with each of the storm types. Once all groups have chosen a storm, explain that each will carry out research, compile information, and make a presentation to the class. This presentation should include a description of their storm type, evidence of any cause-and-effect relationships, and any other information that will help their classmates better understand the type of storm. Provide students with a copy of the **Storm Presentation Rubric** (see Sample 1.9, page 59) to familiarize them with the project requirements and criteria for success. Go over all criteria and allow students to ask questions. As groups begin their research, provide a variety of reading materials on different reading levels to accommodate varying reading abilities. Also, post useful Web sites for the students to explore, and provide a list of other possible resources. Students may need several class periods to complete their research and prepare their presentations.	This research activity was differentiated based on both interest and readiness. I grouped students to work cooperatively based on their interest responses on the **Unit Self-Assessment** and on my knowledge of their readiness levels. In addition, I considered their research skills and placed them in groups with students who had similar skills. Doing so allowed me to provide some groups with the extra assistance they needed to carry out their research, while other groups worked with less assistance from me.
Storm presentations and note-taking with follow-up discussions correlating to unit concepts. Each group should present its storm information on a predetermined day. The rest of the class should take notes about the information presented. To help students determine what to include in their notes, remind them that they are looking for **cause-and-effect** relationships. It would also be a good idea to review important information after each group presentation. You might do this through a quick Think–Pair–Share that encourages students to share their ideas with one another.	I provided students who needed more structure with the **Storm Presentations Note-Taking Template** (see Sample 1.10, page 60). I encouraged students to staple these sheets into their weather journal.

LESSON SEQUENCE AND DESCRIPTION	TEACHER COMMENTARY
Review any **cause-and-effect** relationships noted in the presentations of storm research. As you do so, highlight varying weather conditions and their effects. Can students identify any **patterns** that are characteristic of all storms?	

LESSON 9   **Global Patterns**   *(2 class periods)*

LESSON SEQUENCE AND DESCRIPTION	TEACHER COMMENTARY
Note: For this lesson, you will need a world map series that shows several different types of data. These maps should also show changes over time, including different seasons. I used the GLOBE Earth System Poster developed by the GLOBE Science and Education Program. This poster showed global variations in solar energy, average temperature, cloud cover, precipitation, soil moisture, and vegetation at different points in a calendar year. Any similar set of maps can be used. Post the maps in locations around the classroom.	This lesson highlights the concept of **patterns**. My goal here was to have students notice and interpret weather patterns. In addition, I wanted them to draw conclusions and make predictions.
Introduction to weather maps. Help students familiarize themselves with the formats and characteristics of weather maps by looking at one specific map and the information it presents about a topic (e.g., vegetation in June). Be sure to point out the map scale and have students practice reading the maps.	This lesson required students to synthesize much of what they had already come to understand during the unit. It was important to allow students to lead this activity with their own observations, questions, and insights.
Small-group work interpreting weather maps and looking for patterns, grouped homogeneously by interest and heterogeneously by readiness. Place students in as many groups as you have types of data so that each group will study one set of data on the series of maps. For example, one group might focus on average temperature at different places and at different points in the year, while another group might focus on cloud cover. Have all students turn in a list of the top two topics they'd most like to study. Form groups to coincide with student choices (interest) and to ensure a range of readiness in each group.	I placed students in mixed-ability groups for a couple of reasons: • Previously they had worked with students of similar readiness levels and I wanted to vary my groupings. • I wanted at least one strong critical thinker in each group, as this activity required a lot of data analysis and interpretation.

LESSON SEQUENCE AND DESCRIPTION	TEACHER COMMENTARY
Ask the groups to move about the classroom to find data about their topic on one of the posted maps. When the students are comfortable interpreting their data from a single map, tell them that they're going to be looking at the same type of data over time. Allow the students to make their own observations and draw their own conclusions. Encourage them to look for **patterns** among the different maps. They should begin noting and examining seasonal changes. When groups have had the chance to thoroughly study the maps and explore their specific topics and data, have them write a brief summary of their findings. Good prompts include, "What appears to happen with regard to _____ over time?" "What **patterns** do you see with regard to _____?" Have each group choose one person to share this information with the rest of the class.	I moved among the groups, asking guiding questions when necessary. For example: "What evidence do you see to support your ideas?" "What changes do you see taking place between these two maps?"
Sharing and discussion of results. When each group has examined the maps and written a summary of its findings, bring the class together. Have students sit in a semicircle where they can all see the maps (you may have to move the maps around, as well!). Allow each group's speaker to share the group summary, and using the information provided, discuss how all of the data might be related. How do changes in cloud cover relate to average temperature and changes in vegetation? How are precipitation and soil moisture related? Allow the students' observations and conclusions to guide the discussion.	This discussion allowed students to learn from one another rather than exclusively from me. As a result of their sharing and discussing, they learned much more than they would have from a lecture or another traditional, teacher-directed activity.
Pose the following question: How does all of this relate back to our unit concepts of **cause and effect** and **patterns?**	This closure discussion ensured that everyone in the class shared common understandings.

LESSON 10   Unit Review   *(2 class periods)*

LESSON SEQUENCE AND DESCRIPTION	TEACHER COMMENTARY
Independent review, differentiated according to need for structure. Students review the information presented and collected throughout this unit by going through their weather journals. **Self-selected small-group preparation for review game.** Allow students to work in groups of three to prepare themselves for a class game that will require them to recall information presented during the unit. Set aside one class period for preparation, and tell students that they will not be allowed to use their weather materials during the game.	I provided the **Unit Review Sheet** (see Sample 1.11, page 61) for those students I knew would struggle with determining which information they should definitely know. On this sheet, I included key vocabulary and concepts as well as general questions concerning **cause and effect** and **patterns**. Although some students needed the scaffolding this review sheet provided, others did well with a more open-ended approach to the unit review.

LESSON SEQUENCE AND DESCRIPTION	TEACHER COMMENTARY
Class game for review. Divide the class into two mixed-ability teams. Split questions into rounds, according to difficulty. Ask each team one question per round, and award one point for each correct answer.	I created the two teams based on my knowledge of the students' levels of understanding with regard to the material we had been studying and with an eye toward making the teams as evenly matched as possible. There are, of course, many different games a class can play to review material.

LESSON 11	**Journal Entry**	*(1 class period)*

LESSON SEQUENCE AND DESCRIPTION	TEACHER COMMENTARY
Individual synthesis and self-evaluation. Have students take out and review their weather journals (see Lesson 3). Tell them they are to complete the following assignment in order to pull together and conclude their weather journals:	This final assignment required students to reflect on their own work and observations and to make general statements about them. It also required them to synthesize information to analyze local weather conditions and trends.
1. Look back through your weather journal. Pay close attention to your observations of weather conditions for each day. What **patterns** or trends do you notice? From your notes, what statements can you make about the weather in our area at this time of year? Were there major changes in the weather, or did conditions remain largely the same?	
2. Write a final entry in your journal that compares your observations to what you know about the climate and seasons of this area. Relate this final entry to one or both of our unit concepts.	
3. Finally, choose the notebook entry that you think shows your best work in this unit and explain why you picked it.	By allowing students to choose and write about their best entry, I encouraged self-evaluation.

LESSON 12	**Final Assessment**	*(1 class period)*

LESSON SEQUENCE AND DESCRIPTION	TEACHER COMMENTARY
The final assessment is made up of two parts, both of which should be completed in a 50-minute time frame.	
Part I: Objective test. This consists of true/false, fill-in-the-blank, and short-answer items. Distribute Part I to all students. Explain that they should turn in Part I when they've completed it, at which time you will give them the second part of the assessment.	There were many non-negotiables in this unit—information students were simply required to know. I included this information on the objective portion of the unit assessment.

LESSON SEQUENCE AND DESCRIPTION	TEACHER COMMENTARY
Part II: Tiered essay question, based on readiness. Each student completes one of two essays:	The essay portion asked students to put their knowledge to work, although at different levels of difficulty.
Essay 1 Pretend that a new student has joined our class today. This student has not yet studied weather, but would like to know what we learned during this unit. What can you tell this student about weather to help him or her understand what you have learned? Include as much information as you can about the following topics: air, air pressure, air masses and fronts, the water cycle, clouds, storms, and global trends. Then explain how these topics affect our local weather and climate. Be sure you discuss how the information relates to our unit concepts of **cause and effect** and **patterns.**	I assigned Essay 1 to students working at or below grade level. This essay required them to distill their knowledge and apply it to weather around them.
Essay 2 Choose five cities on the weather maps provided. For each of the cities, explain the type of weather conditions the city is experiencing now. Then predict what conditions each city can expect in the next few days. Fully explain your forecast by incorporating evidence of the **cause-and-effect** relationship and an analysis of **patterns**. Include the aspects of weather that we have studied during his unit. Be specific!	Essay 2 was for my more advanced students. This essay required them to analyze information and apply that analysis to make predictions.

Teacher Reflection on the Unit

The sequencing of this unit was its greatest strength. I was pleased with how the concepts progressed in a way that made sense to the students. The unit included numerous differentiated activities that allowed each student to build an understanding of the concepts based on his or her readiness level. Also, we constantly connected the learning that was taking place inside our classroom to experiences in our environment. The journaling provided a means for students to express their observations and conclusions. And although it required much effort, designating time for whole-class reflection enhanced the learning experience for all students. As I had hoped, the students left the study with a greater appreciation for weather and a deeper understanding of how it affects their lives.

Laura C. Massey most recently taught science in North Carolina. She can be reached at MasseyLaura@aol.com.

SAMPLE 1.1—Graphic Organizer: Cause and Effect

Cause	Effect

SAMPE 1.2—Unit Self-Assessment

Here are some topics that we may study during our exploration of weather. Which of them are you most interested in learning about? Number your choices from 1 (your favorite) to 10 (your least favorite). You may also write-in another weather-related topic that is of interest to you.

_____   sand and dust storms

_____   hurricanes, typhoons, and cyclones

_____   storms at sea

_____   thunder and lightning

_____   rain and hail

_____   tornadoes

_____   famous storms in history

_____   people who work in the weather field

_____   weather forecasting

_____   global patterns and trends

Other idea: _____

Now rate yourself on the following skills and interests. Use a scale of 1–10, with 1 indicating the highest level of skill or interest and 10 indicating the lowest level of skill or interest.

_____   interest in science

_____   interest in weather

_____   understanding of science

_____   understanding of weather

_____   ability to carry out experiments

_____   ability to work in a group

_____   ability to work independently

_____   ability to follow directions

_____   ability to read for information

_____   ability to take notes

_____   presentation ability

SAMPLE 1.3—Differentiated Air Experiments

Experiment A: How Can We Determine Relative Humidity? (1)

Materials:

tape   a rubber band

water   a piece of cardboard

2 identical thermometers   a Relative Humidity Table

gauze (2" x 2")

Procedure:

1. Look up "relative humidity" in your science book.
2. Wrap the gauze around the bulb of one of the thermometers and secure it with the rubber band.
3. Wet the gauze.
4. Tape each thermometer to the edge of a desk, with the bulb just hanging over the edge.
5. Fan both thermometers, using the piece of cardboard. Continue to fan the thermometers until the temperature of the wet thermometer stops decreasing.
6. Record the temperature of both thermometers.
7. Record the difference in temperature between the two thermometers.
8. Look at the Relative Humidity Table. The numbers in the left-hand column represent the difference between the wet and dry reading. Follow your dry bulb temperature reading across the table and follow your difference reading down the column until they intersect. Record this relative humidity reading.

Conclusions:

1. What was the dry bulb reading? What was the difference between the dry bulb and the wet bulb reading?

2. What was the relative humidity?

3. What does this tell us about the relative humidity in our classroom?

4. Who might need to know this type of information?

Experiment B: How Can We Determine Relative Humidity? (2)

Materials:

2 identical thermometers

water

rubber bands

scissors

an empty 1-quart milk carton

a small piece of cotton material

thread

Procedure:

1. Look up "relative humidity" in your science book.
2. Cover the bulb of one of the thermometers with a small piece of cotton material.
3. Secure the material with thread, leaving a small amount of the material hanging off one end.
4. Attach the thermometers to the sides of the milk carton using the rubber bands.
5. Poke a small hole in the milk carton just below the bulb of the covered thermometer.
6. Push the small amount of excess material through the hole so that about a ¼-inch is inside the milk carton.
7. Slowly fill the bottom of the carton with water. Be sure that the water level does not go over the hole, but is high enough to wet the cotton material.
8. Record the temperature on each thermometer.

Conclusions:

1. Which thermometer had the highest temperature?

2. Why do you think this happened?

3. What can this tell us about relative humidity?

4. Of what use is this information?

SAMPLE 1.3—*(continued)*

Experiment C: How Can We Determine the Direction of the Wind?

Materials:

a small flowerpot

a red marker or crayon

dirt

a navigational compass

tape

an index card (3" x 5")

a drinking straw

a straight pin

a pencil (with eraser)

thin wire (or paper clips)

scissors

Procedure:

1. Fill the flowerpot with dirt.
2. Use the scissors to make a 1-inch slit in opposite sides of one end of the drinking straw.
3. Use the scissors to cut an arrow with a tail out of the index card.
4. Slide the arrow into the cut end of the straw. Secure with tape.
5. Mark the other end of the straw with the red marker or crayon two inches below the arrow, and push the straight pin through the straw so that it is parallel to the arrow.
6. Push the pin into the eraser of the pencil. Test the straw to see if it can spin about on the pencil.
7. Cut four pieces of wire, each 3 inches long.
8. Bend the ends of the pieces to form the letters *N, E, S,* and *W,* leaving a tail of wire on each.
9. Wrap the excess wire around the middle of the pencil so that the letters represent the four cardinal directions.
10. Push the point of the pencil into the dirt so that the pencil is firmly supported and pointing straight up. Be sure the pin and the pencil are both perpendicular to the dirt.
11. Take your "weather vane" outside and place it in an open area.
12. Use the compass to orient your weather vane so that the letters *N, E, S,* and *W* are appropriately positioned.
13. Observe and record what happens when the wind blows.

Conclusions:

1. What is the function of a weather vane?

2. How does a weather vane work to determine the direction of the wind?

3. Who would need to know the direction of the wind? Why?

Experiment D: How Does Air Move?

Materials:
talcum powder
a cloth
a lamp

Procedure:
1. Sprinkle a small amount of talcum powder on the cloth.
2. Shake the cloth and observe what happens.
3. Record your observations.
4. Turn on the lamp and give it a few minutes to warm up.
5. When the light bulb is relatively hot, shake the powdered cloth over the lamp and observe what happens to the powder.
6. Record your observations.

Conclusions:
1. How was the movement of the powder different when shaken over the heated lamp?

2. Why do you think this happened?

3. What does this tell us about air?

4. As a result of this experiment, what conclusions can you draw about how the wind blows?

5. Of what use is this information?

SAMPLE 1.3—*(continued)*

Experiment E: Does Air Have Weight?

Materials:

2 large balloons of equal size

string

books

2 yardsticks

a straight pin

Procedure:

1. Lay one of the yardsticks on a table so that most of it is hanging over the edge. Use the books to secure it.
2. Cut a 12-inch piece of string. Tie one end to the yardstick hanging off the table and the other end to the middle of the other yardstick. Adjust the position of the string so that the two yardsticks form a balance and the hanging yardstick rests parallel to the floor.
3. Blow up the balloons so they are the same size, and knot the open ends securely.
4. Attach the balloons to opposite ends of the balanced yardstick with 10-inch pieces of string. After the balloons are attached, be sure that the strings are still of equal length.
5. If necessary, readjust the yardstick so that it is perfectly balanced (parallel to the floor).
6. Use the pin to make a small hole in one of the balloons, close to the knot.
7. Observe what happens as the balloon deflates.
8. Record your observations.

Conclusions:

1. What did you observe?

2. Why do you think this happened?

3. What does this tell us about air?

4. Why is this information important?

5. How is this information useful in the real world?

SAMPLE 1.3—(continued)

Experiment F: Does Air Take Up Space?

Materials:
a handkerchief
a tall glass
a bowl of water

Procedure:
1. Stuff the handkerchief into the bottom of the glass. Be sure that it does not fall out when the glass is turned upside down.
2. Slowly immerse the glass upside down in the bowl of water. Be sure that you do not tip the glass as you place it in the water.
3. Observe what happens
4. Record your observations.

Conclusions:
1. What did you observe? What happened to the water in the bowl? What happened to the handkerchief?

2. What surprised you about the results of this experiment? Why?

3. What does this tell us about air?

4. Of what practical use is this information?

5. What kind of professionals might need this information? Why?

SAMPLE 1.3—(continued)

Experiment G: Does Air Have Movement?

Materials:

a plastic drinking bottle   a balloon

a bowl of hot water   a bowl of cold water

Procedure:

1. Secure the balloon over the neck of the plastic drink bottle.
2. Place the bottle into the bowl of hot water. Be sure to hold it upright.
3. Observe what happens.
4. Record your observations.
5. Repeat the experiment, this time using a bowl of cold water.
6. Record your observations.

Conclusions:

1. What happened in each experiment?

2. Why do you think this happened?

3. What does this tell us about air?

4. Of what practical use is this information?

5. What kind of professionals might need this information? Why?

SAMPLE 1.4—Experiment Steps to Success

1. Read through your set of experiment directions and make sure that everyone in your group understands each step.

2. Read through your experiment sheet's conclusion questions. Remember: Each member of your group must fill out his or her own sheet.

3. Read the list of materials that you will need to complete your task.

4. Pick one person in your group to be the materials manager. That person will collect the materials from the material box.

5. After you gather your materials, read through the instructions again. Do you have everything you need?

6. Follow the directions carefully to complete your task.

7. When you have completed the whole task, work as a group to answer the conclusion questions. Complete your experiment sheet.

8. Have the materials manager return the materials to the materials box. If the materials are wet, be sure to dry them completely before returning them to the box. The rest of the group should tidy up your work area.

9. Select one or two people in your group to share what you did, what the results were, and the implications of the experiment. Help them plan how to do this most effectively.

SAMPLE 1.5—Air Experiment Conclusions and Applications

Name of experiment: _____

Group members: _____

Detailed description of what you did:

Detailed description of what happened:

Explanation of what you learned from this experiment:

Explanation of why it matters:

SAMPLE 1.6—Thinking About Air Pressure Worksheet

Four statements about air pressure:

1.

2.

3.

4.

Using the maps provided, what predictions can you make about the weather in different places around the United States? Make multiple predictions for each of the different regions.

In the space below, using your own words, discuss the importance of understanding air pressure. What examples of cause and effect are related to this understanding?

SAMPLE 1.7—Differentiated Air Masses and Fronts Experiments

Experiment A: What Happens When a Cold Air Mass Meets a Warm Air Mass?

Materials:

cooking oil   water

2 clear plastic cups   a clear shallow pan

Procedure:

This is a two-part experiment. In both, the oil represents the warm air mass and the water represents the cold air mass.

Experiment 1.

1. Fill one clear cup two-thirds full of water.
2. Slowly pour a small amount of oil into one of the cups.
3. Record your observations with words and/or pictures.

Experiment 2.

1. Fill the other clear cup two-thirds full of water.
2. Pour some oil into the pan and tilt the pan slightly so that the oil runs vertically down to the base of the pan.
3. Pour a small amount of water from the second cup onto the elevated side of the pan.
4. Record your observations with words and/or pictures.

Conclusions:

1. How do both experiments display what happens when air masses of different temperatures collide?

2. Of what practical use is this information?

Experiment B: What Happens When Two Air Masses Meet?

Materials:

2 beakers or jars	a thermometer
red food coloring	cold (refrigerated) water
hot water	red pencils or markers

Procedure:

1. Fill one beaker two-thirds full of cold (refrigerated) water. Measure and record the temperature of the water.
2. Fill the other beaker with hot tap water and add several drops of red food coloring. Measure and record the temperature of the water.
3. Gently pour the hot water down the side of the beaker containing the cold water.
4. Observe what happens when the cold and hot water meet. Sketch the results.
5. Measure and record the temperature of the water near the top of the beaker.
6. Put the thermometer deeper into the water and record the temperature near the bottom of the beaker.
7. Observe the beaker for 10 minutes.
8. At regular intervals, sketch a diagram of what is happening to the colored water.
9. After 10 minutes, measure the temperature at the top and bottom of the beaker again.

Conclusions:

1. Write a short paragraph summarizing the temperature readings and the action of the colored water.

2. How does this experiment relate to what happens when a cold air mass meets a warm air mass?

3. Of what use is this information?

SAMPLE 1.7—*(continued)*

Experiment C: How Do Fronts Form?

Materials:

a clear plastic shoebox   red and blue food coloring
red pencils or markers   a freezer bag
a clothespin   blue pencils or markers
ice   a straight pin
warm water

Procedure:

1. Fill the shoebox two-thirds full of warm water.
2. Put several ice cubes in the freezer bag and use the straight pin to punch three small holes in the bottom of the bag.
3. Place the bag at one end of the shoebox and use the clothespin to clip it to the side.
4. Add three drops of blue food coloring to the water directly in front of the bag.
5. Now add three drops of red food coloring to the water at the opposite end of the container.
6. Be sure to keep the container still so the food coloring can disperse naturally.
7. At regular intervals, draw a series of pictures illustrating how the colors moved through the water.

Conclusions:

1. Write a paragraph detailing what you observed.

2. What type of air mass is represented by the blue food coloring?

3. What type of air mass is represented by the red food coloring?

4. How does this experiment relate to what happens when cold and warm air masses meet? What do they form as a result?

5. Why is this information important?

SAMPLE 1.8—Hydrologic Cycle Note-Taking Sheet

Vocabulary To Know:

evaporation

transpiration

condensation

nuclei

nucleation

coalescence

precipitation

Important Information About the Hydrologic Cycle:

SAMPLE 1.9—Storm Presentation Rubric

Clearly described the characteristics of the storm.	20 points
Provided a detailed explanation of the causes of the storm.	30 points
Connected the causes of the storm to the effects experienced.	30 points
Highlighted how this storm affected or could affect the environment.	20 points
Displayed relevant visuals to enhance explanations and descriptions.	20 points
Included extra information to help the audience better understand the storm.	10 points
Presented information in a clear and appropriate manner.	20 points
Contributed to the success of the group.	30 points
Total	**180 points**

SAMPLE 1.10—Storm Presentations Note-Taking Template

Type of Storm	Characteristics	Causes	Effects	How It Relates to Me	Other Interesting Information

SAMPLE 1.11—Unit Review Sheet

Key Vocabulary:

air pressure	air currents
wind	humidity
barometer	thermometer
air mass	front (warm and cold)
forecasting	meteorologist
precipitation	evaporation
condensation	coalescence

Important Questions:

• How does air pressure affect weather conditions?

• Why does wind occur? Can we observe patterns with wind?

• What causes a front to form? What type of weather is the result of warm and cold fronts?

• What are the steps of the hydrologic cycle?

• What are the different types of clouds and how does each affect weather?

• What conditions lead to the different types of storms?

• How do we predict storms?

• What climate trends can we observe?

• How does the ocean affect weather and climate?

• What patterns do we see in our own weather and climate? What patterns can we see in global weather and climate?

It Changed Us All

A Social Studies Unit on the European Exploration and Colonization of America

Unit Developer: Caroline Cunningham Eidson

Introduction

This three- to four-week unit follows the study of Native Americans and precedes the study of the American colonies. It highlights the causes and effects of the exploration and colonization of America by Spain, France, and England during the 16th, 17th, and 18th centuries.

Although many facts are presented during the course of this unit, the unit really focuses on the concept of **movement**. In our highly mobile society, moving from one place to another is a concept that many children can relate to, and they can apply generalizations about movement to all types of geographical moves. Other concepts that relate to this unit and to the concept of **movement** are courage, freedom, change, cause and effect, influence, and culture.

The unit opens with a broad examination of the reasons why people move from one place to another and then examines the exploration and colonization of North America by the Spanish, the French, and the English, in that order. Map skills are addressed as students use maps to show the places being explored. And throughout the unit, students are encouraged to examine the lives of the explorers and colonists.

The texts used in this unit are *The First Americans* and *Making Thirteen Colonies* (both are in the *A History of Us* series by Joy Hakim, published by Oxford University Press) and *Why We Remember: United States History Through Reconstruction* by Herman Viola (published by Scott Foresman-Addison Wesley). Other texts that include similar information may certainly be substituted. (It would be a good idea to establish a "Colonial America" classroom library, as the students will have opportunities to pursue their own interests through independent research.) Text readings are supplemented with research, thoughtful discussions, and reliance on other information sources, such as primary source documents and the Internet.

Teacher Reflection on Designing the Unit

Growing up in Texas, I was almost constantly involved in some study of my state's history, including the various people who had explored and settled there. I recall visiting the German-influenced hill country in Central Texas, and the Greek festival in Houston was one of my family's favorite events. I also enjoyed school field trips to the old missions established by the Spanish, and I fell in love with Spanish architecture and Mexican art.

When I began working on this unit, I knew that I wanted to encourage students to open their eyes to the many cultures represented in our own "American" culture and to see the connection between these cultures and their own lives. I decided to focus on the concept of **movement** because I felt it would be one that many students could easily relate to. Because families are often required to move for financial and work-related reasons, many children find themselves uprooted from friends, neighborhoods, and schools—sometimes on a fairly regular basis. So I settled on the concept of movement as the driving force behind my unit and developed the big ideas about movement that related both to the history of the United States and to students' lives. Ultimately, I wanted my students to see geographical moves as both necessary and difficult, positive and negative. I also wanted them to understand that movement impacts both those who move and those who stay behind.

I looked to state standards as grounding for the unit and combined them into a broad look at the exploration and colonization of America. I knew that I wanted to use independent study in the unit as a way to touch on students' individual interests. I also knew that I wanted to incorporate a couple of strategies for differentiation (Complex Instruction and tiered lessons) that I've grown increasingly comfortable with over the past few years. I recognized that I had to provide for thoughtful discussions throughout the unit so that students would have many opportunities to relate both their lives and their new knowledge to the big idea of movement and its generalizations. Overall, I hoped this approach would help students to transform historical facts about exploration and colonization into a better understanding of the effects human beings can have on one another.

U.S. History Standards Addressed
- The student understands the causes and effects of European colonization in America and is expected to
  — Explain when, where, and why groups of people colonized and settled in America.
  — Describe the accomplishments of significant colonial leaders such as Anne Hutchinson, William Penn, John Smith, and Roger Williams.

- The student will trace the routes and evaluate early explorations of the Americas in terms of
  - — Motivations, obstacles, and accomplishments of sponsors and key expedition leaders from Spain, France, Portugal, and England.
  - — The political, economic, and social impact on the Native Americans.
  - — The economic, ideological, religious, and nationalistic forces that led to competition among European powers for control of North America.

Unit Concepts and Generalizations

Movement (main concept), Courage, Freedom, Change, Cause and Effect, Influence, Culture

- People move geographically for a variety of different reasons.
- Movement from one place to another often results in consequences that can be both positive and negative.
- When people move to a new place, they affect the nature of the new place.
- Movement from one place to another can involve hardships.
- Movement from one place to another can require courage on the part of those who are moving.

Unit Objectives

As a result of this unit, the students will *know*

- The names and accomplishments of key individuals in the exploration and colonization of America (including Juan Ponce de León, Hernando de Soto, Francisco Vasquez de Coronado, Giovanni da Verrazzano, Jacques Cartier, Samuel de Champlain, Sir Francis Drake, Sir Walter Raleigh, Anne Hutchinson, William Penn, John Smith, and Roger Williams).
- The names and locations of important places related to the exploration and colonization of America (including Spain, France, England, Cíbola, Florida, the American Southwest, the Mississippi River, the Northwest Passage, Canada, Roanoke Island ["The Lost Colony"], and Jamestown).
- Important events related to the exploration and colonization of America (de Soto lands in Florida, Verrazzano sails up the North American coast, English colonists land on Roanoke Island, the founding of Jamestown, the defeat of the Spanish Armada).

As a result of this unit, the students will *understand that*

- The explorers and colonists came to America for a variety of different reasons.
- The exploration of America was fueled largely by economic interests.

- The exploration and colonization of America affected the culture and life of Native Americans.
- Many explorers and colonists demonstrated great courage by coming to America.
- The explorers and colonists faced many hardships in America.
- The explorers and colonists came from different parts of Europe and settled in different parts of America.
- Certain individuals had a great influence on the development of the American colonies.

As a result of this unit, the students will *be able to*
- Explain and distinguish between the reasons why various individuals chose to come to America.
- Compare, contrast, and evaluate the impact that Spanish, French, and English explorers and colonists had on Native Americans.
- Compare their own lives to those of the European explorers and colonists.
- Identify important individuals in the exploration and colonization of America and describe their accomplishments.
- Describe the hardships that the explorers and colonists faced in America.
- Locate Spain, France, England, "The New World," and other places important and relevant to the exploration and colonization of America on maps and globes.
- Create maps using geographic information provided.
- Read for information.
- Draw conclusions after synthesizing information read or discussed.
- Plan and carry out independent research.
- Work cooperatively with partners and in groups to achieve common goals.

Instructional Strategies Used

- Complex Instruction
- Independent research
- Learning stations
- Reading buddies
- Tiered assessment
- Gardner's multiple intelligences
- Learning centers
- Pre-assessment
- Think–Pair–Share
- Tiered assignments

Sample Supporting Materials Provided

Unit Overview

LESSON	WHOLE-CLASS COMPONENTS	DIFFERENTIATED COMPONENTS
LESSON 1	Discussion introducing the unit and the unit concept of **movement** *15–20 minutes*	
	Examination and discussion of maps *10 minutes*	
Introduction	Pre-assessment *15 minutes*	
		Self-selected assignment based on multiple intelligences *30 minutes*
	Sharing of products *20 minutes*	
2 class periods	Introduction and preliminary work on independent project assignment *10 minutes*	Students select a research topic based on interest

LESSON	WHOLE-CLASS COMPONENTS	DIFFERENTIATED COMPONENTS
LESSON 2 **The Spanish Arrive and Decide to Stay** *2–3 class periods*	Review of background information (optional) *15–30 minutes*	
		Text assignment on Spanish colonization with reading buddies at a similar reading level *15 minutes* Independent learning center research/ independent project work (anchor activities)
	Discussion of Spanish colonization *10–20 minutes*	
		Complex Instruction activity based on learning profile and readiness *50–80 minutes*
		Assessment based on readiness *10–15 minutes*
	Reading homework *15 minutes*	
LESSON 3 **The French Have Their Turn** *2 class periods*	Discussion of reading homework *10 minutes*	
	Oral reading selection *15 minutes*	
		Self-selected individual assignment based on multiple intelligences *50 minutes*
		Partner-work based on readiness *10–15 minutes*
	Discussion of unit concepts and generalizations *10–15 minutes*	

LESSON	WHOLE-CLASS COMPONENTS	DIFFERENTIATED COMPONENTS
LESSON 4 **The English Jump on the Boat** *4 class periods*	Think–Pair–Share on the reasons for English colonization *20 minutes* Reading and discussion of primary source document *30 minutes*	 Learning station assignments based on reading proficiency *3 class periods*
LESSON 5 **Jamestown 1607** *2 class periods*	 Discussion of text *15 minutes* Discussion of related unit generalizations *15 minutes*	Text assignment on Jamestown with self-selected reading buddies *20 minutes* Small-group activity based on reading proficiency *50 minutes*
LESSON 6 **Important Individuals of the Time Period** *4–5 class periods*	Review of unit generalizations *10 minutes* Sharing of products *20–30 minutes* Journal entry *10 minutes*	Independent research on a key individual based on readiness (reading level and complex thinking skills) *3–4 class periods*
LESSON 7 **Putting It All Together** *2 class periods*	Review for unit assessment *1 class period*	Formal written (tiered) assessment focusing on unit concepts and generalizations *1 class period*

LESSON	WHOLE-CLASS COMPONENTS	DIFFERENTIATED COMPONENTS
LESSON 8 **Sharing What We Learned** *2–3 class periods*	Presentation of independent projects *2–3 class periods*	

Unit Description and Teacher Commentary

LESSON 1	**Introduction**	*(2 class periods)*

LESSON SEQUENCE AND DESCRIPTION	TEACHER COMMENTARY
Discussion introducing the unit and the unit concept of movement. Begin with a group discussion about moving from one place to another using the following types of questions: • Who has moved before? Why did you move? What are other reasons why people might need or want to move? • What were some good things about your move? What were some not-so-good things about it? Was it easy or hard? Why? • If you were planning to move, what would you look for in a new place? Introduce the study of the colonization of North America into the discussion of **movement**. Why might whole groups of people and families want to move at the same time and to the same place? Allow the students to discuss what they already know about the European exploration and colonization of North America and encourage them to ask questions.	Here, I set the stage for upcoming discussions and activities regarding the Europeans' move to North America by encouraging students to talk about the concept of **movement** and what motivates people to move. I wanted students to see the relationship between this concept and their own lives, and I knew that we would be addressing these ideas repeatedly in upcoming lessons. As the discussion continued, I listened for what students already knew about European exploration and colonization of North America. I did not want to teach what my students already knew. Nor did I want to overlook gaps in knowledge. I asked myself, "Do the students already know some facets of European colonization? As a group, do they seem to lack some important information?"

LESSON SEQUENCE AND DESCRIPTION	TEACHER COMMENTARY
Examination and discussion of maps. Distribute maps of the world and ask students to locate Europe and North America on maps and on a globe. Ask: What route do you think the explorers took? How might they have traveled? What do you think the trip might have been like?	I hoped that most students would already have an idea of where Europe is in relation to the United States. This activity served as a quick reminder and as a jumping-off point for discussing the long and difficult journey to the New World.
Pre-assessment. Students will respond in writing to the following question: "Why do you think the colonists wanted to come to America?" They may also illustrate their ideas.	Coupled with the information from the previous discussions, this more formal pre-assessment gave me an idea of students' varying degrees of understanding regarding the exploration and colonization of North America. I waited to give the pre-assessment until after we'd gotten into some discussion in order to give students a chance to remember things they might have forgotten. I hoped the opening discussions would jog their memories so they could tell me more of their prior knowledge on the pre-assessment.
Self-selected assignment based on multiple intelligences. Students will choose and complete one of the following activities: *Option 1: Spatial Intelligence* Think about the moves you have made in your own life. Create a map of your moves, using a key to show your favorite place among them. Which of the moves was the most difficult to complete? Why? Develop an original way to share this information with your classmates. *Option 2: Verbal/Linguistic Intelligence and Interpersonal Intelligence* Create an interview protocol about moving, and carry out an interview with a classmate. What are some important questions you should ask about moving? Be ready to explain why you chose to ask the questions that you did. *Option 3: Logical/Mathematical Intelligence* Create and conduct a moving survey. You might want to focus on how many times people have moved or the reasons why people have moved. What else can you focus on? Survey your classmates and create a graph to illustrate the results.	At this point, I wanted to give the students an opportunity to work with the unit concept, **movement**, in ways that would be comfortable and conducive to success. Thus, I allowed the students to choose an activity from a list of options based on Gardner's theory of multiple intelligences.

LESSON SEQUENCE AND DESCRIPTION	TEACHER COMMENTARY
Option 4: Visual/Spatial Intelligence and Verbal/Linguistic Intelligence Create a list of "moving hints." What should people know before they embark on a move? What are some helpful hints you might give them? Present your final product in the form of a pamphlet you can share with others.	
Sharing of products. Allow students to share their "moving products." Prompt students to speculate on the "big statements" (generalizations) we can make about moving. Lead them to the unit generalizations about **movement** and post these statements in the classroom.	The goal of this last portion of the lesson was threefold: 1) To give students an audience for their products; 2) to encourage students to synthesize the information they processed while completing their products; and 3) to help students develop the big ideas about **movement** emphasized throughout the unit. Posting these big ideas (or generalizations) for all to see helped to ensure that I revisited them in subsequent lessons.
Introduction and preliminary work on independent project assignment. Explain to students that they will be working on an independent project throughout the course of the unit. They will have time to work on their projects in class. Make sure students understand that you will be available to answer questions, provide guidance, and discuss project findings on an ongoing basis. At the end of the unit, each student will present a final product that will demonstrate what he or she has learned. Explain to students that their first task is to select a topic to research—it can be anything that they find interesting within the time period under investigation.	As with any open-ended project, organization is crucial to ensure the students' success. When I decided to incorporate independent projects into this unit, I was aware I might need to vary the amount of support that I would provide to particular students, as some would need more structure and support and others would need less. Because the process of creating the final product is as important (if not *more* important) than the actual product itself, I encouraged the students to do much of their research and product work in class and provided specific times for them to do so. This allowed me to observe the progress that students were making. Although students can often satisfy their interests through learning and interest centers, the independent project component, in which students explore a topic of their choice, is an important aspect of discovery and learning to learn.

LESSON SEQUENCE AND DESCRIPTION	TEACHER COMMENTARY
Have students begin brainstorming possible topics for their research. Stress that over the next few days, you will help them narrow down their topic selection and talk over their project plans.	As students first brainstormed and then honed their ideas, I met with them individually and helped some to rethink unreasonable or inappropriate project ideas.
When students have solidified their choice of topics (either after this lesson, or in the days to come) instruct each to complete the **Independent Project Learning Contract** (see Sample 2.1, page 87).	The student and the teacher should have a copy of the agreed-upon learning contract so that both parties understand project expectations. Because it is a good idea to give students a chance to evaluate their own work, I included a self-assessment component in the independent project. (See the **Independent Project Self-Evaluation Form**, Sample 2.2, page 88.) This piece further clarified what the students should do and how their final products should look.
Continue to set aside time for students to work on these ongoing independent projects throughout the unit and provide individual support and guidance as needed.	This project also served as an anchor activity that students could turn to when finished with individual or group work.

LESSON 2   **The Spanish Arrive and Decide to Stay**   *(2–3 class periods)*

LESSON SEQUENCE AND DESCRIPTION	TEACHER COMMENTARY
Review of background information. Provide the class with necessary background information on Spain's role in the New World, including that by the early 16th century, the Spanish had already established a foothold in Mexico and Peru. In their ongoing search for gold, they decided to look to the north. Spanish conquistadors Juan Ponce de León, Cabeza de Vaca, Hernando de Soto, and Francisco Vasquez de Coronado set out to explore the "borderlands" north of Mexico, an area we now know as the southern United States. As a result, Spain went on to claim more land in America than all the other European countries combined.	Depending on what students have already studied, it may be necessary to spend more time reviewing the conquistadors and their accomplishments and failures. However, not doing so provides opportunity for students to carry out independent research in this area if they are interested in doing so. I created a learning center/reading area (the "Spanish Conquistador Center") with related articles and other resources, and students used these resources to examine the lives and adventures of the conquistadors in greater detail.

LESSON SEQUENCE AND DESCRIPTION	TEACHER COMMENTARY
Text assignment on Spanish colonization with reading buddies at a similar reading level. Students will read "Settling the Borderlands," (pp. 104–106) and "The First Americans" (pp. 100–101) in the assigned text, or a comparable text passage addressing Spanish colonization and its effects on Native Americans. After they finish the reading, the reading buddies will discuss the questions at the end of the selection.	Here, I had students read and work with a classmate on the same reading level ("reading buddies"), and I worked with a small group of struggling readers to ensure that they understood the reading selection.
Independent learning center research/independent project work. When students finish their work, they should visit the Spanish Conquistador Center to get more information or work on their independent projects.	Throughout the unit, the Spanish Conquistador Center and students' independent projects (see Lesson 6) served as anchor activities—activities they could turn to when they finished other work. This allowed other students to finish their work and ensured that the students were continually engaged in meaningful, relevant activities.
Discussion of Spanish colonization. Students reassemble as a large group to discuss the following: Where did the Spanish set up colonies? Why did they choose these places? What impact did this colonization have on the Native Americans who were already living there?	During this discussion, I referenced the generalizations about **movement**. I wanted students to understand that people move for a variety of reasons and that moving has both positive and negative consequences. Specifically, I wanted students to be able to respond to the question "What were the consequences of Spanish colonization for Native Americans?" and to be able to demonstrate empathy with both the Spaniards and the Native Americans.
Complex Instruction activity based on learning profile and readiness. This activity allows students to examine the impact of the Spanish colonization in a variety of different ways. Students will work in small groups of four to six to complete tasks presented on task cards. They should understand that although everyone in the group is expected to help with the completion of all tasks, specific students will be responsible for leading work on specific tasks. They should also understand that all group members must be able to discuss each task at the completion of the activity.	At this point, students had already worked both alone and in pairs. Here, I wanted them to work in small groups. I chose to use the strategy Complex Instruction because it allows for a variety of academic strengths to be addressed while ensuring that all group members are contributing to the final products.

LESSON SEQUENCE AND DESCRIPTION	TEACHER COMMENTARY
Task Card #1 Examine maps of the United States and identify names of cities that are derived from the Spanish language. How many can you find and what states are they in? Are you surprised? Why or why not? *Task Card #2* Through brainstorming and research, identify examples of Spanish heritage in our culture. Create a collage that highlights Spanish influences. It may be helpful to think about the features that make up a culture. *Task Card #3* Research an American city that reflects a great deal of Spanish culture and create a travel brochure for that city that could be used by a person seeking to learn more about Spanish culture. *Task Card #4* The Spanish had an immediate impact on the Native Americans of the Southwest. Think about this impact and write obituaries for a conquistador from both a Spanish and a Native American point of view. *Task Card #5* Create a monologue that illustrates changes in the Native American way of life during the time of Spanish colonization. *Task Card #6* Create a comprehensive chart that shows both the positive and negative consequences of Spanish colonization. Your work should reflect what you have come to understand about Spanish colonization. Once groups have had a few minutes to familiarize themselves with their tasks, meet with each group to discuss the group's plans and expectations for success.	I designed these particular tasks with a variety of abilities in mind: • Spatial ability • Fluency of thought • Creative thinking and production • Reading and researching skill • Logical thinking • Interpersonal skill • Writing ability My role here was to make sure that each student in each group had a leadership role with regard to at least one of the tasks (for example, who was the primary person for Task Card #2?)

LESSON SEQUENCE AND DESCRIPTION	TEACHER COMMENTARY
Groups should maintain work logs that show what they intend to accomplish, what they actually do accomplish during work times, and who is responsible for working on which portions of the tasks. See the **Complex Instruction Work Log** (Sample 2.3, page 89) for a template.	With regard to the work logs, I asked the groups to indicate on their logs who was working on each task and how the group would know when the task had been successfully completed. At the end of each work session, group members met to discuss what they had completed and what still needed to be done.
When all groups have completed their tasks, the whole class should gather to listen to the deliveries of the monologues (Task Card #5). The other products should be displayed around the room, and time should be provided for the students to examine and discuss one another's work.	This part of the lesson gave the groups an opportunity to share their products with one another and to learn from one another.

Assessment based on readiness. Students will write in response to one of the following differentiated journal prompts:

Prompt A
Imagine that you are a newspaper editor in Spain at the time of the Spanish colonization of America. Write a brief editorial about the colonization. What are your opinions of it? Why?

Prompt B
Imagine that you are a member of a committee responsible for determining the extent to which Native American tribes should be compensated for their treatment during Spanish colonization. Prepare a short statement about the nature of the colonization and its effect on the Native Americans that encompasses both sides of the story. What will your recommendation to the committee be?

Here, I wanted to give students a chance to show me what they had come to understand about Spanish exploration and influence. However, I knew that the students operated on different levels of complexity and that I could not give them all the same assessment. Both these journal entries require students to synthesize information from this lesson, and I found that responses to both prompts gave me insight into which students understood the causes and consequences of Spanish colonization and which did not. However, notice that Prompt A calls for a less complex response than Prompt B, in that it does not ask the student to consider both sides of the story of Spanish colonization. I assigned each student either Prompt A or Prompt B, based on the student's previous study of Spanish colonization and on my observations of his or her ability to synthesize information.

LESSON SEQUENCE AND DESCRIPTION	TEACHER COMMENTARY
Reading homework. Have the students read pp. 124–129 in *The First Americans* ("From Spain to England to France" and "France in America: Pirates and Adventurers") or a similar selection that introduces the French and English colonization of what would become the United States.	This reading assignment gave students an idea of what was going on back in Europe at this time and explained England's interest in America. It served as a good lead-in to our next activities. I chose to assign it for homework, but it could also serve as quiet and independent class work.

LESSON 3   **The French Have Their Turn**   *(2 class periods)*

LESSON SEQUENCE AND DESCRIPTION	TEACHER COMMENTARY
Discussion of reading homework. Begin this lesson with a discussion to make sure students understand what they read for homework. Questions might include • Why did the English call Queen Mary "Bloody Mary"? • Who became queen of England after Mary? • What was Verrazzano looking for and why? • Why did the French decide to go to Florida? • Who were the Huguenots?	Throughout this unit, it was important to keep track of which students were recalling and understanding the material. I used this discussion as a means of informal assessment and kept a clipboard nearby with a list of the students' names so that I could take quick notes regarding their grasp of the material. The questions I asked served primarily as a review of their homework and as an introduction to this lesson.
Oral reading selection. Discuss why the French initially came to the Americas (to find gold and the Northwest Passage). As a group, read about and discuss New France (use pp. 108–110 in the Viola text or a similar selection).	Here, I wanted to ensure that students understood the motivations behind the French exploration of North America.
Self-selected individual assignment based on multiple intelligences. Following the reading and discussion, the students will choose to complete one of three activities. These activities address the hardships that the French explorers faced and are based on Gardner's theory of multiple intelligences.	My goal for this differentiated activity was to help students develop an understanding of what exploration might have been like for the French explorers. I allowed students to choose which task to complete so that they could "put their best foot forward." As with an earlier activity (see Lesson 1), I based the students' options on multiple intelligences so that students could opt to work in ways most effective for them.

LESSON SEQUENCE AND DESCRIPTION	TEACHER COMMENTARY
Option 1: Spatial Intelligence and Mathematical/Logical Intelligence Using the resources available in the classroom and the blank maps provided, map the routes taken by the following French explorers: Giovanni da Verrazzano, Jacques Cartier, Samuel de Champlain, and Robert La Salle. Based on topography, distance, and obstacles along the way, who do you think took the best route? Why? Find and map a better route for each explorer on another blank map. Be sure your product shows evidence that you understand the hardships that the French explorers faced in America.	Before students began their work, I distributed the **Product Evaluation Rubrics** (see Sample 2.4, page 90), which shared the criteria I would be using to evaluate each activity's product. At that time, I also stressed that all products should show evidence of an understanding of the hardships that the French explorers faced in America. Specific evaluation criteria for Option 1's product included consideration of multiple criteria, evaluative thinking, insightfulness, accuracy of mapping, and neatness.
Option 2: Verbal/Linguistic Intelligence Read *The First Americans*, page 136 (or a similar selection). Imagine that you are Louis Joliet making your way along the Mississippi River. Create a travel log of your adventures. Include at least four entries, and be sure to discuss why you decided to turn back. What did you think about the journey? What was going through your mind when you realized that your trip was a failure? What might you have done differently? Be sure your product shows evidence that you understand the hardships that Joliet faced in America.	Evaluation criteria for this product included insightfulness, imagination, factual understanding, range and depth of entries, and clarity.
Option 3: Spatial Intelligence Choose one of the French explorers (Giovanni da Verrazzano, Jacques Cartier, Samuel de Champlain, Robert La Salle, or Louis Joliet) and create a scrapbook of his travels. Be sure your scrapbook demonstrates both high and low points along the journey from your explorer's point of view and shows evidence that you understand the hardships that the French explorers faced in America.	This activity is much like Option 2 in its focus; however, students who chose Option 3 selected which French explorer to focus on and illustrated his frame of mind through images rather than words. Evaluation criteria for this product included insightfulness, imagination, factual understanding, appropriate and meaningful use of images, and neatness.
When students have completed their products, allow them to share with their classmates one thing that they learned about the French exploration. To avoid repetition of ideas, have students write two to three ideas down on index cards before any ideas are shared with the class. They should only share an idea that others have not already shared.	

LESSON SEQUENCE AND DESCRIPTION	TEACHER COMMENTARY
Partner-work based on readiness. Using the resources provided in the classroom, students will work with partners to compare and contrast the Spanish and French relationships with the Native Americans. Whose treatment showed greater fairness to Native Americans? Why? Students should devise a way to show their ideas in a visual manner (such as a Venn diagram or a compare-and-contrast chart). Display students' work in the classroom.	I wanted students to work in pairs during this portion of the lesson because two heads are often better than one. I partnered students who had similar degrees of content knowledge and abstract thinking ability because I wanted to be sure they collaborated on the task. In addition, students had just completed individual products, and many wanted the chance to work with someone else.

This activity required students to recall information about the Spanish treatment of the Native Americans and apply their understanding of that information as they compared it to the French treatment of the Native Americans. I gave pairs who needed extra support a blank **Graphic Organizer** (see Sample 2.5, page 93) instead of requiring them to come up with their own ways to show their ideas. |
| **Discussion of unit concepts and generalizations.** As closure for this portion of the unit, lead a whole-class discussion about the Spanish and French colonization as they relate to the unit's generalizations. For example, what can we say about the reasons the French and Spanish came to the New World? How did their reasons differ? What positive and negative consequences did their explorations and colonization have for those involved? Make sure that students can relate the generalizations concerning **movement** to the Spanish and the French. | As during earlier discussions, I repeated the big statements about **movement** that I wanted the students to understand, and I took notes on their grasp of these generalizations as they relate to Spanish and French exploration and colonization. The questions I asked here were designed to bring closure to the activities the students had just completed and encourage them to relate new knowledge and understanding to what they had learned in the unit's previous lessons. |

LESSON 4	The English Jump on the Boat	*(4 class periods)*

LESSON SEQUENCE AND DESCRIPTION	TEACHER COMMENTARY
Think–Pair–Share on the reasons for English colonization. Begin this lesson with a Think–Pair–Share that generates hypotheses on the motives behind English movement to the Americas.	This discussion sparked connections between what students already knew and what they did not yet know. I like to use Think–Pair–Share to begin

LESSON SEQUENCE AND DESCRIPTION	TEACHER COMMENTARY
Ask students to respond to this question: Based on what we already know about the Spanish and the French, why do you think the English decided to come to America? Students first think quietly about their answer, then share their thoughts with a partner. Finally, some students share their response or their partner's response with the whole class.	discussions like this one because it encourages greater thought among the students (again, two heads are better than one!) and because it gives reluctant speakers a chance to share in a "safer" way (not in front of the entire class if they're not comfortable doing so). Think–Pair–Share allows students to choose a partner with whom they are comfortable, or if they wish, just to work with someone nearby.
Reading and discussion of primary source document. Distribute copies of Hakluyt's "Reasons for Raising a Fund to Settle America" (one of many relevant primary source documents available online through sources such as historyteacher.net). Explain that this is a primary source document—a document created during the time period students are studying. As a large group, read and decipher (decode) the document with the following questions in mind: Why did Richard Hakluyt believe that England should colonize America? What reasons does he state? Do you think that most English people agreed with his position? Why or why not? Would you have been convinced by his arguments? Why or why not?	This particular activity served several key purposes: • It introduced students to the reasons that England decided to try its luck in America. • It exposed students to a primary source document and gave them an opportunity to learn from a primary source. • It exposed students to the English language of the period being studied and gave them practice reading it. Many students needed to use this "deciphering" skill later in the unit.
Learning station assignments based on reading proficiency. Once students have completed the primary source activity, introduce them to the learning stations set up in the classroom. Each station addresses (and provides different readings on) one of the four following topics: • The Lost Colony • Queen Elizabeth I • Sir Francis Drake and the Sea Dogs • The Spanish Armada	I like to use learning stations to make efficient use of time and to encourage students to be more responsible for their own learning (a must in a differentiated classroom). These stations were very simple in design and organization and were intended to give students a broad range of background information concerning England's early colonization of America in a relatively quick and flexible manner.

LESSON SEQUENCE AND DESCRIPTION	TEACHER COMMENTARY
Students are to visit each of the stations, where they will select one reading (thus, they will read a total of four selections—one on each topic). Afterward, they will synthesize the information in the four readings to create one of the following products: • A newspaper article or journal entry from the time period • A comic strip • A time line • A graphic organizer Products should incorporate information from *each* of the four stations and should be displayed around the classroom. Allow time at the end of this activity for students to look at and discuss each other's work.	Readings in the stations covered a range of reading levels from text and other sources so that weak readers would not be overwhelmed and advanced readers would not be bored. Although it took a while to collect the reading materials, I knew that I would reuse them whenever I taught this particular unit. Among the resources I used were • *Sir Francis Drake and the Struggle for an Ocean Empire* by Alice Smith Duncan (advanced readers) • *Sir Francis Drake: His Daring Deeds* by Roy Gerrard (struggling readers) • *Elizabeth I* by Alan Kendall (advanced readers) • *Queen Elizabeth I* by Robert Green (grade-level readers) • *Good Queen Bess: The Story of Elizabeth I of England* by Diane Stanley and Peter Vennema (grade-level text, but in a picture book format). It was necessary in some cases to steer students to reading selections that were most appropriate for them. In addition, I found that these readings served to encourage deep interest in some of the topics and inspired some students to purse these topics independently. Concerning the products, I required that they demonstrate the student's grasp of both the information presented in each of the four stations *and* each topic's overall relationship to English colonization. For example: How was The Lost Colony representative of English colonization? What was Drake's role in the colonization?

| LESSON 5 | Jamestown 1607 | *(2 class periods)* |

LESSON SEQUENCE AND DESCRIPTION	TEACHER COMMENTARY

Text assignment on Jamestown with self-selected reading buddies. As an introduction to this lesson, students will read pp. 25–28 in *Making Thirteen Colonies* ("English Settlers Come to Stay") with reading buddies. This reading concerns the arrival of three English ships at the Chesapeake Bay and describes the founding of Jamestown, the first successful English settlement in America. You may substitute a similar selection from another text.

This introductory reading gave students information on the Jamestown settlement and the difficulties settlers encountered there.

Discussion of text. Following the reading, pose the following kinds of questions to the whole class: What were the English really looking for and why? Where did they ultimately choose to settle? Was Jamestown a good choice? Why or why not? What were the settlers like? Who ultimately became their first effective leader?

As with earlier large-group discussions, it was important to assess students' understanding during this discussion, and I did so by listening to and taking notes on their individual responses. The questions I asked were designed to ensure that students understood what they had read. The questions also served as a lead-in to the next activity.

Small-group activity based on reading proficiency. When the discussion is complete, assign students to groups of four, where they will examine instructions given to the Jamestown colonists by the Virginia Company of London.

Give groups of less advanced readers a paraphrased copy of the instructions. Give groups of more advanced readers the primary source copy.

Groups at *both* levels complete the following tasks:

1. Restate in a list the instructions given to the colonists.
2. Illustrate the type of place the colonists were instructed to settle.
3. Write job descriptions for the tasks to be assigned to the colonists.
4. Write an argument for why these particular instructions were the ones given to the colonists.
5. Fill in the gaps: What instructions were not provided that might have been helpful to the Jamestown colonists? Write them for the colonists.

As I looked back at the previous activities, I realized that students had been working on the same tasks and in the same ways for a while. Thus, it was time for a differentiated set of tasks, and here I decided to differentiate the materials that the students would be using. My objective in this portion of the lesson was to give all of the students the opportunity to work with interpreting and analyzing the same information. So I provided the information (the instructions to the Jamestown colonists) in a differentiated manner and grouped students based on reading proficiency.

LESSON SEQUENCE AND DESCRIPTION	TEACHER COMMENTARY
	I didn't differentiate the way in which the students would work with the reading material. Rather, I gave students a product assignment that required them to *comprehend, apply,* and *evaluate* the instructions given to the Jamestown colonists. I asked more advanced students to apply the deciphering skills they practiced during Lesson 4. When evaluating the groups' products, I sought evidence that students understood both the instructions and their impact on the colonists. How did the instructions relate to the success of Jamestown as a new settlement?
Discussion of related unit generalizations. Following the completion of the differentiated activity, assemble the class as a large group and discuss the generalizations concerning **movement** as they pertain to the English colonists. For instance, why did they move as a group and as individuals? What were the hardships that they faced? In what ways did they demonstrate courage?	As with previous discussions, the idea here was to provide closure for the activity and to ensure that students understood the unit generalizations and could apply them to information they were exploring and learning.

LESSON 6   **Important Individuals of the Time Period**   *(4–5 class periods)*

LESSON SEQUENCE AND DESCRIPTION	TEACHER COMMENTARY
Review of unit generalizations. Begin this lesson by reviewing once more the generalizations about **movement**. Explain to students that they are going to apply some of these generalizations to individuals who lived during the time of the European exploration and colonization of North America . . . and that they will be doing so independently.	Again, it was important to ensure that students understood the big ideas presented in this unit.
Independent research on a key individual based on readiness (reading level and complex thinking skills). Students will choose a research subject from the following list (add to the list as appropriate): • William Bradford • George Calvert • Mary Dyer • Thomas Hooker • Anne Hutchinson • William Penn • John Smith • Roger Williams • Edward Winslow • John Winthrop	This assignment gave students the chance to relate the unit's big ideas to the lives of individuals who influenced events during this time period.

LESSON SEQUENCE AND DESCRIPTION	TEACHER COMMENTARY

Students will research one of the listed individuals and complete three common tasks and one differentiated task. To give students further direction and extra motivation, tell them that they will be putting their research to use with partners or in groups later in this lesson.

Research sources should include a variety of books and reference materials provided in the classroom, including the Internet and appropriate computer software. Presenting limited background information about each of the people on the list will help students choose whom they want to research further.

Common Tasks
1. Create a time line, enhanced with either words or illustrations, of the individual's life.
2. Create a graphic organizer that provides the following information about the individual: reasons for coming to America, hardships faced, significant acts of courage, and contributions to the colonization of America.
3. Create a "wanted" poster that might have been distributed by the individual's opposition.

Differentiated Tasks
Each student will complete *one* of the following tasks (as assigned):

Task A
With a partner and using your research, develop a list of characteristics about the individuals who influenced the colonization of America. How would you describe these people? Next, think about some famous people today. What hardships have they had to overcome, and what acts of courage have they demonstrated? Create a list of people from current times who you think resemble those you have studied from the past. Be ready to defend your choices.

I provided grade level, below grade level, and above grade level reading material about the individuals to be researched in order to accommodate a range of reading abilities (again, this was a lot of work at the beginning but the payoff was that the students were able to work independently and at their own levels). I put the reading selections in colored folders according to reading level and assigned each student the appropriate color in which to find materials on their research subject. In this way, I made sure advanced readers were not deliberately choosing material that was too easy for them.

I decided that I wanted students to look for and use much of the same types of information about their historical figures. Thus, I required all students to complete these three tasks. I found that some students needed a blank **Graphic Organizer** (see Sample 2.6, page 94) provided for them so they could successfully complete the second task. I chose a graphic organizer in chart form, although a web would have been equally appropriate.

I assigned students to one of these tasks based on their readiness to analyze and evaluate information and to think critically. Although both tasks were high-level and engaging and both required students to create justifications for their choices and use the available information to defend their choices before their classmates, the second task asked students to think more deeply about the concept of courage. In addition, it required the students to work together to solve a problem. I have found that some of my more advanced students often need opportunities to practice working with others at their ability level.

LESSON SEQUENCE AND DESCRIPTION	TEACHER COMMENTARY
Task B Working in groups of three or four and using your research, assume you are a member of a committee assigned the task of awarding a medal for courage to only one of the people the members of your group have researched. What factors should you consider in awarding this honor? What questions must be considered? List them, and then use them to select the award recipient. Be ready to defend your choice.	
Sharing of products. The small groups will share their products with the rest of the class. After the presentations, ask the class questions such as these: Based on our research, what can we say about the individuals who impacted the colonization of America? How do the choices they made and the lives they lived reflect our generalizations about **movement**?	As with earlier lessons, I recognized the fact that my students stand to learn as much from one another as from me, and I wanted them to hear the different ideas their classmates had developed.
Journal entry. Provide closure for the lesson by asking students to respond in their journals to this prompt: How are you similar to and different from the individual you researched today? In what way(s) would you like to be more like that person? What specific things can you do to become more like that person?	The objective of this journal assignment was to encourage students to relate what they had learned to their own lives and to see themselves as courageous or capable of courageous acts. This was an affective goal on my part.

LESSON 7   **Putting It All Together**   *(2 class periods)*

LESSON SEQUENCE AND DESCRIPTION	TEACHER COMMENTARY
Review for unit assessment. Hold a class review session during which the students will review and take notes on the information that they have studied during the unit. Ask students to look back through their work and reexamine the products displayed around the classroom. They should focus on the following questions: • Why did the Spanish, French, and English want to explore and colonize America? What were their goals? • What obstacles and hardships did they face, and what influences did they have on the people who were already here? • How can we characterize the explorers and colonists, and who were some significant figures during this time period? During the review session, students should take notes to help themselves prepare for the unit assessment to follow.	Because the students were required to know the information I reviewed during this lesson, I found it necessary to provide guidance for those I knew would have difficulty taking notes. The **Unit Review Note-Taking Template** (see Sample 2.7, page 95) provided major headings such as "Reasons for Exploration" and "Courageous People" that students could use to help them focus on relevant information. This scaffolding helped to ensure that they would be successful both with this activity and with the final unit assessment.

LESSON SEQUENCE AND DESCRIPTION	TEACHER COMMENTARY
Formal written (tiered) assessment focusing on unit concepts and generalizations. This assessment is provided on two different levels to accommodate learning differences among students.	After providing a series of differentiated activities during the course of our study, it just didn't make sense to give all students the same assessment. Thus, I differentiated this as well.
Level 1 Assessment Given each of the unit generalizations concerning **movement**, provide at least three examples from the time period studied to support each of the generalizations. Examples must be detailed and directly related to the generalizations that they support. You may present them in the form of a list or other graphic representation.	The Level 1 Assessment was differentiated to place less emphasis on writing ability and greater emphasis on the *breadth* of the student's understanding.
Level 2 Assessment Choose two of the generalizations concerning **movement** and write about how the events and people in the time period studied support that generalization *and* the ways in which the generalizations are related. Be sure to provide appropriate justification for the generalizations you discuss. Responses must be written in essay form and must be detailed and insightful.	The Level 2 Assessment was differentiated to place greater emphasis on writing ability and greater emphasis on the *depth* of the student's understanding. I kept student learning differences in mind when I evaluated their responses to the assessment questions.

LESSON 8　　　　　**Sharing What We Learned**　　　　　*(2–3 class periods)*

Presentation of independent projects. Have each student share the product of his or her independent learning project with classmates. After each presentation, ask students questions to help them link what was presented to the unit concepts and generalizations. Evaluate students' products based on the agreed-upon criteria set out in the learning contracts.	Independent projects offer students the opportunity to express their interests and learning styles. Some students needed more support than others in designing and in carrying out their research, but all enjoyed the chance to share what they had learned. The self-assessment aspect of this project was particularly rewarding. Students were able to reflect on what they learned about doing research as well as what they learned about themselves during this process. This connection of cognitive and affective education is so important to learners of all ages.

Teacher Reflection on the Unit

There are a couple of things that I particularly like about teaching this unit. First, my students can relate to the concept of movement. By looking at movement conceptually, they begin to see that they can also relate in some ways to the experiences of the American explorers and colonists. It's not always easy to get students to see how history might relate to them, and this unit invites them to see how their lives might be similar in some ways to the lives of those who came before. My students enjoy seeing that connection. And, for me, it makes teaching history that much easier.

Second, I like the variety of instructional strategies in this unit. When teaching history, it's easy to get bogged down in textbook facts. This unit feels a bit more alive to me because the students are engaged in so many different types of activities. Each activity is different from the next, and the texts are part of a collection of resources rather than the primary sources for information. Teaching this way invites my own creativity and challenges me to find ways to make learning irresistible for my students. When I can get excited about a unit because creating it caused me to think out of the box, I can be assured that my students will also be excited about the unit. This was an engaging unit for both my students and me.

Caroline Cunningham Eidson has taught in North Carolina and Virginia. She can be reached at ceidson@nc.rr.com.

SAMPLE 2.1—Independent Project Learning Contract

Please spend time thinking about what you want to research before you sign this contract. This contract binds you to the project that you choose, so be sure that you have chosen something that interests you strongly.

Today's Date: _____

Student's Name: _____

Topic of Interest: _____

Project Product: _____

Presentation Format: _____

Steps to Take to Complete Product (what you need to do in order to produce an exceptional product):

Criteria for Evaluation (the qualities that will make your product exceptional):

Project Due Date: _____

I agree to stay on task while working on this project and to put forth my best effort toward completing it successfully.

Student's Signature _____ Date _____

I agree to offer help and feedback throughout the completion of this project.

Teacher's Signature _____ Date _____

SAMPLE 2.2—Independent Project Self-Evaluation Form

Name: _____

Topic: _____

Date: _____

Met all student-created criteria (5 points)   _____

Well-organized, interesting format (20 points)   _____

Used time wisely in class (15 points)   _____

Presentation (10 points)   _____

Completed on time (5 points)   _____

Total   _____

What new information have you learned from completing this project? Think about what you have learned about your topic *and* what you have learned about yourself.

What skills did you have to use to complete this project?

SAMPLE 2.3—Complex Instruction Work Log

Date	Day's Goal(s)	Person(s) Responsible	Actual Progress	Next Step(s)

SAMPLE 2.4—Product Evaluation Rubrics

The French Explorers: Rubric for Option 1's Product

Criteria for Success	3 = Excellent	2 = Satisfactory	1 = Poor
CONSIDERATION OF MULTIPLE CRITERIA topography of land, distance, obstacles, climate	Product includes detailed attention to many different criteria in the evaluation of the routes taken and in the creation of an original route.	Product includes some attention to different criteria regarding the routes taken, and only a few criteria are applied to a new possible route.	Product includes limited attention to the different criteria that might have been influential in the choices of routes OR includes irrelevant criteria.
INSIGHTFULNESS original ideas, depth and breadth of thought	Presents a logical, detailed, and well-thought-out approach to analyzing and creating routes. Many possibilities are considered.	Presents a clear approach to analyzing and creating routes, but does not exhibit "new" thinking. Limited possibilities are considered.	Ideas lack logic, thought, and originality. Limited possibilities are considered.
ACCURACY OF MAPPING ability to read and interpret necessary maps and to locate places on them	Very accurate and detailed.	Somewhat accurate but lacking detail.	Lacking in both accuracy and detail.
NEATNESS ability to show various routes on one map, clean product	Product reflects organization. Colors are used appropriately to distinguish between routes. Product is easy to read.	Product is somewhat sloppy, making it difficult to read some places and discern some routes. Color is used but is somewhat confusing.	Product is extremely sloppy, making it impossible to distinguish various routes. Color is not used.

Teacher's Comments:

SAMPLE 2.4—*(continued)*

The French Explorers: Rubric for Option 2's Product

Criteria for Success	3 = Excellent	2 = Satisfactory	1 = Poor
INSIGHTFULNESS original ideas, depth and breadth of thought	Thoughtful and original ideas are explored in detail. New theories are presented.	Thoughtful and original ideas are expressed, but other ideas seem "recycled."	Ideas are limited to ones that have been posed earlier and product does not provide any new theories.
IMAGINATION fluency and elaboration of ideas	Product displays detailed attention to a variety of possibilities and perspectives.	Product displays attention to detail, although ideas are limited in terms of creativity.	Little imagination or creativity is expressed. Few ideas are explored.
FACTUAL UNDERSTANDING accuracy in terms of time period and geography	Ideas are supported by facts and are clearly based on the reality of the time and place.	Key ideas are reality-based, but lesser ideas are not supported by the facts of the time and place.	Ideas are not related to the reality of the time and place.
RANGE AND DEPTH OF ENTRIES amount and types of information included	Product includes at least 5 entries that address a wide variety of details and a range of information. Each entry incorporates different information.	Product includes 3–4 entries that present an adequate scope of information. Entries display a variety of information.	Product includes fewer than 3 entries, and the entries present a limited scope of information.
CLARITY expression of ideas	Ideas are expressed clearly and eloquently.	Ideas are expressed directly but without attention to style.	Ideas are not expressed clearly, causing confusion for the reader.

Teacher's Comments:

The French Explorers: Rubric for Option 3's Product

Criteria for Success	3 = Excellent	2 = Satisfactory	1 = Poor
INSIGHTFULNESS original ideas, depth and breadth of thought	Thoughtful and original ideas are explored in detail. New theories are presented.	Thoughtful and original ideas are expressed, but other ideas seem "recycled."	Ideas are limited to ones that have been posed earlier and product does not provide any new theories.
IMAGINATION fluency and elaboration of ideas	Product displays detailed attention to a variety of possibilities and perspectives.	Product displays attention to detail; however, ideas are limited in terms of creativity.	Little imagination or creativity is expressed in product. Few ideas are explored.
FACTUAL UNDERSTANDING accuracy in terms of time period and geography	Ideas are supported by facts and are clearly based on the reality of the time and place.	Key ideas are reality-based, but lesser ideas are not supported by the facts of the time and place.	Ideas are not related to the reality of the time and place.
APPROPRIATE AND MEANINGFUL USE OF IMAGES effectiveness at conveying meaning	Images communicate ideas clearly and effectively and demonstrate careful thought and planning.	Images seem disconnected and do not clearly express ideas. Limited thought and planning demonstrated.	Images are confusing to viewer and do not adequately convey meaning or understanding. Thought and planning not evident.
NEATNESS production and organization of images	Product is clean and well-organized. Images are placed neatly.	Product is somewhat clean but lacks organization. Images are placed in a careless manner.	Product is sloppy and does not reflect care in production. Looks as if it were completed at the last minute.

Teacher's Comments:

SAMPLE 2.5—Graphic Organizer

Spanish and French Relationships with the Native Americans

Spanish

French

SAMPLE 2.6—Graphic Organizer

Important Individuals of the Time Period

Important Individual: _____

Reasons for Coming to America	Hardships Faced During Exploration and/or Colonization	Significant Acts of Courage During Exploration and/or Colonization	Major Contributions to the Colonization of America

SAMPLE 2.7—Unit Review Note-Taking Template

Reasons for the Exploration and Colonization of America

Spanish	French	English

Consequences of Exploration and Colonization

Positive	Negative

Hardships Faced by the Explorers and Colonists

Courageous People/Acts

3

What Makes a Region?

A Social Studies Unit on Regional Characteristics and Variance

Unit Developer: Holly C. Gould

Introduction

This three- to four-week unit helps students develop an understanding of how the regions of the United States are defined and what makes each region unique. Unit activities culminate in an independent project requiring students to apply what they have come to understand about the field of geography and the uniqueness of each U.S. region. Activities ongoing throughout the unit include a process log used for accountability and evaluation and a study of current events in different regions.

Prerequisite skills for this unit include 1) experience using print resources, books, and the Internet to conduct research; 2) ability to read for main ideas and information; 3) ability to summarize ideas in complete sentences; 4) expository writing skills; 5) experience using primary and secondary sources; and 6) experience creating PowerPoint, ClarisWorks, or Hyperstudio presentations. In addition, students working on this unit should have studied the history of their own city or town.

The unit opens with a review of basic map skills and terminology and then examines the concept of **region.** The primary question for students to consider is, "What makes a region a region?" Following this portion of the unit, the students explore the causes of changes within regions by examining the history of their own city or town. Finally, the students begin their independent projects, in which they are asked to think and behave as geographers do. The product-based approach allows all students to make sense of and apply key information, concepts, and understandings, which will serve them well throughout the year (and beyond). During the time students spend researching and working on their products, the teacher can meet with individuals and small groups to reteach, reinforce, or extend specific understandings and skills. The product-based approach also enables the teacher to help students with their independent learning skills.

Teacher Reflection on Designing the Unit

I needed to develop a unit about the regions of the United States. After examining my social studies textbook, I decided that it emphasized many facts, but offered little that would help my students develop a deep understanding of regions and regional differences. It also seemed that the textbook offered surface-level knowledge that my students would be unlikely to remember for long. Thus, I began a search for good, sound curriculum that I could first defend and then differentiate.

To move beyond the text, I sought guidance from my state standards for geography and the National Curriculum Standards for Social Studies. I decided to address a few essential objectives as thoroughly as possible by encouraging my students to think and behave as geographers do. After examining the standards, I looked back to the textbook to determine what it highlighted, and I asked myself, "What is really important for my students to know and understand about geographical regions?" I decided it was essential they understand that the United States includes a variety of regions, each differing in ways both natural and human-made. Other important ideas flowed from that central understanding. By using the textbook as a resource rather than as the centerpiece of the social studies curriculum, I was able to look more deeply at the field of geography and at the importance of geographical regions. Examining several textbooks on world geography helped me gain a better grasp of what a geographer needs to know, understand, and be able to do in the context of real-world applications. It also helped me determine the vocabulary that would add to my students' understanding of geography.

At this point, I was working on developing sound and high-quality curriculum, but in the back of my mind, I was already starting to match my plans to learner needs. How would I differentiate this unit to help all my students achieve the greatest possible gains in understanding and skill? Still, I knew that spending time developing a meaningful and engaging unit was my first role. Not only is it easier to differentiate instruction when a solid unit is in place, but the resulting differentiation is far more likely to have the intended goal of maximizing student learning.

Geography and Social Studies Standards Addressed

- Use maps and other geographic representations, tools, and technologies to acquire, process, and report information.
- Understand that people create regions to interpret the world's complexity.

- Understand how culture and experience influence our perception of places and regions.
- Understand the processes, patterns, and functions of human settlement.
- Understand how human actions modify the physical environment.
- Understand how physical systems affect human systems.
- Understand the changes that occur in the meaning, use, distribution, and importance of resources over time.

Unit Concepts and Generalizations

Region, Interaction, Variation

- Geographic regions are divided by variations in landforms, climate, and natural resources.
- Regions vary with regard to development of natural resources, art, architecture, literature, customs, religion, economics, and transportation.
- The characteristics of a region can change.
- People interact with their physical environment.
- People's interactions with their physical environment affect cultural and economic development.

Unit Objectives

As a result of this unit, the students will *know*

- Specific vocabulary terms, including *globe, map, atlas, latitude, longitude, equator, Prime Meridian, distortion, legend, key, relief, contour line, compass rose, cardinal directions, map scale, political units, plain, plateau, mountain, hill, elevation, erosion, natural resources,* and *economics.*
- Basic map skills, including how to find absolute location using latitude and longitude, how to use cardinal directions, and how to identify places using a legend or key.

As a result of this unit, the students will *understand that*

- The United States is made up of regions that are unique and that vary in both naturally occurring and human-made ways.
- We can learn to appreciate others by studying regional differences and similarities.
- People can modify their physical environments.
- The characteristics and distributions of human populations are always changing.
- The movement of people, goods, and ideas occurs through various modes of transportation and communication.
- Geographers examine more than just the physical geography of places.

As a result of this unit, the students will *be able to*

- Demonstrate an understanding of the spatial concepts related to reading, using, and creating maps.
- Recognize and use appropriate geographic tools and technology.
- Explain how humans affect their environments.
- Describe, compare, and contrast the physical, cultural, and economic characteristics of regions.
- Describe how the physical characteristics of a region affect human behavior.
- Analyze changes in regions over time.
- Work independently to complete a project.
- Work cooperatively with others to reach a common goal.

Instructional Strategies Used

• Brainstorming	• Flexible grouping
• Independent research	• Jigsaw
• Metacognitive thinking	• Pre-assessment
• Self-assessment	• Tiered assignments

Sample Supporting Materials Provided

Sample #	Title	Page
3.1	Independent Project Assignments	109
3.2	Independent Project Evaluation Rubric	112
3.3	Independent Project Self-Evaluation	114

Unit Overview

LESSON	WHOLE-CLASS COMPONENTS	DIFFERENTIATED COMPONENTS
Preparation	Pre-assessment of map skills *30 minutes*	
LESSON 1 **Map Skills** *1–2 class periods*	Group brainstorming session on the importance of map skills *15 minutes*	Tiered assignment based on readiness *40–50 minutes*
	Group discussion about maps and map skills *15 minutes*	

LESSON	WHOLE-CLASS COMPONENTS	DIFFERENTIATED COMPONENTS
LESSON 2 **What Makes a Region a Region?** *2 class periods*	Introductory presentation and discussion of regions *15–20 minutes*	
	Individual or small-group activity on regions *25–30 minutes*	
	Discussion of activity results and correlation to unit concepts *20 minutes*	
	Presentation and discussion of new information concerning regions *15–20 minutes*	
	Introduction of independent projects *10 minutes*	Students select a region to study based on interest
LESSON 3 **Regional Changes over Time** *2 class periods*	Discussion of unit generalizations *20–30 minutes*	
		Jigsaw activity based on interest *40 minutes*
	Discussion of Jigsaw and unit generalizations *30 minutes*	
LESSON 4 **What Does a Geographer Do?** *4–6 class periods*		Independent project work based on interest and readiness
		Mini-lessons and coaching based on readiness *4–6 class periods*
LESSON 5 **Regions Fair** *1–2 class periods*	Presentation and viewing of research project products *1–2 class periods*	
	Self-evaluation *10 minutes*	

Unit Description and Teacher Commentary

Preparation	
DESCRIPTION	TEACHER COMMENTARY
Pre-assessment of map skills. Before beginning the unit, measure students' current knowledge and understanding of the different types and uses of maps and students' basic map skills, such as finding absolute location using latitude and longitude, using cardinal directions, and using a legend or key to identify places.	This pre-assessment may be either teacher-created or taken from a social studies teacher's manual. You might want to use a textbook post-test that addresses the highlighted map skills and vocabulary.

LESSON 1	Map Skills	*(1–2 class periods)*

LESSON SEQUENCE AND DESCRIPTION	TEACHER COMMENTARY
Group brainstorming session on the importance of map skills. Begin with a whole-class brainstorming session. Ask: Why might map skills be important to you personally?	I find that students participate more enthusiastically in learning activities when they understand how such activities relate to their own lives.
Tiered assignment based on readiness. Assign students to one of two activities focused on map skills:	I tiered these activities based on the pre-assessment results. Those students who demonstrated a solid grasp of basic map skills and vocabulary by scoring 90 percent or higher on the pre-assessment completed the second activity. Those who needed further practice with map skills and vocabulary completed the first activity before they moved ahead to application tasks.
Activity 1 Examine the maps provided. What kind of maps do you think they are and for what might they be used? Why do you say so? What information do they show? Create a chart that shows the similarities and differences among all of the different types of maps. Be sure to use the correct vocabulary to describe each map.	This first activity offered students who needed it additional practice with the vocabulary of maps and with map reading. I provided a variety of maps, including relief maps, navigational maps, contour maps, and road maps, along with resources students could use to look up key vocabulary. I encouraged students in this group to work together so that they could share ideas and discuss their growing understanding.

LESSON SEQUENCE AND DESCRIPTION	TEACHER COMMENTARY
Activity 2 Using what you know about map symbols and terminology and about types of maps, create two different maps of the school grounds. Each map should serve a different purpose, and you should be able to explain these purposes clearly. In addition, your maps should be accurate and attractive enough to be useful to someone visiting the school for the first time.	This activity allowed students who had a firm grasp of the language and characteristics of maps to apply that understanding by mapping a familiar place. The criteria helped to ensure that students created high-quality products. Students in this group worked either in pairs or small groups. A parent volunteer monitored students as they worked in and around the school building.
Group discussion about maps and map skills. Conclude the lesson by asking students to share their charts and maps and to further discuss the importance of maps. Why do we need maps? What characteristics make a map really useful?	Here, I wanted the students to listen to one another talk about maps and the importance of maps. Students who worked on Activity 1 talked about different types of maps and also gave feedback to their classmates by examining the maps of the school and trying them out.

LESSON 2   What Makes a Region a Region?   *(2 class periods)*

LESSON SEQUENCE AND DESCRIPTION	TEACHER COMMENTARY
Introductory presentation and discussion of regions. Begin by covering necessary background information, including that a **region** is an area that has key characteristics in common. Some regions are defined by one characteristic, such as government or landform types; others are defined by the **interaction** of many characteristics, such as language, ethnic group(s), and environment. Areas that form a region do not have to be contiguous.	I found it was necessary to go over the definition of a region before beginning the next activity, and I made sure students could explain the concept of **region** before we went any further. Also, this discussion helped me find out what they already knew about geographical regions in the United States.
Focus student discussion on the following questions: If you had to divide the United States into only seven sections (or **regions**), what would they be and why? How would you determine where to divide them? What are the positive and negative consequences of creating such sections or regions?	I required the students to explain the reasoning behind their thinking. My primary question was, "Why do certain regional divisions make more sense to you than others?"
Individual or small-group activity on regions. For this activity, students will need maps of the United States that do not show political boundaries but do show landforms. They may work either independently or in small groups.	During this part of the lesson, I provided maps without regional divisions because I wanted the students to propose their own. I was interested in finding out how they would divide the country and the justification they would provide for their decisions.

LESSON SEQUENCE AND DESCRIPTION	TEACHER COMMENTARY
Directions: You have been hired to redivide the 50 states into only 7 regions. How you decide to do this is up to you, but you must provide a well-reasoned rationale for your decisions. In order to complete your job, you must do the following: 1. Present a map of the United States that clearly shows your newly developed regions. 2. Write a statement that fully explains how you decided to develop and define the regions. This statement must describe characteristics of the regions you created and the criteria you used to make your decisions. 3. Create a list of the problems that you encountered as you developed your regions. What issues did you have to solve? How did you solve them?	My goal here was critical thinking. Specifically, I wanted students to consider two questions: • How are regional divisions created? • What criteria might be considered in creating them? I required the students to elaborate on the reasoning behind their decisions so they would use metacognitive skills, and I asked them to maintain a list of the problems they encountered during this activity to give them an idea of issues involved in creating regional divisions.
Discussion of activity results and correlation to unit concepts. When the students have completed the activity, allow them to share their regions and the reasoning behind their regional division decisions with the rest of the class. What problems did they run into as they created their regions? What similar and different criteria did the groups use to create regions?	During this discussion, I introduced the unit generalizations concerning the characteristics of and **variations** between **regions.**
Presentation and discussion of new information concerning regions. Provide students with maps showing the "true" regions of the United States. Discuss the criteria that were used to create these regions. Ask students what they think of this way of dividing the country. Invite students to share what they already know about the various regions and write their ideas on the board. As students share their ideas, be sure to note misconceptions, which you'll want to address as the unit progresses.	After I gave students a map with the "true" U.S. regions (Alaska, Hawaii, Southeast, Southwest, Northwest, Midwest, Northeast), I asked the students to compare their ideas to "reality." During this discussion, I shared some interesting facts about each region, with the goal of helping students to select regions of interest for their upcoming independent projects.
Introduction of independent projects. Conclude the lesson by introducing the upcoming research project and asking the students to write on an index card the two U.S. regions they would be most interested in studying in depth. Explain to the students that over the next few weeks, they will be researching a single region of their choice in order to understand important ideas about all regions of the United States.	Allowing the students to select a region helped to give them a more personal connection to the upcoming project. Thus, the project was differentiated partially on student interest.

LESSON SEQUENCE AND DESCRIPTION	TEACHER COMMENTARY
	When some students remained undecided about which regions they were interested in studying, I encouraged them to spend some time doing preliminary research (talking to others, reading short selections about a couple of regions, watching videos on various regions) in order to determine an interest.

LESSON 3   **Regional Changes over Time**   *(2 class periods)*

LESSON SEQUENCE AND DESCRIPTION	TEACHER COMMENTARY
Discussion of unit generalizations. Begin this lesson by asking students to consider the impact people have on places. How do humans affect their environments? How do we cause change in environments over time? How does population growth impact a place? Ask students to provide examples to support their ideas. What general statements can students create regarding the **interaction** of people and their environments? Post their statements in the classroom for continued reference.	I introduced the unit generalizations concerning people and the environment and asked students to provide evidence to support these ideas.
Jigsaw activity based on interest. For this activity, students will first work in self-selected groups to complete one of six possible tasks. Explain that every member of the group must participate in and contribute to the group's work and that every member will be asked to share the information the group discovers with other students. In addition, every group member must have his or her own copy of the group's final product.	This activity relates to the unit concept of **interaction**. Students had studied the history of their city prior to this unit, and I wanted them to apply the unit generalizations to a familiar location before applying them to places with which they were less familiar.
	I like using the Jigsaw technique for several reasons:
	• As a grouping strategy, it encourages cooperation among the students.
	• It gives each student a chance to be a "resident expert" within a small group. This is extremely powerful for those students who seldom find themselves in the "expert" role.
	• It encourages students to take shared responsibility for the learning that takes place in the classroom.

LESSON SEQUENCE AND DESCRIPTION	TEACHER COMMENTARY
	• It takes the spotlight off of me as the sole source of information. • I find that requiring every student to have a copy of the final product helps to ensure student accountability in group-work situations.
Task 1 Create a chart showing our city's population growth since settlement. When did the greatest number of people come to the city? What might explain this population growth?	For this activity to work, all tasks needed to be completed by at least one group. To ensure that all tasks were addressed, I asked students to give me their top two choices, as well as any topics they were definitely *not* interested in. From that information, I was able to form groups that worked well for individual and class needs.
Task 2 Why did people move to our city in the past and why do they continue to do so? Develop a clear and organized way to show what you learn.	
Task 3 When was our city connected to other cities, through what modes of transportation, and for what reasons? Develop a creative way (for example, newspaper headlines and articles from the time period) to show the city's early ties to other places.	After I had assigned groups of students to particular tasks, I stressed that they each needed to have a very solid grasp of the information gained from their tasks because they would be teaching this information to each other. I also explained that the skills they would be using on these tasks were similar to the ones they would need to complete their
Task 4 When did our city gain telephone and television technology? Compare and contrast the city before and after the arrival of this technology.	independent projects. This was a way for students to practice these skills in groups before setting off to use them on their own.
Task 5 What hazards existed in the past and continue to exist today for people living in our city? What has been done and could be done to lessen these hazards? Create an organizer to show your information and ideas.	During both the initial research portion of the task and the Jigsaw portion, I moved around the room, listening to conversations, asking questions, and taking notes on what I heard. This helped me monitor student understanding as well as group function.
Task 6 How have people changed the physical makeup of our city over time? Use a "before and after" approach to answer this question and develop an interesting way to show your ideas.	
Once students have completed their work on the tasks, they will Jigsaw—be regrouped so that each new group will have one representative from each of the six task groups. In the new groups, students will share with one another what they have learned about the changes in their city and about ways people have affected their city over time.	I required students to take notes and ask questions as they listened to one another share the information generated from the various tasks. This helped to keep the students focused.

LESSON SEQUENCE AND DESCRIPTION	TEACHER COMMENTARY
Discussion of Jigsaw and unit generalizations. Following the completion of the Jigsaw activity, lead a whole-class discussion of what students learned about the changes in their city over time. Do these sorts of changes occur in other places? Is there a relationship between people and their environments? Why or why not? Ask students to defend their responses. Use your insights from this discussion and your monitoring of the activities to ensure that students have correct and similar understandings about terms, concepts, and skills.	As we completed this activity, I referred back to the unit generalizations, and I asked students to explain how their new information about their city related to the generalizations.

LESSON 4   **What Does a Geographer Do?**   *(4–6 class periods)*

LESSON SEQUENCE AND DESCRIPTION	TEACHER COMMENTARY
Independent project work based on interest and readiness. Students will arrive in class having already selected the region they wish to study. Now, they will receive their research role assignment, differentiated for readiness. (See the **Independent Project Assignments,** collected in Sample 3.1, beginning on page 109.) Assign each student to work independently in one of three roles:	Because my students performed at different levels during the previous activities, and because I recognized that some of them needed more concrete learning experiences, I tiered the independent project assignments and assigned students to the project roles that seemed best suited to their readiness levels.
Physical Geographer (Struggling Learners)	The Physical Geographer role required students to use many of the same skills and much of the same information they had used previously in the unit, but the role called for them to analyze and apply these understandings and skills. Thus, even though it was the most familiar and concrete of the three roles, it still required high-level thought.
Cultural Geographer (On-Target Learners)	The Cultural Geographer role was more demanding than Physical Geographer because it was more abstract in terms of the information students were to seek and required slightly more complex research skills. However, this role required students to examine aspects of society that they could see around them all the time.

LESSON SEQUENCE AND DESCRIPTION	TEACHER COMMENTARY
Economic Geographer (Advanced Learners)	This was the most complex and abstract of the roles, as it addressed economics, an area of society few of my students had been exposed to. In addition, the role required students to combine ideas and information from two different fields (geography and economics) and draw conclusions based on the relationship between the two. I assigned to this role students who could think abstractly, had a large storehouse of information, and could grasp new ideas and concepts quickly.
Introduce the three different types of geographers and ask the students to consider the different approaches and skills involved. What does each type of geographer probably study? What kinds of data must they work with? What sorts of questions do they seek to answer? Following this whole-group discussion, introduce the project requirements and assign the students to their particular projects. Students will work on their projects both as class work and homework during the project time span.	Although the roles varied in complexity, all three required students to simulate behaviors and thinking of geographers, to keep a daily process log, to create products that demonstrated an understanding of regional differences, and to show how these differences relate to the unit concepts and generalizations concerning **region, interaction,** and **variation.**
Mini-lessons and coaching based on readiness. Provide consultation and assistance during the research process as necessary. Throughout the project work span, offer mini-lessons on specific roles, research strategies, presentation techniques, using the rubric to guide work, and so on. You should probably invite some students to attend particular sessions, based on your observation of their needs. It is also wise to open the workshops to any student who feels attendance would improve the quality of his or her understanding and work.	I provided the **Independent Project Evaluation Rubric** (see Sample 3.2, page 112), a simple checklist for success that students could use to guide their own work and their feedback on their peers' projects. On such rubrics, it's helpful to include some criteria that all class members must address and some "negotiated criteria"—specific criteria either added by individual students to reflect their own goals and interests or designated by the teacher *for* an individual student to encourage growth in that learner. I included blank cells in this project's evaluation rubric to provide write-in space for negotiated criteria.

LESSON SEQUENCE AND DESCRIPTION	TEACHER COMMENTARY
Continue to monitor students' understanding and progress as they work on their independent projects. You can do this through mini-workshops, with end-of-class discussions, through question-and-answer sessions as class begins, through required journal or process log entries, and by sitting with and coaching individuals and groups as they work.	At this age, most students will need "guided" independent study rather than total independence. It is the teacher's role to provide the structure necessary to help students succeed.

LESSON 5   **Regions Fair**   *(1–2 class periods)*

LESSON SEQUENCE AND DESCRIPTION	TEACHER COMMENTARY
Presentation and viewing of research project products. Following the completion of the independent projects, provide time for the students to share their products with the class *or* set up the student projects in the classroom, computer lab, or other central place, such as the media center. (If there aren't enough computers available to play all the multimedia presentations, students should print out hard copies of their presentations for display.)	
Divide the class into two groups so that half the students are "experts" on the displays and the other half are "visitors." Visitors should circulate among the projects, asking questions and providing feedback to the experts. The next day, have students switch expert/visitor roles.	Students who play the visitor role can use the **Independent Project Evaluation Rubric** (see Sample 3.2) as one means of providing feedback. If you ask other guests (parents, teachers, other classes, community members) to view the exhibits, you might also want to ask them to complete rubrics for the products they view.
Self-evaluation. Be sure students complete the self-evaluation form provided (see the **Independent Project Self-Evaluation,** Sample 3.3, page 114).	The ability to reflect on and assess one's own work is an important skill in becoming a more self-directed learner.

Teacher Reflection on the Unit

The thing that pleased me the most about this unit was that the students didn't feel like they were being grouped *only* by readiness. The students grouped themselves based on the region they were interested in, and then I provided additional grouping by giving them assignments within that interest group based on readiness. This approach gave them an opportunity to work on a region of interest, yet be challenged at an appropriate level. I was also pleased with the connection to the real world of the geographer that this unit offered.

Holly C. Gould most recently taught in Alaska. She can be reached at gould@virginia.edu.

SAMPLE 3.1—Independent Project Assignments

Physical Geographer

You are a physical geographer. Physical geographers study the natural landscape and the ways in which people change land, bodies of water, climate, soil, and vegetation. For example, physical geographers study the soil erosion that results from the plowing of steep slopes. They consider the effects of strip mining on land and vegetation and the way burning fossil fuels sends large quantities of carbon dioxide into the atmosphere, changing rainfall patterns.

The United States government is developing a project to help new immigrants to the country understand how the United States is grouped into regions.

Your tasks:

1. Research your region of interest from the perspective of a physical geographer.

2. Create a map of your region that incorporates the areas you research. Your map must show landforms, climate conditions, natural resources, vegetation and wildlife, types of terrain, and natural hazards.

3. Using a variety of resources and media, research current events occurring in your region that relate to physical geography. Develop a way to illustrate these events, and be ready to explain how they represent and impact the physical geography of your region.

4. Create a multimedia presentation that highlights what you have learned about the physical geography of your region. You must include a summary of your ideas as well as pictures, film clips, sound bites, and any other information that will help others understand the physical geography of your region. What makes your region unique? You must also discuss how people have affected the physical environment of your region over time and how the region has been changed as a result.

5. Maintain a daily process log for the duration of the project. Your log should include your thoughts about your research and what you are learning about your region. How do your ideas change? What new information seems important and perhaps surprising to you? Why? How are you feeling about the research process? What parts of the process do you like and what parts seem troublesome to you? What problems do you run into and how do you solve them? Be sure to include your thoughts on how your research affects your understanding of the unit concepts and generalizations concerning **region**, **interaction**, and **variation**.

Cultural Geographer

You are a cultural geographer. Cultural geographers attempt to learn about the people of a particular region. They study the land on which people live, how people have changed the land, and how people have used available resources in order to survive. Cultural geographers study people in order to gain insight into how societies can solve problems and examine the lifestyles and traditions of societies.

The United States government is developing a project to help new immigrants to the country understand how the United States is grouped into regions.

Your tasks:

1. Research your region of interest from the perspective of a cultural geographer.

2. Create a clear way to show the following information about your region: ethnicity of the people who live there; customs, traditions, and celebrations; locations of major cities; regional art and architecture; regional literature; and religions.

3. Using a variety of resources and media, research current events occurring in your region that relate to cultural geography. Develop a way to illustrate these events, and be ready to explain how they represent and impact the culture of your region.

4. Create a multimedia presentation that highlights what you have learned about the cultural geography of your region. You must include a summary of your ideas as well as pictures, film clips, sound bites, and any other information that will help others understand the culture of your region. What makes your region unique? You must also discuss how people have affected the physical environment of your region over time and how the region has been changed as a result.

5. Maintain a daily process log for the duration of the project. Your log should include your thoughts about your research and what you are learning about your region. How do your ideas change? What new information seems important and perhaps surprising to you? Why? How are you feeling about the research process? What parts of the process do you like and what parts seem troublesome to you? What problems do you run into and how do you solve them? Be sure to include your thoughts on how your research affects your understanding of the unit concepts and generalizations concerning **region**, **interaction**, and **variation**.

SAMPLE 3.1—(continued)

Economic Geographer

You are an economic geographer. Economic geographers study the geographic distribution of the people's economic activities. They examine production, secondary production, retailing, the consumer sector, goods and services, and employment.

The United States government is developing a project to help new immigrants to the country understand how the United States is grouped into regions.

Your tasks:

1. Research your region of interest from the perspective of an economic geographer.

2. Create a clear way to show the following information about your region: cultivation of natural resources; production of goods; services offered; jobs unique to the region; income of people; unemployment rates; and population statistics.

3. Using a variety of resources and media, research current events occurring in your region that relate to economics. Develop a way to illustrate these events, and be ready to explain how they represent and impact the economy of your region.

4. Create a multimedia presentation that highlights what you have learned about the economic geography of your region. You must include a summary of your ideas as well as pictures, film clips, sound bites, and any other information that will help others understand the economy of your region. What makes your region unique? You must also discuss how people have affected the physical environment of your region over time and how the region has been changed as a result.

5. Maintain a daily process log for the duration of the project. Your log should include your thoughts about your research and what you are learning about your region. How do your ideas change? What new information seems important and perhaps surprising to you? Why? How are you feeling about the research process? What parts of the process do you like and what parts seem troublesome to you? What problems do you run into and how do you solve them? Be sure to include your thoughts on how your research affects your understanding of the unit concepts and generalizations concerning **region**, **interaction**, and **variation**.

SAMPLE 3.2—Independent Project Evaluation Rubric

Criteria	5 = Excellent	3 = Satisfactory	1 = Poor
Research	Used a variety of high-quality primary and secondary resources that would be used by a geographer. Derived interesting and defensible conclusions. Addressed the uniqueness of the region from a geographer's perspective.	Used different primary and secondary resources. Sometimes addressed the uniqueness of the region as a geographer would. Drew limited conclusions that showed understanding of the region.	Used only secondary resources. Did not address the uniqueness of the region as a geographer would. Drew no conclusions, or drew conclusions that did not show understanding.
Presentation	Multimedia presentation was informative and thought provoking. Summarized ideas and covered important aspects of the research. Presented information in a way that was logical, interesting, and easy for the audience to follow.	Multimedia presentation addressed the required areas. Information was accurate, but not always interesting or insightful. The audience could follow and understand the presentation.	Multimedia presentation was weak. Information was presented in a disorganized and illogical way. The audience could not always follow or understand the presentation.
Visuals	Visuals were very neat, well organized, and accurate. High-quality artistic effort evident. Incorporated detail that was helpful, not distracting. Clearly labeled.	Visuals were neatly drawn. Artistic effort evident. Incorporated some detail. Labeled adequately for identification.	Visuals were difficult to read and interpret. Minimal artistic effort evident. Incorporated little detail. Inadequately labeled.

SAMPLE 3.2—(continued)			
Criteria	**5 = Excellent**	**3 = Satisfactory**	**1 = Poor**
Process Log	Log contained daily entries. Clearly discussed the process of researching, developing, and testing ideas about unit concepts and generalizations concerning **region**, **interaction**, and **variation**. Thinking about thinking is evident.	Log contained 2–3 entries per week. Evidence of thinking about the process was often present. Included meaningful discussion of unit concepts and generalizations concerning **region**, **interaction**, and **variation**.	Log was incomplete and showed little evidence of thought or working through problems. Unit concepts and generalizations concerning **region**, **interaction**, and **variation** were not discussed or were not discussed in a way that showed understanding.
*			
*			

*Note: Add criteria as desired. (For example: organization, creativity, mechanics.)

SAMPLE 3.3—Independent Project Self-Evaluation

Complete the following sentences:

1. My project was

2. The resources I used to develop my project were

3. Important things I learned as a result of my project were

4. The most difficult part of this assignment for me was

5. The part of the project that I am most proud of is

6. If I could do the project again and do it differently, I would

Using the criteria listed below, evaluate your project and your work on it. Place an X on the number that indicates your evaluation of the specific criterion. The lowest possible score is 1, and the highest possible score is 5. Your teacher will do the same for each criterion by circling a number so that you can compare the evaluations.

Validity of Resources	1	2	3	4	5
Accuracy of Information	1	2	3	4	5
Quality of Thought	1	2	3	4	5
Presentation Effectiveness	1	2	3	4	5
Authenticity of Role	1	2	3	4	5
Efficient Use of Time	1	2	3	4	5

4

Finding a Voice

A Language Arts Unit on Writer's Voice

Unit Developer: Holly L. Hertberg

Introduction

This two- to three-week unit focuses on developing students' understanding of voice in writing, with an eye toward creating fluid and more powerful writers. Students explore the elements and function of voice in both their own and published writers' work. Through a focused study of a wide variety of professional writers' voices, students develop and apply a set of principles to guide the effective use of voice in their own writing.

The unit begins with an exploration of the sound of writing, examining the connections between music and writing to illustrate how rhythm and tone can be created through words. Students consider, through analysis of the writing of professional essayists, poets, and fiction writers, what makes these individual writers' voices unique. Students next examine how word choice, tone, and rhythm contribute to a writer's voice, and then apply these understandings to their own writing. At the end of the unit, students choose from a variety of product assignments to apply their understanding of the elements and function of **voice**.

Throughout the unit, students respond to a series of woven journal prompts designed to illustrate the powerful connections that exist between their lives and the literature with which they are engaged. These journal prompts provide an illustration of how readers interact with texts in unique ways (according to their personal experiences and backgrounds). They are tied to the concept of voice in writing in that they illuminate for students the validity of using personal experiences as the basis of thinking—and writing—about important ideas.

This unit works well for students with special education Individual Educational Plans (IEPs). There is enough flexibility in the way students work to allow the classroom teacher (or a special education specialist) to work easily with students on

115

basic writing and vocabulary goals. For example, it's natural to talk about descriptive words as a part of voice and to have students practice description as a part of their work with the concept. It's also easy to have all students draw on their own experiences in this unit as they set personal goals for writing and collaborate with a variety of peers to achieve these goals. You'll note that the key concepts and principles on which the unit is based apply to all learners.

Teacher Reflections on Designing the Unit

I have found that this unit works really well when used near the beginning of the year. Calling attention to voice is a crucial way of letting students know that their individual voices are valued in the classroom and that each voice is necessary to bring richness and texture to the learning in which they are all engaged. Certainly, students will not master the concept of **voice** in this unit; mastery may take years, as voice is an incredibly complex and difficult concept. However, this unit provides students with the beginning of a common literary vocabulary. It also allows students to explore their own and each other's backgrounds; allows them to recognize their own and others' areas of knowledge and expertise; and shows them that their voices have an authority in the classroom—an authority their classmates and I acknowledge, value, and seek.

Language Arts Standards Addressed
- The student will read a variety of fiction and nonfiction and
    - Describe how the author's voice elicits emotional response from the reader.
    - Compare and contrast authors' voices.
- The student will read and write a wide variety of poetry and describe how word choice, rhythm, and tone elicit a response from the reader.
- The student will write narratives, descriptions, and explanations and
    - Use a variety of planning strategies to generate ideas.
    - Select vocabulary to enhance the central idea, tone, and voice.

Unit Concepts and Generalizations
Voice (main concept), Rhythm, Style, Tone
- A writer's voice is unique and personal.
- A writer's background, culture, and experiences contribute to the uniqueness and power of his or her voice.
- A powerful voice is a crucial component of effective, compelling writing.

Unit Objectives

As a result of this unit, the students will *know*

- Vocabulary related to voice, including *tone, word choice,* and *rhythm.*
- What makes a writer's voice unique—the components of voice in writing.
- How to create and use a rubric.

As a result of this unit, the students will *understand that*

- Rhythm, tone, and word choice contribute to a writer's voice.
- A writer's voice is unique and personal.
- A writer's background, culture, and experiences contribute to the uniqueness and power of his or her voice.
- A powerful voice is a crucial component of effective, compelling writing.

As a result of this unit, the students will *be able to*

- Describe how an author's voice elicits emotional response from a reader.
- Compare and contrast writers' voices, including their own, those of their classmates, and those of published writers.
- Use rhythm, tone, and word choice in their own writing to elicit a response from a reader.
- Use the works of published writers as a model for their own writing.
- Use a variety of planning strategies to generate ideas for writing.
- Select vocabulary to enhance the central idea, tone, and voice of their writing.
- Connect the concept of voice/style in writing to the concept of voice/style in other disciplines.
- Synthesize information to construct new concepts.

Instructional Strategies Used

- Flexible grouping
- Independent projects
- Mini-lessons for review
- Peer critiques
- Rubric assessment
- Self-evaluation
- Tiered assignments
- Varied product assignments

Sample Supporting Materials Provided

Unit Overview

LESSON	WHOLE-CLASS COMPONENTS	DIFFERENTIATED COMPONENTS
Preparation	Pre-assessment	
Unit Alternative **Independent Project** *2–3 weeks*		Alternate independent project assignment based on readiness (independent study skills, reading, and writing)
LESSON 1 **Introduction** *1 class period*	Journal Prompt 1 and response discussion *20 minutes*	
	Introduction to the unit *10 minutes*	
	Informal interest and resource inventory *10 minutes*	
	Discussion of the culminating product assignment *10 minutes*	Products differentiated by interest
LESSON 2 **The Sound of Music** *2 class periods*	Journal Prompt 2 and response discussion *15 minutes*	
	Presentation/journal responses to various pieces of music *20 minutes*	
	Presentation/discussion of the elements of musical style *10–15 minutes*	
	Small-group sharing of journal responses *15 minutes*	
	Brainstorming of a class list of distinguishing musical elements *10 minutes*	

LESSON	WHOLE-CLASS COMPONENTS	DIFFERENTIATED COMPONENTS
	Introduction and explanation of the oral narrative assignment *10 minutes*	
	Planning time for the oral narrative assignment *20–30 minutes*	Optional mini-lesson on interviewing techniques *20–30 minutes*
LESSON 3 **The Sound of Writing** *2 class periods*	Journal Prompt 3 and response discussion *15 minutes*	
		Group reading and discussion based on reading readiness *30–40 minutes*
	Discussion and listing of insights gained *15–20 minutes*	
	Project work *30 minutes*	Mini-lesson for struggling learners on the elements of writing *30 minutes*
LESSON 4 **Writers' Voices** *2 class periods*	Pre-assessment (optional) *10 minutes*	
		Poetry reading activity based on readiness *10–15 minutes*
	Journal Prompt 4 and response discussion *20 minutes*	
		Small-group work on **voice** based on readiness *30–45 minutes*
	Sharing of student writing *15–20 minutes*	
LESSON 5 **Oral Narratives** *1–2 class periods*	Journal Prompt 5 and response discussion *15 minutes*	

LESSON	WHOLE-CLASS COMPONENTS	DIFFERENTIATED COMPONENTS
	Self-selected small-group sharing and discussion of oral narratives *30–40 minutes*	
	Creation of class rubric for writer's voice *30–40 minutes*	
		Homework using class rubric to evaluate reading (based on interest) *20 minutes*
LESSON 6 **Tying It Up** *2 class periods*	Journal Prompt 6 and response discussion *15–20 minutes*	
	Discussion and refinement of class rubric on writer's voice *30 minutes*	
	Discussion of product assignment progress *10–15 minutes*	
		Peer feedback on product assignment plans, grouped by readiness *40–50 minutes*
LESSON 7 **Working on Products** *2–3 class periods*	Independent work on products and peer feedback opportunities *2–3 class periods*	
LESSON 8 **Product Presentations** *2–3 class periods*	Sharing and discussion of products *2–3 class periods*	

Unit Description and Commentary

Preparation	
DESCRIPTION	TEACHER COMMENTARY
Pre-assessment. Prior to beginning this unit, pre-assess the students' use of **voice** in their writing.	For this pre-assessment, I looked at a few samples of student writing. Don't rely upon just one piece of writing.

Unit Alternative	**Independent Project**	(2–3 weeks)

DESCRIPTION	TEACHER COMMENTARY
Alternate independent project assignment based on readiness. Students whose pre-assessments indicate that they have a strong command over voice in writing will complete this assignment as an alternative to the majority of regular unit work (see Sample 4.1, **Independent Project Guidelines**, page 137). These students should, however, participate in the regular woven journal prompts.	The alternative unit assignment requires a high level of independent study skills. Students assigned to this project should be strong in this area and should be advanced writers and readers. Nonetheless, these students will need and benefit from teacher time and attention as they work. They should receive coaching and direction from the teacher, as should all students in the class.
Distribute and discuss the **Independent Project Checklist for Success** (see Sample 4.2, page 138).	Providing students with a checklist for success clarifies the teacher's expectations for the independent project and its final product and helps promote student self-assessment.

LESSON 1	**Introduction**	(1 class period)

LESSON SEQUENCE AND DESCRIPTION	TEACHER COMMENTARY
*Guiding question: What does it mean to have a **voice**?* The purpose of this lesson is to introduce unit concepts and develop an understanding of students' strengths/interests in relation to the unit.	I like to begin each lesson by providing students with a guiding question, written on the board. It helps them—and me—to focus on the purpose of the lesson.
Journal Prompt 1 and response discussion. As students come into class, ask them to get their journals and to respond to the following prompt:	

LESSON SEQUENCE AND DESCRIPTION	TEACHER COMMENTARY
What does it mean to have a voice? What do we gain by having a voice? How does having a voice give us power? What would it be like not to have a voice? Students should discuss their responses to the journal prompt as a large group, developing a classwide preliminary understanding of what voice is and why it matters.	This series of woven journal prompts continues throughout the unit. Its purpose is to encourage students to mine their experiences to identify possible topics for future writing projects. Even if students don't choose to pursue one of these topics for the unit's final product, the process will give them ideas for later writing projects. This particular journal prompt also serves the purpose of getting students in touch with what they know—with the idea of beginning writing from a point of authority. (We are all great authorities on ourselves!) Students who need scaffolding can audiotape their journal prompt responses. In addition, prompts can be easily modified for students with IEPs.
Introduction to the unit. Explain to students that over the next few weeks, they will be working on developing their own voices as writers by studying music, art, literature, their own writing, and the stories of their family members. Let them know they will be studying the *sound* of writing. Introduce immediately the generalizations that will inform the rest of the unit: • A writer's **voice** is unique and personal. • A writer's background, culture, and experiences contribute to the uniqueness and power of his or her **voice**. • A powerful **voice** is a crucial component of effective, compelling writing.	Make certain to emphasize throughout the unit that writers' own experiences are often the substance of their writing—whether they're writing fiction or critical essays. Stress to students how important their areas of expertise are—not only to their writing, but also to the classroom knowledge base.
Informal interest and resource inventory. Ask students if any of them know a lot about a particular musical form or musical instrument, and if any of them have any particular interest in music. If so, tell those students that tomorrow's lesson deals with music, and that their knowledge would be welcomed to add depth to the discussion. Ask students if they or their parents know any artists, musicians, or writers who live in the area. Keep a record of the names of these possible resources for students who may choose to include interviews of experts in their final products.	It's a great idea to find out at the beginning of the unit what particular talents and interests students have that the unit could tap into. It is also important to identify students' areas of expertise so that you can involve "experts" in broadening the knowledge of their fellow students. Compiling a database of available resources/contacts/experts is invaluable. These experts may be able to come in to talk about their experiences as professionals. Even if they don't visit during this unit, they may be useful resources later on in the year.

LESSON SEQUENCE AND DESCRIPTION	TEACHER COMMENTARY
Discussion of the culminating product assignment. Tell students that if they are really interested in music, they should consider pursuing it further in their unit product. Also mention that for students who are interested in art, there is a similar product assignment. Let students look over the four options for the **Culminating Product Assignment** (collected in Sample 4.3, beginning on page 139). Ask students to start thinking about which product they would like to complete. Tell those who think they might choose Product Assignment 1, 2, or 4 that they should start as soon as possible, as their products involve making appointments with other people.	I wanted students to start (and continue!) thinking about their final product assignment now, as many of the products required interviews and advanced planning. I developed these particular product assignments to allow students to investigate the concept of **voice** through a variety of lenses. Although the products are differentiated according to interest, all require students to engage in thoughtful consideration of how individual authors create and develop a voice as well as the ways in which an author's experiences affect the development of his or her voice. Additionally, when I was designing these product assignments, I wanted students to produce something they could share with the class to broaden the whole class's understanding of the unit concept.
Distribute and discuss the **Culminating Product Assignment Checklists for Success** (collected in Sample 4.4, beginning on page 144).	I included the various checklists for success because I have found the quality of products improves when students have the opportunity to self-assess before turning the products in.

LESSON 2	The Sound of Music	*(2 class periods)*

LESSON SEQUENCE AND DESCRIPTION	TEACHER COMMENTARY
Guiding question: What makes individual pieces of music unique? The purpose of this lesson is to help students develop an understanding of what makes music unique—an understanding that they can apply to their own and others' writing.	
Journal Prompt 2 and response discussion. Open the lesson by asking students to respond to the following prompt: Make a list of your most memorable personal experiences. Just keep listing them! You don't have to give details; just be clear enough so that when you look back at this list, you'll know what you meant.	In this prompt, I wanted students to begin brainstorming a list of rich personal experiences from which they will draw in later lessons.

LESSON SEQUENCE AND DESCRIPTION	TEACHER COMMENTARY
When the journaling time is up, ask students who feel comfortable doing so to share their memorable personal experiences with the class.	
Presentation/journal responses to various pieces of music. To introduce students to the concepts of rhythm, style, and tone (all of which are important in developing a strong writing voice), play a variety of musical selections—classical, jazz, salsa, rap, hard rock, folk, new age, and so forth. Ask students to respond in their journals to each of the selections while they are listening to them. Provide this prompt: What does this selection remind you of? What pictures/scenes does it create in your head? Imagine that this is a soundtrack to a movie. What's going on in the movie right now?	Play each selection of music long enough for students to get a feel for its rhythm, style, and tone and then to record their responses in their journals. You don't need to play entire songs, but short snippets aren't sufficient to give students a sense of music that may be unfamiliar to them.
Presentation/discussion of the elements of musical style. Next, play two very different types of music, one right after the other—perhaps classical and rap, folk music and jazz—and ask students to point out how the pieces are different from one another. What are the specific elements that *make* them different?	This comparison works best when there is a strong juxtaposition of music types. You may want to ask students what they think would clash the most and play the selections they suggest.
Small-group sharing of journal responses. Students assemble in small groups to share what they visualized during the musical selections and to discuss the elements that distinguish one type of music from another.	Divide students into heterogeneous groups, making sure to evenly distribute music "experts" if possible. Move between groups to validate their findings, pose questions to further their thinking, and keep them on task.
Brainstorming of a class list of distinguishing musical elements. After students have discussed their ideas in small groups, have them share with the whole group their ideas about what specific elements make one genre of music different from another. Ask one person to be the class recorder and to keep track of the list of elements the class generates.	Because some students will be pursuing the elements of music that contribute to style in greater depth (and presenting those findings to class), it is not necessary here to use the correct musical terms to describe what students noticed when they were listening to the music, although you certainly may do so. (You may wish to consult the music specialist on your faculty for this information.)

LESSON SEQUENCE AND DESCRIPTION	TEACHER COMMENTARY
	The most important thing is for students to brainstorm about what makes different styles of music sound different from one another—beat, rhythm, instrumentation, tempo, mood, etc. Later, in Lesson 3, students will compare this list to parallel elements in writing, so it is important to generate *lots* of ideas.
Introduction and explanation of the oral narrative assignment. Distribute the instruction sheet for the **Oral Narrative Assignment** (see Sample 4.5, page 148). Explain to students that they will work on this task at home and that it will be due in one week. Go over the assignment, emphasizing that we write best about what we know. Our families are often the things we know best, so that's a great place to start.	This assignment requires students to interview a family member. For students whose family members do not speak English, recording and transcribing the interview in their native language is fine—and, in fact, will expose other students to the different rhythms of other languages and prompt deeper discussion.
✳ **Optional mini-lesson on interviewing techniques/Planning time for the oral narrative assignment.** A quick mini-lesson on interviewing techniques may be appropriate here, depending on student need. These skills are required to complete the homework assignment, and many students will also be interviewing people as part of their final products. Students who already know how to conduct interviews may begin working on prompts to extract narratives from a family member.	I held this mini-lesson after the discussions of the culminating product assignment and the oral narrative assignment because I wanted students to understand *why* they needed to know interviewing techniques.

| **LESSON 3** | **The Sound of Writing** | *(2 class periods)* |

LESSON SEQUENCE AND DESCRIPTION	TEACHER COMMENTARY
*Guiding question: What makes a writer's **voice** unique? What do the sound of writing and the sound of music have in common?* This lesson has two purposes: 1) to help students make connections between the sound of music and the sound of writing, and 2) to expose students to a variety of effective writers from a wide diversity of cultural backgrounds.	In this lesson, students apply the understanding they've developed about the differences in musical genres by comparing differences in musical genres to differences in writing.

LESSON SEQUENCE AND DESCRIPTION	TEACHER COMMENTARY
Journal Prompt 3 and response discussion. Open the lesson by asking students to respond to the following prompt: Go back to the list of memorable experiences you made yesterday. Choose the two that you can remember most clearly. Write down everything you know about these experiences. Look around in your memory and include as much detail as you can. Who was there with you? When was it? What was it like outside (or inside, depending upon where you were)? How did you feel? What was going on around you? What were other people doing? What sensory information can you recall—any particular images, sounds, tactile sensations? Allow students who wish to do so to share a portion of their descriptions with the class. Tell students that today they will be "listening" to writing. Their goal is to hear *how* each writer sounds different from the others and identify *why* each writer sounds different from the others. Tell students that these unique sounds are called **voices**.	In this prompt, students begin a detailed analysis of two personal experiences. I wanted students to get in the habit of using information gathered through all five senses to enhance their descriptions.
✴ **Group reading and discussion based on reading readiness.** Divide students into three groups to read passages written by a wide variety of published writers. Give each group a different set of passages, which are differentiated according to the students' facility with reading.	Make group assignments based on student facility with reading. All groups will be engaged in responding to the same questions, but their reading material will be different. It is possible to use the same authors for the different groups, simply by choosing more or less complex passages from their works. Also, note that using writers from a variety of cultural and ethnic backgrounds is crucial to this assignment, as it gives richness to the variety of voices students will encounter. Some writers I'd recommend for the richness of their voices as well as the variety of their backgrounds include Sandra Cisneros, Gabriel Garcia Marquez, Toni Morrison, Langston Hughes, James Thurber, Garrison Keillor, and Mark Twain.

LESSON SEQUENCE AND DESCRIPTION	TEACHER COMMENTARY
Group 1: Struggling Readers Students listen to a series of passages from books-on-tape. Select passages from writers who have particularly strong and distinctive voices and who are from diverse ethnic and cultural backgrounds.	Here, I wanted students who were struggling readers or who were in the beginning phases of learning English to encounter the richness of the writers' voices without the distraction of decoding.
Group 2: On-grade Readers Students take turns reading aloud selected passages by writers who have particularly strong and distinctive voices and who represent a variety of ethnic and cultural backgrounds. Because students are reading aloud, these passages should not contain too many unfamiliar vocabulary words or complicated sentence constructions.	On-grade readers may read the same passages that the students in Group 1 are listening to, or you may choose to have them read more complex passages.
Group 3: Advanced Readers Students take turns reading aloud selected passages by writers who have particularly strong and distinctive voices and who represent a variety of ethnic and cultural backgrounds. These readings should be challenging, but not so challenging that students cannot pick up the music of the language.	Students in this group should be very comfortable reading challenging material aloud.
When the readings are complete, ask groups to discuss the following questions about each of several passages of their choice: 1. What immediately struck you about the way this writer's voice sounded? Explain why you felt as you did. 2. Judging from this writer's voice, if this writer were an animal, what kind would he or she be? Why? Quote a line or a couple of lines that made you think this. 3. Which type of music that you listened to in class (or know from experience) did this passage remind you of? Why? What's similar? What's different? 4. How does rhythm in writing work differently from rhythm in music? How do they work similarly?	Whenever I ask students to work in groups, I make sure to have individual task cards prepared for each group. I often color-code these task cards to make it easy for me to identify which card belongs to which group. This way, I don't have to waste the whole group's time by giving directions for each separate group.
Discussion and listing of insights gained. Students reassemble as a large group and discuss what they discovered about the relationship between a writer's voice and music.	Here, you may want to solicit additional information from students who know a lot about music, particularly if these students are generally quiet during class discussions. Knowledgeable students may be able to make really interesting and unexpected connections between music and the elements of writing.

LESSON SEQUENCE AND DESCRIPTION	TEACHER COMMENTARY
Have yesterday's recorder write the brainstormed list of musical elements (see Lesson 2) on the board. Ask students to match an element of writing to each of the identified elements of music, and write the writing element next to the matching musical element on the board. (For example, students might say that beat in music is like syllables in writing.) Remind students that it is the unique way these elements are used that makes one writer's voice distinguishable from another's. Tell students that some of their classmates are pursuing this relationship in greater depth for their culminating product, and at the end of the unit, they will present their findings to the class. Ask another student to be class recorder and to take down the list when it is finished. This list will serve as the foundation for the class rubric on writer's voice (see Lesson 5).	
If the class is having difficulty coming up with a variety of elements of writing, prompt them by reading a passage and asking them specific questions to further their thinking. Here are several recommendations for discussion starters:	You will get a sense of whether the class is struggling by the students' silence, their looks of confusion, or their off-the-mark responses.
• What about the writer's word choice struck you? Is it different than the other writers you've read recently? How? What are some of the different ways that writers can choose words to develop a **voice**? • Listen to the way the writer uses sentence lengths. When does he or she use short sentences? How about long ones? Sentences of alternating lengths? What do these different sentence lengths accomplish? • What is the tone, or mood, of this piece? How do you know that? How does that contribute to this writer's voice and make it unique?	You might want to contrast Shel Silverstein with Robert Frost as an example.
Mini-lesson on the elements of writing/Project work. If only a few students are struggling with these concepts, hold a mini-lesson while the other students work on formulating an idea for their final product.	Because these are relatively abstract concepts, it is important to determine if there are some students who are confused, and then, to work through the concepts with them in a more applied, concrete manner.

LESSON 4	**Writers' Voices**	*(2 class periods)*

LESSON SEQUENCE AND DESCRIPTION	TEACHER COMMENTARY
*Guiding question: How do we apply what we've learned from other writers to create powerful **voices** in our own writing?*	Students will be transferring what they've learned from studying other writers' writing to their own writing.

LESSON SEQUENCE AND DESCRIPTION	TEACHER COMMENTARY
The purpose of this lesson is to expose students to a wide variety of poetry and to reading poetry for pleasure and to give them the opportunity to apply and reinforce their understandings about the elements of **voice** in their own writing.	A poetry reading activity serves as the jumping-off point for the day's journal prompt. Remember that students working on the independent project assignment are also participating in the woven journal prompts, and so should be included in the poetry reading exercise as well.
Pre-assessment (optional). Before beginning this lesson, you may wish to do a quick written assessment of students' understanding of **voice** and its components by having students write about what elements contribute to a writer's voice and how they would define these elements.	This pre-assessment is probably best given at the beginning of class, before students get into their poetry reading groups, so that you may look over the assessment while students are engaged in reading poetry and writing in their journals.
Poetry reading activity based on readiness. Divide the class into two groups according to poetry reading readiness. Each group should have access to a large number of poems	Make your group assignments based on your knowledge of students' past experiences with poetry—or their understanding of other complex and abstract material.
For readers who struggle with poetry, choose poems that are grade-level appropriate and have vibrant but easy-to-decipher language and images. For the more advanced poetry readers, search for poems that are slightly less straightforward, but still relatively easy to decode, again focusing on those with vibrant language and images.	Be sure to provide a wide variety of poetry for each group.
The purpose of this exercise is *not* for students to analyze the poetry, but instead to read the poems for enjoyment and to listen to their rhythms. Ask students to look through the collection of poems and find the line that they like best.	From time to time, remind students that they are reading for pleasure, not for analysis.
Journal Prompt 4 and response discussion. When students have located their favorite line, they should respond to the following journal prompt: Write down the line of poetry that you liked best (as well as the name of the poem and the poet from which it came so you can find it later). What about this line do you like? How would you describe the poet's **voice** in this line? How did you identify the poet's voice (that is, what elements of writing did he/she use to create his or her voice?) (Check our class list!) Invite students to share their responses in pairs.	I wanted students to note the differences and similarities between the use of voice in poetry and prose and to begin to analyze what it is about voice that attracts the reader.

LESSON SEQUENCE AND DESCRIPTION	TEACHER COMMENTARY
Small-group work on voice based on readiness. At this point, students should be ready to practice playing around with sentence length, word choice, tone, and rhythm in their own writing. Divide the class into two readiness groups. Assign students who seem to be struggling with the concept of **voice** to Group 1, which will review the concept and work on a structured application of voice. Assign students who seem to be grasping the concept well to Group 2, where they will work on a less structured application.	
Group 1: Students Struggling with the Concept of Voice Work closely with students to read and analyze a short piece of fiction, nonfiction, or poetry (their choice) to identify tone, word choice, and rhythm and how these elements contribute to a writer's voice. Then have the students practice using these different elements to develop different voices. Have them respond to the following questions:	Work with Group 1 students as a whole group, explaining in detail what tone, word choice, and sentence construction mean. Read passages out loud to students and point out places where the writer varies sentence length and construction and word choice to create a tone.
1. If a turtle could write, what do you think his tone would sound like? What would the tone of a bear sound like? An alligator? A hyena? 2. What kind of words do you think an elephant would use? (Long, short, hard-to-understand, simple, funny, polite, rude?) What about a hippopotamus? A pig? A goat? 3. What kind of sentences would a woodpecker use? (Long and involved? Short and to the point? A combination?) What about an owl? A jackrabbit? 4. Now choose an animal—one of the ones mentioned above or one of your own choosing—and write a paragraph about anything you think that animal might be interested in, using the tone, word choice, and sentence construction (or rhythm) that you think that animal would use. You are trying to recreate that animal's **voice**.	I chose animals here, but you can use almost anything—types of cars, TV characters, buildings, and so forth. Chose your topic according to the dynamics of the group, or let the students choose.
Group 2: Students Who Seem to Grasp the Concept of Voice Direct students to use what they know about what contributes to a writer's **voice** (appropriate use of tone, sentence construction, and word choice) to do the following:	Students in Group 2 should work on their assignments independently. If any express confusion over the assignment, have them join Group 1, as they may need clarification on goals and terms.
1. Think about what the **voice** of thunder might sound like. What about a light rain? A gentle breeze? A big gust of wind? Molasses? Diamonds?	

LESSON SEQUENCE AND DESCRIPTION	TEACHER COMMENTARY
2. Write a short paragraph or poem, using the voice of one of your favorites from above (or of your own creation), about any topic you think that thing would be interested in writing about. Remember, you are writing as though you *are* this thing—use the first person.	
Sharing of student writing. After students have completed the assignment, have volunteers share what they wrote with the rest of the class. Ask students to think about—and share, if they wish—which animal or thing's voice most resembles their own and why.	
Remind students that their oral narratives are due the following day.	

LESSON 5	Oral Narratives	*(1–2 class periods)*

LESSON SEQUENCE AND DESCRIPTION	TEACHER COMMENTARY
*Guiding question: What do oral narratives have to teach us about **voice** in writing?* The purpose of this lesson is to explore the similarities and differences between spoken and written **voice**, to deepen understanding of the elements of a writer's voice, and to develop a preliminary rubric.	Oral narratives help students hear the different rhythms of people's spoken voices—which can help students identify the value of their own stories and their own voices in their writing. It's also important for students to consider how oral language differs from written language and to think about why the two forms of communication are so different.
Journal Prompt 5 and response discussion. Open the lesson by asking students to respond to the following prompt: Look at the two memorable experiences you identified as your favorites from the list in your journal. Choose the one you would most like to write about. Think (and write) about *why* this memorable experience means so much to you. How did it help shape you into who you are today? Conduct a class discussion of why certain events are more memorable than others.	This prompt directly relates to the unit generalizations about the relationship between a writer's background and his or her **voice**.
Self-selected small-group sharing and discussion of oral narratives. Students break into self-selected small groups and read their oral narratives to each other. After all narratives have been read, students should discuss in their small groups the differences and similarities between the many voices they heard. Next, they should analyze the oral narratives to see what patterns they notice in oral language that they did not notice in written language.	As they listen to the various voices, ask students to consider the wide variety of stories people have to tell and the different ways in which they tell them. Also tell them that oral language and written language have different conventions, and ask them to think about what these may be and why.

LESSON SEQUENCE AND DESCRIPTION	TEACHER COMMENTARY
Creation of class rubric for writer's voice. Students reassemble as a large group to reexamine the class list of elements of style in writing that correspond to elements of style in music. Encourage students to add or delete items that no longer seem to fit. During this discussion, use questions like the following to prompt students' exploration of the differences between speaking and writing: • Why is writing sometimes harder than speaking? • When is it harder to speak than to write? • Do we speak for different reasons than we write? What are the purposes of each? • How might these different purposes affect the conventions for each? Students should adjust the list of characteristics of a writer's voice to reflect what they discover during this discussion. When they feel satisfied with the list, guide them in creating a descriptive rubric (e.g., powerful voice, adequate voice, whisper) to assess a writer's use of voice in a piece of writing. Tell students to jot down the rubric in their notebooks, as they will be using it for their homework.	
Homework using class rubric to evaluate reading (based on interest). Students choose their own reading to do for homework. Their task is to consider the **voice** of the piece as they read, apply the rubric, and assign a grade.	Tell students to choose to read something they enjoy; it doesn't have to be "school reading."

LESSON 6	**Tying It Up**	*(2 class periods)*

LESSON SEQUENCE AND DESCRIPTION	TEACHER COMMENTARY
*Guiding question: How do we decide what makes **voice** powerful?* The purpose of this lesson is to help the students to refine their rubric and to assign support teams for culminating products.	
Journal Prompt 6 and response discussion. Open the lesson by asking students to respond to the following prompt: Look at the line of poetry that you wrote down in response to Journal Prompt 4. Then reread your response to Journal Prompt 5 about why the memorable experience that you chose means so much to you. What connections do you see between the line of poetry that you chose and the memorable experience (and its meaning for you) that you wrote about?	It is important that students see and feel the connection between writing and the concepts of self-discovery or self-understanding.

LESSON SEQUENCE AND DESCRIPTION	TEACHER COMMENTARY
Write about this connection—think deeply about it! What do you think this connection means? What does this connection tell you about yourself? What new insights about yourself and this experience do you have? Ask willing students to share their new insights.	
Discussion and refinement of class rubric on writer's voice. Have students share what they read the night before, commenting on what they thought of the voice in the selection and how the voice rubric worked as a tool to think about the selection. What do students feel should be added to the rubric to make it more useful? What are some weaknesses of the rubric? How does it need to be adjusted before using it to grade student work? Provide guidance as necessary to help students refine the rubric.	The point is to have students refine the voice rubric so that it will be a more useful tool for examining their own writing. Explain that this rubric will be used throughout the year to evaluate their use of voice in their writing—with modifications, of course, as the year continues and the class understanding of voice becomes more refined. Type up the final version of this rubric and hand it out to the students during the next class session.
Discussion of product assignment progress. By this point, all students should have decided which **Culminating Product Assignment** they would like to pursue (see Sample 4.3, page 139). Go around the room and ask students what they have decided to do and what progress they have made so far.	
✳ **Peer feedback on product assignment plans, grouped by readiness.** Based on student responses, divide the class into three groups, differentiated according to student status relative to thinking about/working on their products: • Group 1 should consist of students who know what they would like to do and have begun working on their products. • Group 2 should consist of students who are pretty sure of what they want to do, but have not started work on their products. • Group 3 should consist of students who are unsure of what they want to do for their culminating product assignment. Once students are in their groups, distribute guidelines for their feedback sessions.	Tell students that they are sharing their ideas for product assignments to help them clarify their own thinking about their projects and get ideas from other people. Tell them that they may solicit advice/help from other students and allow time for this. It is useful for students to hear from classmates at all progress stages, but it is also useful for them to work (and partner with) other students who are at or near the same stage they are. With this approach, groups and partners can serve as a peer supports for one another throughout the product completion stage.

LESSON SEQUENCE AND DESCRIPTION	TEACHER COMMENTARY
Group 1 Group 1 students should pair up and talk briefly about the products they're working on—how they are progressing, what they are doing, and what challenges they are facing. In pairs, students should devise time lines for completing their products. Check in briefly with Group 1 students to see if they need any guidance or questions answered, then let them continue working on their products.	Assigning partners within this group gives students a sounding board and a guide, and makes the process of completing the project less over-whelming. You may want to model a few sample partner conferences prior to dividing up the groups to give students an idea of how to conduct these conferences themselves.

Group 2
Pair students and have them talk with one another about what they *think* they would like to do. You should model for students the types of questions to ask of each other to clarify their thinking about their products—questions that ask for specific information. For example:

- "That idea sounds interesting. How do you imagine the end product looking? What steps would you need to take to get there?"
- "What challenges are you facing in thinking about how to complete this project? How might you get past these challenges?"
- "What resources are you going to need? Where can you get those resources?"

In pairs, students should construct time lines for their projects, all the way through product completion.

Group 3
Have students meet as a group. Each student should list the product options that appeal to him or her, and briefly discuss the reasons for their uncertainty. Some students may express a need for time to think on their own; they may opt out of the group discussion time. This time (spent either in discussion with the group or thinking alone) may spark a decision in some students. Afterward, you should meet individually with students who are still unsure to discuss their options and to lay out steps they will need to complete the product. Once students have chosen a product, assign them a partner to develop time lines for completion of their products. Students who need a great deal of structure should develop their time lines with you.

Teacher Commentary (continued):

It is particularly important to have students in Groups 2 and 3 develop realistic time lines. While students will be creating time lines with partners, you may want to ask students to share these time lines with you to make sure that they are viable and contain all the necessary steps. The time lines can serve as a "contracts" between you and individual students.

The fact that the current product choices allow work in several modalities, including oral tradition, makes them appropriate starting places for most students. However, students with IEPs who cannot work effectively with the current product assignments can work on writing or other language tasks appropriate to their goals. You can work with the students individually or in a small group, as can the special education specialist. The process we use with these students is very much like that used with all students. There are also opportunities for these students to share their work with peers. The four product options are also easy to modify for students with particular learning needs.

LESSON 7	Working on Products	(2–3 class periods)

LESSON SEQUENCE AND DESCRIPTION	TEACHER COMMENTARY
Guiding question: How do writers benefit from both self-reflection and peer reflection on their work? The purpose of this lesson is to give students time to develop their products, to help them develop their time management skills, and to foster a feeling that the class is a community of writers working together.	
Independent work on products and peer feedback opportunities. Reserve class time each day for students to share their progress with other students. On these occasions, begin class by going quickly around the room and having students tell what they are doing, what challenges they are facing, and so forth. It's wise to alternate whole-class and small-group feedback sessions. Invite students working on the independent project assignment to join the class for these feedback sessions.	Hearing about their classmates' progress and setbacks helps students to maintain focus, get ideas for their own products, and gain insight about how to manage their time. I like using feedback sessions because they provide students an opportunity to articulate their thinking before an audience, which often can help them clarify ideas they're struggling with.

LESSON 8	Product Presentations	(2–3 class periods)

LESSON SEQUENCE AND DESCRIPTION	TEACHER COMMENTARY
The purpose of this lesson is to allow students to share their products and (if you desire) to help them devise a plan for where they might take their products next.	
Sharing and discussion of products. Students, including those students who completed independent project assignments, share and discuss their products either in a whole-class format (where, depending on class size, each student might have five minutes or so to present an important part of what he or she has discovered, learned, and created) or in small "sharing and response" teams of five or six students. You (or the students) might also identify other appropriate audiences for student products, and elect to share with those groups rather than with class members. For example, students who created children's books may want to read their books at a local school or childcare center.	It is extremely important that all students share at least a portion of their final product with the class. This way, students do not think of the teacher as the only audience for their work. To some students, small-group sharing may seem "safer" than whole-class sharing. Small-group sharing also saves time. If you use the small-group format, I suggest providing each group with sample follow-up questions for a brief discussion after each student shares his or her work. Another option is to appoint a student with strong group leadership skills to act as a lead discussant.

Teacher Reflection on the Unit

What I like best about teaching this unit is the students' reactions to it. At first, they are reluctant to accept that they can use their own experiences as the foundation for their in-school writing, but once they do, their writing blossoms! Freed from writing about *what* they think their teacher expects and in the *style* that they think the teacher expects, students write more naturally, more powerfully, and more colorfully. An additional benefit that arises from this unit is that students become more aware of their own and other students' personal histories and cultures and the influence that these backgrounds have on individual perspectives.

Having students choose from a variety of product assignments has its advantages and disadvantages. The students love having options, but it forces me to be much more organized and to keep clear and up-to-date records of what each student is doing. I found that keeping a small, separate notebook with me at all times during class (in which I jot notes on what individual students are doing, how they are progressing, what questions they have, and what sorts of twists and turns their projects are taking) allows me to stay on top of where each student is in the process.

Another aspect of this unit that I really like is that it inevitably sparks discussion of individual *differences* (in cultures, in writing style, in interests), which sets up a perfect, natural time to begin talking about why we differentiate instruction for individual students. This is particularly effective when the unit falls at the beginning of the year. I like to follow this unit with one focused on adjusting voice according to a piece of writing's purpose and its intended audience.

Holly L. Hertberg has taught in Connecticut and Virginia. She can be reached at hertberg@virginia.edu.

SAMPLE 4.1—Independent Project Guidelines

During the next few weeks, you will be extending your understanding of the concept of **voice** in writing by pursuing independent reading in a variety of genres, choosing one writer whose style and voice you find particularly powerful, and analyzing his or her work to glean lessons that will help you strengthen your own writing. You will be using this writer as a "mentor" or guide for your own writing.

Note: Although you will not participate in most class activities during this unit, plan to participate in the woven journal prompts and in the product presentations at the end of the unit.

The following steps are suggested to guide your progress over the next few weeks. Be sure to read all instructions before you begin your work.

Steps:
1. Keep a process log throughout your independent study. This process log is a document of the thinking, reading, and writing that you do for your project. You should record your thoughts about **voice**, note powerful passages from your reading, and comment on your reading, writing, and so on. This will help you develop your thinking about your chosen writer, about voice, and about your own writing. You will be turning in your process log for my review periodically.
2. Go to the library and immerse yourself in books—all kinds of books—fiction, nonfiction, science fiction, poetry, biography, and so on. Read lots of first pages, perhaps some first chapters, maybe even more, until you find a writer you absolutely *love*. Even if you come to this project with a writer you love in mind, give some other writers a chance. What you find might surprise you. There is *nothing* that so improves our writing as reading broadly from other writers. They all have something to teach us. **In your process log,** keep a record of what you're reading and investigating and your reactions to these works. Highlight a few—you don't have to mention every book whose binding you crack.
3. Once you decide on the author, poet, or playwright you would like to study in-depth and have an idea of which of the writer's works you'd like to read, meet with me so that we can develop a timeline for progress on this independent study. **This meeting is required.** You're likely to find it very helpful!
4. Next, read as much of the writer's work as you can. This isn't a race, however; savor what you read, looking for the writer's style and *how* he or she creates the voice that you enjoy so much. While you are reading, keep in the back of your mind the idea that you are reading these works as a model for your own writing. Take notes on the way that the writer uses word choice, sentence construction, rhythm, and tone to create his or her voice—and to create an effect on the reader.
5. Read part of an autobiography or biography about your chosen writer, so that you can get an idea of his or her background and what contributed to his or her success as a writer.
6. Do your own writing. Use the readings that you have been doing as a model, drawing lessons on voice from your chosen author, poet, or playwright. Make lists of ideas for pieces that you would like to write as they occur to you.
7. Choose one of the ideas you generate to develop into a longer piece of writing that you will turn in as your final product. This piece may take any form you wish, but it should exhibit the understanding of **voice** that you developed from your independent study.

SAMPLE 4.2—Independent Project Checklist for Success

Student Name: _____

Product Name: _____

Use the following checklist to make sure that you have included all the elements that you need to include in your final product. Please complete this checklist and turn it in with your final product.

Process Log:

_____ includes evidence of the development of my thinking about voice.

_____ includes a list of all the books/writers that I consulted during my independent study project.

_____ includes my reactions to and thoughts about the works I found most interesting/helpful/ thought-provoking during my independent reading.

_____ includes my notes about my focus writer's style and voice, how he or she uses word choice, sentence construction, rhythm, and tone (and other devices that you notice) to affect the reader.

_____ includes my notes about the autobiography/biography I read about my focus writer—particularly notes on this writer's background and what contributed to his or her success as a writer.

_____ includes the writing I did while reading. (These don't have to be finished pieces.)

Product Format:

My product . . .

_____ shows evidence of careful proofreading.

_____ looks like a "finished product."

Product Content:

My product . . .

_____ exhibits my understanding of **voice** developed during my independent study. (Please fill out and attach the class-created rubric on writer's voice.)

_____ is a fully-developed, "finished" piece of writing. (Please submit all drafts of the piece).

SAMPLE 4.3—Culminating Product Assignments

Product Assignment 1: Music Expert

How is "style" created in music? How much is style in music a result of the rhythm, chosen instruments, and other technical aspects of music, and how much is it a result of the musician's background and personality? How does this relate to style (or **voice**) in writing? How can you teach your classmates (and future students) about styles in music that will help them not only learn more about music, but also improve their own writing?

Your final product may take any form you wish—a presentation, an essay, a children's book, a chart, etc.— but its purpose is to serve as a classroom resource that will teach other students about the stylistic elements of music and how they might apply that information to improve their own writing.

Steps:

1. Keep a process log of your thinking about your product as it develops. (This will also help you track your progress). Date your entries.
2. Make arrangements to interview two musicians (musicians are everywhere!). Meet with a member (or members) of a local band, a singer in a church choir, a professor of music at a nearby college, the high school band director . . . or whomever else you can think of. Although you are only required to interview two people, you may wish to interview more; your findings will probably be richer and more interesting. *You may find that you can interview a musician via e-mail. This is a perfectly satisfactory method of conducting an interview.*
3. To prepare for your interview, consult at least one biography or autobiography of a musician to see what they have to say about style. This will help you formulate your interview questions.
4. Write your interview questions. You want to understand what goes into developing a musician's style and what it's like to be a musician or a person who studies music. Among other questions, you'll want to ask your interviewee about his or her background/personal history and how this has influenced his or her musical style or musical preferences. *Make sure that you have developed a written list of interview questions before going to the interviews. You may stray from these questions, but make sure to have them prepared. If you wish, you may meet with me or a trusted partner to go over the questions prior to the interviews (highly recommended).*

SAMPLE 4.3—*(continued)*

Product Assignment 1: Music Expert *(continued)*

5. Conduct your interviews and take complete notes during each interview. Be sure to ask good follow-up questions so you'll have plenty of information to work with.

6. Read over the notes from your interviews. What themes do you notice about style in music? What seem to be the common ideas about how style is developed in music? How are your interviewees' views on style different?

7. Talk about what you think you've discovered with someone (another student pursuing the same topic, one of the musicians or music experts you interviewed, me) to clarify your thinking.

8. Think about what we've discussed in class about how style—or **voice**—is developed in writing (for help, refer to the list that we have created). What parallels/differences beyond those we have discussed in class do you notice between style in writing and style in music?

9. Design and complete your final product. Reread the statement about the product's purpose at the top of this handout. Be sure your product shows *clear evidence of your learning throughout this unit,* particularly with respect to the unit generalizations concerning **voice**.

SAMPLE 4.3—(*continued*)

Product Assignment 2: Art Expert

How is "style" created in art? How much is style in art a result of the medium, the colors chosen, and other technical aspects of art, and how much is style a result of the artist's background and personality? How does this relate to style (or **voice**) in writing? How can you teach your classmates (and future students) about styles in art that will help them not only learn more about art, but also improve their own writing?

Your final product may take any form you wish—a presentation, an essay, a children's book, a chart, etc.—but its purpose is to serve as a classroom resource that will teach other students about the stylistic elements of art and how they might apply that information to improve their own writing.

Steps:
1. Keep a process log of your thinking about your product as it develops. (This will also help you track your progress). Date your entries.
2. Make arrangements to interview two artists (artists are everywhere!). Meet with your art teacher, a local painter, a high school art student, a student or professor at a local college, or whomever else you can think of. Although you are only required to interview two people, you may wish to interview more—your findings will probably be richer and more interesting. *You may find that you can interview an artist via e-mail. This is a perfectly satisfactory method of conducting an interview.*
3. To prepare for your interview, consult at least one biography or autobiography of an artist to see what they have to say about style. This will help you formulate your interview questions.
4. Write your interview questions. You want to understand what goes into developing an artist's style and what it's like to be an artist or a person who studies art. Among other questions, you'll want to ask your interviewee about his or her background/personal history and how this has influenced his or her artistic style or artistic preferences. *Make sure that you have developed a written list of interview questions before going to the interviews. You may stray from these questions, but make sure to have them prepared. If you wish, you may meet with me or a trusted partner to go over the questions prior to the interviews (highly recommended).*
5. Conduct your interviews and take complete notes during each interview. Be sure to ask good follow-up questions so you'll have plenty of information to work with.
6. Read over the notes from your interviews. What themes do you notice about style in art? What seem to be the common ideas about how style is developed in art? How do your interviewees' views on style differ?
7. Talk about what you think you've discovered with someone (another student pursuing the same topic, one of the artists or art experts you interviewed, me) to clarify your thinking.
8. Think about what we've discussed in class about how style—or **voice**—is developed in writing (for help, refer to the list that we have created). What parallels/differences beyond those we have discussed in class do you notice between style in writing and style in art?
9. Design and complete your final product. Reread the statement about the product's purpose at the top of this handout. Be sure your product shows *clear evidence of your learning throughout this unit,* particularly with respect to the unit generalizations concerning **voice**.

Product Assignment 3: Memorable Personal Experience Narrative

We have been looking at how **voice** is developed in a writer's writing. A large part of the power of an individual's voice comes from writing about what one knows. Whom do you know better than you know yourself? Writing autobiographical pieces allows us not only to write about things that we know really well and are definite authorities on, but also allows us to get to know ourselves better.

Steps:
1. Return to the woven journal prompts that you have been working on throughout this unit. Reread the entire sequence of responses, thinking in particular about your final few entries. You have already identified some key details about a memorable personal experience and thought about how it has shaped you as an individual. As a result, you have probably developed new insights about yourself.
2. If possible, interview a key participant in your memorable experience to enrich your memory and understanding of the event.
3. Develop the memorable experience that you chose to focus on in your journal—and your thoughts about how this experience has affected your life and your development—into a completed piece of writing that shows off your own personal voice. Your piece of writing may take one of several forms:
   • *Tell your memorable experience in children's book form.* Your illustrations (if you choose to use them) may be pictures you draw yourself, pictures from a magazine or the Internet, or pictures you generate on the computer. Look at some of the samples provided for ideas about how to construct your book. Use the rubric on voice to give you hints about how to make your writing voice powerful and interesting.
   • *Write about your memorable experience in a collection of poems.* In your poems, provide different perspectives on the memorable experience, varying your voice according to the perspective you assume. For example, one poem might recount the experience from your perspective. Another poem (or poems) might recount the experience from the perspective of another person (or people) involved. Another poem might be from the perspective of an inanimate or nonhuman object involved in that experience (a chair, a tree, a squirrel, a piece of paper). To get your writing started, read some of the poetry that we have in the classroom. (Often, reading other people's work helps get the creative juices flowing.) Use the rubric on voice to give you hints about how to make your writing voice powerful and interesting. For hints on how to adjust your voice to capture the perspective of various people or things, refer to your notes from our "Thunder and Lightning" or animal voices exercise (Lesson 4).
   • *Write about your memorable experience in essay or story form.* Look at some of the sample autobiographical essays provided for ideas on how to construct these narratives. Use the rubric on voice to give you hints about how to make your writing voice powerful and interesting.
   • *Pursue another idea you have.* You must obtain my approval before you begin.
4. As you develop your final product, keep a process log in which you record your reactions to the sample products you consult, your thoughts on developing your own writer's voice for this product, and a timeline of your progress.
5. Annotate your finished piece of writing to explain how it reflects your own writer's voice, particularly with respect to the unit generalizations concerning **voice**.

Product Assignment 4: Oral History Narrative

Did you enjoy collecting the oral narrative from someone you knew? You may, if you wish, continue to work on that project. You must keep a process log in which you note your thoughts, reactions, ideas, and insights along the way. Your process log will also serve as a timeline and record of your progress on the project.

Steps:

1. Collect oral histories from various members of your family. (Or, if you wish, you may choose to collect oral histories from another group of people. For example, you might interview a group of people who lived through the bombing of Pearl Harbor, and collect their memories of that event, or you might interview a group of people who all love baseball and collect their stories of the most memorable baseball game they ever watched. It's up to you! Choose something you find interesting!) You should interview four or five people to get a broad and interesting range of perspectives.

2. Once you've collected the narratives, analyze the interviews and look for the rhythms in the various speakers' speech patterns, the type of vocabulary they use, their tones, and so on. (For help with this, consult the rubric on voice we created in class.)

3. Now decide how you will put the narratives together into a final product. There is a range of possibilities, including (but not limited to) the following:

   • *Write a play that interweaves the stories of the people you interviewed.* Be sure that when each character "speaks" you can clearly identify them based on their "voice."

   • *Create a narrative about the event that interweaves your interviewees' stories.* Describe the event through their various voices. Be sure that when each character "speaks" you can clearly identify them based on their "voice."

   • *Write an article for a newspaper that uses the voices of the people you interviewed as "sources."* Be sure that when each character "speaks" you can clearly identify them based on their "voice."

   • *Write a series of brief public radio commentaries about the event.* Be sure that when each character "speaks" you can clearly identify them based on their "voice."

   • *Pursue another idea you have.* You must obtain my approval before you begin.

4. Include with your finished product a brief discussion of how the voices of the people you interviewed differ from one another, particularly with respect to the unit generalizations concerning **voice**.

SAMPLE 4.4—Culminating Product Assignment Checklists for Success

Product Assignment 1: Music Expert

Student Name: _____

Product Name: _____

Use the following checklist to make sure that you have included all the elements that you need to include in your final product. Please complete this checklist and turn it in with your final product.

Process Log:

_____ I have included my process log. My process log contains dated entries that trace the development of my thinking about my product. I feel that my process log provides evidence of the thought and work that I put into creating my product.

Product Research:

_____ I have included my notes/transcripts from my interviews with two or more musicians.

_____ I have included my interview questions from my interviews with two or more musicians.

_____ I have included my notes about style from the musician biography or autobiography that I consulted during my product research.

Product Format:

My product . . .

_____ is in an easy-to-use, understandable, interesting format that other students can use to learn about how style in music relates to voice in writing.

_____ shows evidence of careful proofreading.

_____ looks like a "finished product." (Remember, your creation will be used in the classroom for years to come—it should be reflective of care!)

_____ presents a theory about the elements of style in music.

_____ explores the connections between a musician's background and personality and his or her musical style.

_____ shows how the elements of style in music relate to the elements of voice in writing.

_____ shows evidence of my developing writer's voice. (Please fill out and attach a copy of the class-created rubric on writer's voice.)

Product Annotation:

My product . . .

_____ contains an explanation of how my product reflects my own writer's voice.

_____ explores how the unit generalizations concerning voice are reflected in my product.

SAMPLE 4.4—(continued)

Product Assignment 2: Art Expert

Student Name: _____

Product Name: _____

Use the following checklist to make sure that you have included all the elements that you need to include in your final product. Please complete this checklist and turn it in with your final product.

Process Log:

_____ I have included my process log. My process log contains dated entries that trace the development of my thinking about my product. I feel that my process log provides evidence of the thought and work that I put into creating my product.

Product Research:

_____ I have included my notes/transcripts from my interviews with two or more artists.

_____ I have included my interview questions from my interviews with two or more artists.

_____ I have included my notes about style from the artist biography or autobiography that I consulted during my product research.

Product Format:

My product . . .

_____ is in an easy-to-use, understandable, interesting format that other students can use to learn about how style in art relates to voice in writing.

_____ shows evidence of careful proofreading.

_____ looks like a "finished product." (Remember, your creation will be used in the classroom for years to come—it should be reflective of care!)

_____ presents a theory about the elements of style in art.

_____ explores the connections between an artist's background and personality and his or her artistic style.

_____ shows how the elements of style in art relate to the elements of voice in writing.

_____ shows evidence of my developing writer's voice. (Please fill out and attach a copy of the class-created rubric on writer's voice.)

Product Annotation:

My product . . .

_____ contains an explanation of how my product reflects my own writer's voice.

_____ explores how the unit generalizations concerning voice are reflected in my product.

Product Assignment 3: Memorable Personal Experience

Student Name: _____

Product Name: _____

Use the following checklist to make sure that you have included all the elements that you need to include in your final product. Please complete this checklist and turn it in with your final product.

Process Log:

_____ I have included my process log. My process log contains dated entries that trace the development of my thinking about my product. I feel that my process log provides evidence of the thought and work that I put into creating my product.

Product Research:

_____ I have included all of my woven journal prompt responses.

_____ I have included the notes from my interviews with a key participant in this experience.

_____ I have included a list of all the works/sample products I consulted when creating my product.

Product Format:

My product . . .

_____ shows evidence of careful proofreading.

_____ looks like a "finished product."

Product Content:

If you have chosen to create a children's book, a personal narrative, or a story . . .

My product . . .

_____ has an identifiable beginning, middle, and end.

_____ contains a conflict and a resolution.

_____ shows evidence of my developing writer's voice. (Please fill out and attach a copy of the class-created rubric on writer's voice.)

If you have chosen to create a poem . . .

My product . . .

_____ contains varied perspectives on my chosen event.

_____ contains a poetic voice that shifts according to the poem's perspective.

_____ shows evidence of my developing writer's voice. (Please fill out and attach the class-created rubric on writer's voice.)

Product Annotation:

My product . . .

_____ contains an explanation of how my product reflects my own writer's voice.

_____ explores how the unit generalizations concerning voice are reflected in my product.

SAMPLE 4.4—*(continued)*

Product Assignment 4: Oral History Narrative

Student Name: _____

Product Name: _____

Use the following checklist to make sure that you have included all the elements that you need to include in your final product. Please complete this checklist and turn it in with your final product.

Process Log:

_____ I have included my process log. My process log contains dated entries that trace the development of my thinking about my product. I feel that my process log provides evidence of the thought and work that I put into creating my product.

Product Research:

_____ I have included the notes/transcripts of the oral histories I collected from the people I interviewed.

_____ I have included my analysis of the speakers' speech patterns, use of vocabulary, tones, etc. (Remember to consult your rubric on voice to help you with this analysis.)

Product Format:

My product . . .

_____ shows evidence of careful proofreading.

_____ looks like a "finished product."

Product Content:

My product . . .

_____ contains the perspectives/stories of all the people I interviewed.

_____ presents clearly identifiable "voices" for each "character" in the final product.

_____ pulls together the various narratives into a unified whole.

_____ shows evidence of my developing writer's voice. (Please fill out and attach the class-created rubric on writer's voice.)

Product Annotation:

My product . . .

_____ contains a discussion of how the voices of the people I interviewed differ from one another.

_____ contains an explanation of how my product reflects the different voices of people I interviewed.

_____ explores how the unit generalizations concerning voice are reflected in my product or factored in the process of creating my product.

SAMPLE 4.5—Oral Narrative Assignment

Homework: Oral Narrative

Interview a member of your family about an important family event. Audiotape the conversation. (If you do not have a tape recorder, you may borrow one. Sign-ups will be posted). Type (or handwrite) five minutes of the conversation. (You don't have to transcribe the whole conversation unless you want to; transcribing takes a long time.)

As you listen to the interview, transcribe the audiotape, and read the transcript, think about the language patterns you are noticing in the speaker's voice. Think about how these patterns are similar to and different from the ones we notice in written language. Think about how oral language patterns and written language patterns are different. Why do you think this is true?

You don't have to write anything about this, although you may wish to jot down a few notes to remind yourself. Just think about it and be prepared to discuss it in class.

5

Line 'Em Up!

*A Pre-Algebra/Algebra I Unit
on Constant Change*

Unit Developer: Nanci Smith

Introduction

This four-week mathematics unit focuses on the concept of **change.** Its primary
purpose is to examine ways in which change is represented both graphically and lin-
early. Throughout the unit, students examine sets of data represented in a variety of
forms and work to apply their new knowledge to an ongoing, independent project
that builds as they gain more information. Topics covered during this unit include
constant versus variable change, linear graphing, regression lines, slope, and linear
equations.

The unit opens with a broad look at the concept of change, and then quickly
immerses students in the skills of interpreting and creating graphic representations
of data. This unit assumes that the students have been pre-assessed (either formally
through a pre-test or informally through observation and discussion) for learning
styles and readiness levels with regard to reading tables and graphs. It also assumes
that the students have been exposed to reading and using tables and graphs,
although they may demonstrate various readiness levels with regard to these skills.
The centerpiece of the unit is the independent project on change. It is designed to
span the four-week unit so that students can apply new information and understandings developed through each lesson. Although the project incorporates specific requirements that all students must meet, it is easily modified for specific
students and can be differentiated based on both readiness and interest.

Teachers should provide in-class time for work on the independent project so
that they can meet with students to discuss project progress and better assess the
processes students are using. Finally, it is imperative that all students have a firm

grasp of what the independent research project assignment is asking them to do, as they will be critiquing one another's projects toward the end of the unit.

Teacher Reflection on Designing the Unit

As I started thinking about teaching this topic to beginning Algebra students, what first came to mind is that lines don't seem to matter to students. Most students, even those who can complete a graph or find a slope, never seem to *understand* very much about linear functions. (I am regularly amazed at the number of my Pre-Calculus students who cannot automatically graph a line from its equation.) Therefore, the overwhelming drive behind this unit was to help students understand lines by tying linear functions to real-world concepts. I chose the concept of **change** because it describes linear functions well and has many real-world applications on which to draw.

I began planning by looking through my textbook and thinking about traditional treatments of line units. I knew I would need to incorporate all the text's information concerning lines, as it would be included on district and state assessments, and that this would cover the basic "knowledge" and "skill" categories I wanted my students to master. But I found little in the textbook that addressed understanding.

The first step I took to structure the unit was to consider the factual and global understandings I wanted students to have as a result of this unit. Some of these were stated explicitly in my textbook, and I added others I thought were important. I took each subtopic within the textbook's unit on lines and placed it within a grid ranging vertically from discrete facts to global understandings and horizontally from basic to abstract. This both reminded me of the variety of content present in this unit and helped me plan an order for unit activities. Then I took a look at each subtopic and thought about my students and the wide variety of ways they could learn and demonstrate their learning. Once I had differentiated the class activities, the formative assessments fell into place pretty logically.

For a final assessment, I knew that I wanted more than just a test. I created an ongoing project that I would assign on the very first day of the unit and ask students to work on over the course of instruction. The project involved independent research, and to complete it, students would need to apply an understanding of every subtopic addressed in the unit. I outlined the basic requirements that I would look for and decided to vary some of the specific requirements for students in order to encourage individual growth. I decided to negotiate these goals individually with each student. Also, I wanted to develop the final scoring guide as a class. I find that doing so gives students a sense of ownership of the assessment process. Although scoring guides might vary somewhat from class to class, students are usually quite adept at identifying what I would consider to be the essential and non-negotiable aspects of quality work. Of course, I gently guide them in the right direction when necessary!

Finally, this unit began as a collaboration with my friend Gene Day many years ago, before I knew anything about differentiation. I appreciate the thought and help our discussions provided in framing the unit.

Pre-Algebra/Algebra Standards Addressed

- Analyze functional relationships to explain how a change in one variable results in a change in another.
- Distinguish between linear and nonlinear relationships through investigations.
- Distinguish between linear and nonlinear functions, given graphic examples.
- Describe, represent, and analyze patterns and relationships using shapes, tables, graphs, data points, verbal rules, and standard algebraic notation.
- Produce the rule (function) that explains the relationship (pattern) between the numbers when a change in the first variable affects the second variable (T-chart, 2-row table, or input/output machine).
- Solve simple linear equations and inequalities using a variety of methods (e.g., informal, formal, graphical) and a variety of manipulatives.
- Describe the concepts of variables, expressions, equations, and inequalities.
- Graph given data points to represent a linear equation, using (x, y) coordinates using all four quadrants of a coordinate grid.

Unit Concepts and Generalizations

Change

- Change can be represented in multiple ways.
- Change is all around us.
- Change can be analyzed.
- Usually, one thing changes with respect to another (e.g., distance and time).

Unit Objectives

As a result of this unit, the students will *know*

- The difference between variable and constant change.
- The difference between independent and dependent variables.
- The parts of tables and graphs.
- The definition of slope and ways to calculate it.
- The slope-intercept formula and other formulas related to graphing data.

As a result of this unit, the students will *understand that*

- Change in one thing is usually dependent on another thing.
- The usability of information can be dependent on how that information is represented.

- Data can be estimated with a regression line.
- Slope analyzes rate of change.
- The slope of a specific line is always the same.
- The cardinality of slope depends on how quickly change occurs.
- You can graph a line using only a point and the line's slope.
- Different forms of a line represent the same line whether they are a graph, an equation, or a point and a slope.
- Having one form of a line enables you to create other forms of the same line.
- If a point lies on a line, then the coordinates of the point are a solution to the equation of the line.
- Equations and graphs of lines can be used to represent situations in the real world.

As a result of this unit, the students will *be able to*
- Represent change in multiple formats.
- Analyze change as constant or variable.
- Distinguish between dependent and independent variables.
- Create scatter plots.
- Draw and use regression lines to make predictions.
- Find the slope of a line.
- Graph lines.
- Explain and apply the slope-intercept formula.
- Solve problems using equations and graphs of lines.
- Create various forms of linear equations.
- Work cooperatively in groups to solve problems.
- Work independently to synthesize information in the creation of a product.

Instructional Strategies Used

- Flexible grouping
- Independent research
- Tiered assessment
- Gardner's multiple intelligences
- Sternberg's triarchic intelligences
- Visual, aural, and kinesthetic learning

Sample Supporting Materials Provided

Sample #	Title	Page
5.1	Guidelines for the Independent Research Project on Change	180

Unit Overview

LESSON	WHOLE-CLASS COMPONENTS	DIFFERENTIATED COMPONENTS
LESSON 1 **Introduction** *1–2 class periods*	Discussion of **change** and how it relates to and is represented in math *15 minutes*	
		Small-group activity looking at real-world changes, based on learning profile (multiple intelligences) *30–45 minutes*
	Sharing of discoveries and ideas *30 minutes*	
	Introduction/preliminary work on the independent research project *15 minutes*	Independent projects differentiated based on readiness and interest
	Journal prompts *5 minutes*	
LESSON 2 **Tables and Graphs** *1–2 class periods*	Examination of sample data and discussion of the merits of various formats (tabular and graphic) *15 minutes*	
	Discussion of how **change** relates to students' lives and how these changes may be represented in a uniform way *10 minutes*	
		Review of scatter plots and regression lines based on need *10 minutes*
		Scatter plot and regression line application activity based on readiness *30–40 minutes*
	Discussion of results *20 minutes*	

LESSON	WHOLE-CLASS COMPONENTS	DIFFERENTIATED COMPONENTS
LESSON 3 **Introduction of Slope** *1–2 class periods*	Review of graphing and introduction of slope *10 minutes*	
		Small-group discovery learning activity to determine how to find the slope of a line, based on learning profile (modality) *20–30 minutes*
		Jigsaw activity (heterogeneous groups) to present results of discoveries and related insights *20–30 minutes*
	Discussion of results and generation of slope formula *20 minutes*	
	Review of key concepts about slope *10 minutes*	
LESSON 4 **Discovering Slope Through Technology** *(Optional)* *1 class period*	Demonstration/practice with Calculator-Based Laboratory (CBL) or Calculator-Based Ranger (CBR) technology (if available) *20–30 minutes*	
	Small-group (random) discussion of results *10–15 minutes*	
	Sharing of conclusions and how they relate to slope *10 minutes*	
LESSON 5 **Differentiated Quiz** *1 class period*	Review for quiz *5 minutes*	
		Quiz on concepts and formulas related to slope, based on readiness *45–50 minutes*

LESSON	WHOLE-CLASS COMPONENTS	DIFFERENTIATED COMPONENTS
LESSON 6 **Graphing with a Point and a Slope** *1–2 class periods*	Review of how to determine the slope of a line *5 minutes*	
	Presentation of graphing a line from a given point and slope *15 minutes*	
		Small-group graphing activity based on learning profile (modality) *20 minutes*
	Journal response synthesizing understandings of slope and related graphing exercises *10 minutes*	
LESSON 7 **Exploring the Equation of a Line in Slope-Intercept Form** *2–3 class periods*	Review of previous learning and presentation of slope-intercept form *30–40 minutes*	
		Small-group discovery learning based on readiness *30–40 minutes*
	Sharing of results and discussion of various equations studied *10–15 minutes*	Discussion questions targeted to readiness groups
LESSON 8 **The Relationship Between the Equation of a Line and the Points on a Line** *2 class periods*	Review of slope-intercept form and presentation on working backward from a graph to the equation of a line *30 minutes*	
	Application exercises in two (random) groups and discussion of results *20 minutes*	
	Independent practice *20 minutes*	
		Small-group summarization activity based on learning profile (multiple intelligences) *25 minutes*
	Review *5 minutes*	

LESSON	WHOLE-CLASS COMPONENTS	DIFFERENTIATED COMPONENTS
LESSON 9 **Solving Real-World Problems Using Lines** *1 class period*	Review of scatter plots, regression lines, slope, and appropriate graphing *10 minutes* Presentation of related real-world problems *20 minutes* Real-world application problems in heterogeneous (random) groups *15 minutes* Discussion of how to best set up and solve the problems *10 minutes*	
LESSON 10 **Relating the Many Forms of Equations of Lines** *2–3 class periods*	Review slope, slope-intercept, and the significance of dependent and independent variables *10 minutes* Lecture on equations for a line *30–40 minutes* Sharing of small-group work and discussion of the need for various equations *30–40 minutes*	Note-taking sheets distributed to some students based on readiness Small-group processing activity based on learning profile (triarchic intelligences) *45–50 minutes*
LESSON 11 **Peer Critiques of Independent Research Projects** *1 class period*	Independent project presentations and feedback in heterogeneous small groups *40–50 minutes*	

LESSON	WHOLE-CLASS COMPONENTS	DIFFERENTIATED COMPONENTS
LESSON 12 **Presentation of Independent Research Projects** *2–4 class periods*	Presentation of independent research projects *2–4 class periods*	
LESSON 13 **Unit Test Review** *1 class period*	Test review with learning stations *40–50 minutes*	Some station assignments based on teacher knowledge of student need related to unit skills
LESSON 14 **Unit Test** *1 class period*	Test *40–50 minutes*	Portions of the test based on readiness

Unit Description and Teacher Commentary

LESSON 1	**Introduction**	*(1–2 class periods)*

LESSON SEQUENCE AND DESCRIPTION	TEACHER COMMENTARY
Discussion of change and how it relates to and is represented in math. Begin with a whole-class discussion of **change** as it occurs in the real world. What changes do the students see around them all the time? Discuss constant change (the change is always the same) and variable change (the degree or amount of change can vary). Have the students generate ideas about things that change and tell them to categorize their examples of change as either constant or variable. Tell them that the unit they are starting focuses on constant change and on how mathematicians view, represent, and analyze this type of change.	Here, I wanted the students to examine **change** in their own lives and worlds. I was hoping to create a connection for them.

LESSON SEQUENCE AND DESCRIPTION	TEACHER COMMENTARY
Small-group activity looking at real-world changes, based on learning profile (multiple intelligences). Put the students in small groups of three or four, based on their intelligence preference. Each group will complete one of the following tasks:	This sense-making activity allowed students to work in ways most comfortable for them. Early in the year, my students complete several learning profile assessments. (We add information as the year progresses.) I used my knowledge of each student's learning profile to assign him or her to the appropriate group. My goals were to
Task 1: Logical/Mathematical Learners Given a set of data that changes over time, such as the population of your city or town, decide on several ways to present the information. Make a chart that shows the various ways you can present the information to your classmates. Discuss as a group which representation you think is most effective. Why is it most effective? Is the **change** you are representing constant or variable? Which representation best shows this? Be ready to share your ideas with the class.	• Promote connection (among students and with important ideas). • Match tasks to students. • Ensure that students really understood the important ideas. • Promote student success (to motivate further success). • Provide variety in students' daily learning experiences. • Promote group interaction among peers.
Task 2: Interpersonal Learners Brainstorm things that **change** constantly. Generate a list. Discuss which of the things change quickly and which of them change slowly. What would graphs of your ideas look like? Be ready to share your ideas with the class.	
Task 3: Visual/Spatial Learners Given a variety of graphs, discuss what **changes** each one is representing. Are the changes constant or variable? How can you tell? Hypothesize how graphs showing constant and variable changes differ from one another. Be ready to share your ideas with the class.	
Task 4: Verbal/Linguistic Learners Examine articles from newspapers or magazines about a situation that involves **change,** and discuss what is changing. What is this change occurring in relation to? For example, is this change related to time, money, etc.? What kind of change is it—constant or variable? Write a summary paragraph that discusses the change and share it with the class.	
Sharing of discoveries and ideas. After the small groups have had enough time to complete their tasks, have them share their discoveries and ideas about **change** with the class. What new ideas about change do they have? What conclusions can they draw about change?	

LESSON SEQUENCE AND DESCRIPTION	TEACHER COMMENTARY
Introduction/preliminary work on the independent research project. Distribute the **Guidelines for the Independent Research Project on Change** (see Sample 5.1, page 180) and review project elements and requirements. This ongoing project extends throughout the four-week unit. It requires all students to select, research, and reach data-based conclusions about a real-life issue involving **change.** It also includes a peer evaluation component.	I differentiated this project by meeting with students individually to negotiate project details and criteria based on readiness and interest.
Areas for differentiation include	Note that the number of data points depends on the research topic. If data are difficult to come by, five data points might be sufficient. If projects incorporate survey data or tracking temperatures, prices, or similar components, 10 to 20 data points would be more appropriate.
• Topic chosen (based on readiness). • Number of required data points (based on readiness). • Number of conclusions required (based on readiness). • Depth level expected (based on readiness). • Additional areas of exploration or extensions required (based on readiness and interest).	
Explain to students that over the next several weeks, you will be available to work with them individually and in small groups to help them iron out the details of their project plans and support their success. You also will expect them to apply what they are learning in class to their project work.	Students may need your help selecting a topic to study. It's a good idea to think of several sample topics in advance and use them as examples during this initial introduction.
Throughout the four-week period, meet with students to discuss specific parts of the project, to set due dates for specific pieces, and to assess the students' progress with the project as a whole.	I gave students regular reminders to work on their projects and to apply the information I was presenting in class. I also talked about developing quality project elements with the class as a whole and with individuals and small groups.
Journal prompts. Close the lesson by asking students to respond individually to the following journal prompts:	This provided another chance for students to make sense of the ideas discussed, this time individually.
• Is all **change** the same? • Why do mathematicians care about **change**?	

LESSON 2　　　　　**Tables and Graphs**　　　　*(1–2 class periods)*

LESSON SEQUENCE AND DESCRIPTION	TEACHER COMMENTARY
Examination of sample data and discussion of the merits of various formats (tabular and graphic). As a whole class, examine a set of data represented in both tabular and graphic form. Discuss the "readability" of both and students' preferences for both. Which type can you interpret more easily? From which one is it easier to make predictions? Why?	This opener served both as a review of what the students already knew and as an introduction to possible new materials. Here, I wanted to try to "even the playing field" a little bit.

LESSON SEQUENCE AND DESCRIPTION	TEACHER COMMENTARY
Discussion of how change relates to students' lives and how these changes may be represented in a uniform way. Introduce the subject of dependent and independent variables by asking students if they are "dependent" on their parents. Who pays for rent and food? (Students are the dependent variables, and parents are the independent variables.) To further explain the two types of variables, discuss "what" depends on "what" for **change.** How about grades and time spent on studying? In general, which depends on which? Lead the students to an understanding that grades are dependent on time spent studying. (Thus, time spent studying is the independent variable and grades are the dependent variable.) Point out that, in general, time is almost always the independent variable in a change that involves time. Tell the students that when graphing, the independent variable is shown on the (horizontal) x-axis and the dependent variable is shown on the (vertical) y-axis.	As in the previous lesson, I wanted the students to relate the information to their own lives. Thus, we were moving from concrete to more abstract thinking.
Ask the class: Why do you think it is important to be able to represent data in a uniform way?	I was encouraging critical thinking here.
Review of scatter plots and regression lines based on need. At this point, if necessary, provide a review of how to scatter plot a set of data or show a scatter plot of roughly linear data. Explain to the students that most real data do not make a perfect line when graphed. This is why we use scatter plots. Sometimes it is necessary to sketch a line through the data to best represent the majority of points. Show this on the board or on an overhead. Point out that the sketched line is called a *line of best fit* or a *regression line.* Explain that there are precise ways to determine the line, but that for now, we will just sketch a line that hits as many points as possible and that divides the remaining points evenly above and below the line. Make your explanations as you model this on the board or on an overhead. Explain that the sketched line can be used to make predictions about data that are not available. Show how to extend the line, pick a point on it, and interpret what that point would mean.	My teacher-directedness here led up to a more student-centered approach later. First, I needed to make sure that we were all on common ground and introduce new vocabulary (regression line). I allowed students who already had a clear understanding of this concept to begin their application activity at this time.
Scatter plot and regression line application activity based on readiness. The students will complete the following tasks in four small groups based on readiness levels with regard to their ability to read, analyze, and create graphs of data.	I based my groupings on previous observations of the students' readiness levels as demonstrated through formal assessments (quizzes, tests), large-group discussions, small-group work, and individual work.

LESSON SEQUENCE AND DESCRIPTION	TEACHER COMMENTARY

Task for Group 1

Given a line graph of a company's sales (real or fictional), determine what is changing with respect to what. Decide which is the independent variable and which is the dependent variable. Write a marketing report describing the sales trends, making sure to use specific data points as references. When are the sales increasing? Decreasing? Staying the same? How do you know? Comment on when the **change** is fastest and slowest, and explain how you determined this. Assume that the sales pattern continues and make a prediction about the company's future sales. Choose a point where the sales pattern changes. What would have happened if the sales had not changed at that point?

Task for Group 2

Given a price plan (real or fictional) for a health club (initiation fee plus a monthly charge), plot a scatter plot of the total money paid over a period of 12 months. Assume that Month 0 is the initiation fee and Month 1 is the first monthly payment. Label the correct axes with the independent and dependent variables, and draw an accurate scale. Sketch a line of best fit for your data. Use the line to determine how much money will have been paid in total after 15 months and 24 months. Make a table of values for Months 0–12. Write a brief summary of the cost of belonging to the health club and how the cost **changes** over time. Make a recommendation for a different plan that would be fair to the health club but less expensive for the consumer. How would that affect the graph?

Task for Group 3

Given a city's (real or fictional) population data in a table, make a scatter plot. Be careful to determine the independent and dependent variables, place them on the correct axes, and label the axes. Clearly show the scale on the axes. Sketch a line of best fit for your data. Use the line to predict the population for at least five different years for which there is no data. Write a population analysis for the city's planners. Describe when the population **changed** the fastest and the slowest, and explain how you determined this. Include in your analysis a prediction of the population growth in the next 10 years and 50 years, and add anything else that you think the planners need to know.

TEACHER COMMENTARY

These group activities move from

- Less complex to more complex.
- Requiring less interpretation to more interpretation.
- Requiring less independence to more independence.
- Less open-ended to more open-ended.

LESSON SEQUENCE AND DESCRIPTION	TEACHER COMMENTARY
Task for Group 4 Form a table of data showing number of items purchased and total prices paid, then make a scatter plot of this data. Label the correct axes with the independent and dependent variables, and draw an accurate scale. Sketch a line of best fit to represent the data. Predict how much would be paid for numbers of items not specifically in the table. Write a paragraph describing your predictions and how you came up with them. How accurate do you think the predictions are? Why?	I made up the data that Group 4 used in this activity. For example, I provided a table of a number of CDs and their prices: 1 CD was $15, 2 CDs were $30, 3 CDs were $45, etc. Depending on the group, sometimes I made the data obviously linear (as the CD example is) and sometimes I gave "package deals" like those for a health club membership or cell phone plan so that the data were not linear.
Discussion of results. After the groups have successfully completed their tasks, have them share their work with the whole class. Then, lead a whole-class discussion that addresses the following questions: • How did the groups determine what the independent and dependent variables were? • What are the strengths and weaknesses of using a line of best fit for making predictions? • Did the groups prefer using tables or graphs or did it depend on the situation?	My questions here required metacognitive evaluation.

LESSON 3   Introduction of Slope   *(1–2 class periods)*

LESSON SEQUENCE AND DESCRIPTION	TEACHER COMMENTARY
Review of graphing and introduction of slope. With the whole class, review what students have discussed and learned about **change** and how change can be represented on a graph. Explain that how something is changing is called "a rate of change" and that if change is constant, then the rate of change is described by the *slope* of the line of best fit. Slope can be thought of as the "steepness" or slant of a line. Do not demonstrate how to determine the slope of a line as the students will be grouped based on learning modalities to discover this on their own.	
Small-group discovery learning activity to determine how to find the slope of a line, based on learning profile. The students will complete the following tasks in small groups based on learning modality:	Discovery is critical to real learning! When students figure out what an idea means or how a skill works, it's likely to be more useful and memorable to them.

LESSON SEQUENCE AND DESCRIPTION	TEACHER COMMENTARY
Activity 1: Visual Learners Complete a worksheet that requires you to determine slope based on linear graphs. Afterward, summarize how to find the slope of a line using a graph. Hypothesize what lines would look like with positive, negative, and zero slope, and draw sketches of these. *Activity 2: Tactile Learners* Given several equations of lines in the form $y = mx + b$, use graphing calculators to graph the lines and then sketch the graphs on paper. Discuss how the "slant" of the lines changes from equation to equation. Hypothesize where the slope is found in the equation of a line and how that number affects the slant of the line. *Activity 3: Aural Learners* From linear graphs with clearly labeled axes, work with the teacher to find the slopes of lines. Discuss what changes the slopes represent. For example, a slope of miles/gallons is the gas mileage of a car (miles per gallon). Suggest other types of changes that can be represented by a similar type of graph. What kinds of changes do the slopes represent?	My goals here were to • Provide discovery learning. • Promote group interaction. • Connect tasks to individual learning modalities. • Promote success. • Facilitate understanding.
Jigsaw activity (heterogeneous groups) to present results of discoveries and related insights. When the students have completed their tasks, use Jigsaw to regroup the students into groups of three so that each new group includes a student from the previous groupings. Thus, each group should include a visual, tactile, and aural learner. Have the students "teach" their group mates what they discovered through their particular tasks.	I like to give the students opportunities to be the "experts." Jigsaw grouping is great for that.
Discussion of results and generation of slope formula. When the Jigsaw activity is complete (meaning that the students have had enough time to share their discoveries), work with the whole group to generate the slope formula. How can we find the slope of a line? What information do we need to use? How do we use this information? Can we generalize a way to find the slope between any two points? Lead the students to the formula for finding slope (m): $$\begin{aligned} m &= \text{rise / run} \\ &= \text{change in } y \text{ / change in } x \\ &= \triangle y\, /\, \triangle x \\ &= (y_2 - y_1)\, /\, (x_2 - x_1) \\ m &= (y_2 - y_1)\, /\, (x_2 - x_1) \end{aligned}$$	

LESSON SEQUENCE AND DESCRIPTION	TEACHER COMMENTARY
Review of key concepts about slope. Close the lesson by reviewing unit generalizations (see page 151) and posting them in the classroom. The students should leave this lesson with these understandings: • Slope is a number that describes the rise over run from one point to another on a line. • The coefficient of the x-variable in the equation of a line is the slope of the line. • Slope describes a rate of **change.** • The sign of the slope can be determined by whether or not the line rises from left to right (positive slope) or falls from left to right (negative slope). If a line is horizontal, the slope is 0. • The magnitude of the number determines how quickly the change occurs (the steepness of the line). • The sign of the slope determines whether the change is increasing or decreasing.	I kept the students' "big ideas" or generalizations posted around the classroom so that the students and I could refer back to them frequently.

LESSON 4   **Discovering Slope Through Technology***   *(1 class period)*

LESSON SEQUENCE AND DESCRIPTION	TEACHER COMMENTARY
Demonstration/practice with Calculator-Based Laboratory (CBL) or Calculator-Based Ranger (CBR) technology. With the whole class, demonstrate the DT-Match (Distance-Time) or similar program on the CBL or CBR unit. In groups (if enough units are available) or as a whole class, have students take turns trying to match the given graphs. One student should be the "hiker" and the rest of the group should coach him or her on how fast to move, which direction to move, when to stop, and so forth.	This activity was a great way to incorporate technology into the unit in a meaningful way that enhanced understanding. It got us to move beyond only calculators. In addition, it included a kinesthetic element that allowed the students to get up and move while they learned.
Small-group (random) discussion of results. After several practice runs, put the students into small, heterogeneous groups to discuss how the "hiker's" movements affected the graphs. The students should arrive at the following conclusions: • The faster the hiker moved, the steeper the graph. • Standing still made horizontal lines. • Moving toward the motion detector made the lines go down. • Moving away from the motion detector made the lines go up. Have the students discuss how they arrived at their conclusions.	

*Note: Lesson 4 is optional, as it depends on the technology's availability.

LESSON SEQUENCE AND DESCRIPTION	TEACHER COMMENTARY
Sharing of conclusions and how they relate to slope. Provide closure for the lesson by asking the groups to share their conclusions and how they came up with them. Continually relate the discussion back to the concept of slope, asking, "How does what you found today relate to what we already know about slope?"	I wanted the students to see how they were building upon their prior knowledge.

LESSON 5 **Differentiated Quiz** *(1 class period)*

LESSON SEQUENCE AND DESCRIPTION	TEACHER COMMENTARY
Review for quiz. Lead a brief, whole-class review of what the students have learned so far about concepts and formulas related to slope.	
Quiz on concepts and formulas related to slope, based on readiness. There are two parts to this assessment. All students complete the first group of tasks. The teacher assigns the final tasks.	This differentiated assessment was in line with my differentiated instruction without sacrificing my need to measure students' grasp of the information presented thus far.
Part I: Whole-Class • Calculate slope given a graph. • Calculate slope given two points. • Identify slope given the slope-intercept form of an equation. • Create a scatter plot graph from given data. • Identify independent and dependent variables. • Sketch a regression line for a scatter plot. • Make predictions or estimations from a regression line.	
Part II: Differentiated *Task 1: Struggling Learners* Determine slope using additional graphs and points. Describe in words how to find the slope given a graph and an equation. *Task 2: Grade-level Learners* Given a line graph with multiple **changes**, describe the changes shown in the graph in terms of rate of change and numerical slope. Predict what the graph would look like if a certain change in the graph had not occurred. *Task 3: Advanced Learners* Write a letter to a friend who will take this class next year and explain slope. Be sure to include what it represents, how it affects a graph, and all the ways to find it. Give examples and provide any other significant information. Be clear!	I gave my struggling and grade-level students tasks much like ones they had worked with already, while I required my advanced students to transform their knowledge and create something novel.

| LESSON 6 | Graphing with a Point and a Slope | *(1–2 class periods)* |

LESSON SEQUENCE AND DESCRIPTION	TEACHER COMMENTARY
Review of how to determine the slope of a line. Conduct this whole-class review by asking students to explain the process for determining the slope of a line from a given graph. Explain that the reverse process, graphing a line from a given point and a slope, is also possible. Remind the students that the slope is rise over run, or $$m = y_2 - y_1 / x_2 - x_1$$ Thus, from the point that is given, go up or down based on the numerator (up if positive, down if negative), and go to the right based on the denominator.	Here, I allowed many students to explain their thinking. Often they learned as much from one another as they did from me.

Presentation of graphing a line from a given point and slope. Use a graph on an overhead transparency to explain the process further.

Begin by explaining that the given point (1, 5) is on the line and $m = 2/3$. Plot the point (1, 5). Next, count up from the point two places (the numerator of the slope) and to the right three places (the denominator of the slope). This puts you at the point (3, 8). Plot this point. For practice and to double check work, repeat the process for a third point. You should now be at (5, 11). Plot this point. All three points should be on the same line. Draw in the line.

Point out to the students that "run" should always move to the right. If the slope is negative, move down on the rise instead of moving up. It is important to keep the run consistent so that it always goes to the right. Remind the students to look at the line to make sure it is logical. A line with a positive slope goes up when reading from left to right, and a line with a negative slope goes down when reading from left to right.

✴ **Small-group graphing activity based on learning profile (modality).** Assign the students to one of three activities based on their preferred learning modalities.

Activity 1: Visual Learners
Students in this assignment group may work individually or in pairs. Given a point and slope, they will graph lines on graph paper. They should plot the given point in one color, use a second color to show the rise from the point, and use a third color to show the run from the point. They should then plot the resulting point in a fourth color. The students should repeat the same process to find a third point on the line.

This activity was my response to the fact that my students needed to learn in different ways. My goals here were to

- Provide group interaction.
- Promote sense making.
- Connect tasks to individual learning modalities.
- Promote success.
- Facilitate skill development.

LESSON SEQUENCE AND DESCRIPTION	TEACHER COMMENTARY
Finally, using a fifth color, they should sketch the line containing all three points. The students will then apply their understanding of the process using a problem such as the following:	

Josh buys his first pack of baseball cards for $3, the next two packs for $4 more, and the next three packs for $6 more. Show the line that predicts how much Josh will pay for nine packs altogether.

Activity 2: Tactile Learners
Students should work in small groups of five or six. Each small group will begin by acting out the process for graphing a line with a point and a slope. On a large grid on the floor, one student stands at the original point. A second student walks the rise and run from the original point to the next point on the grid, counting aloud while doing so. Another student begins where the second student is standing and repeats the process to find a third point. The students repeat this process until all the students represent points on the line. They then create the line by holding string between them. Finally, students will apply this same process to a problem similar to that in Activity 1.

Activity 3: Aural Learners
Students may work individually or in pairs to practice graphing several lines given initial points and slopes. After practicing, they will create a news bulletin that explains the process and implications of this type of graphing and will share their bulletins with the class.

Journal response synthesizing understandings of slope and related graphing exercises. Each student will respond in writing to the following prompts:	This activity was another chance for the students to process the information individually after working with it in groups. In addition, the journal responses served as a quick and informal assessment of their understanding so far.

- How do you graph a line given a point and a slope?
- When doing so, what do you have to be careful of?
- What questions or concerns do you still have about this process?

| LESSON 7 | Exploring the Equation of a Line in Slope-Intercept Form | (2–3 class periods) |

LESSON SEQUENCE AND DESCRIPTION	TEACHER COMMENTARY

Review of previous learning and presentation of slope-intercept form. With the whole class, review what they have learned about graphing lines and slopes thus far. Make sure they recall that a line can be graphed given a point and a slope and that slope can be determined using the equation of a line in slope-intercept form. Tell the students that there are different ways to graph a line given an equation and that during this lesson they will examine two of these ways.

Again, I wanted the students to build upon their previous understanding and skills.

Explain that equations of lines come in many forms, and each form has its own name. During this lesson, the students will work with the slope-intercept form. Begin by explaining the first method for using equations to graph lines. Place a picture of a T-chart on the overhead and demonstrate how to generate an x-value and substitute in to find the corresponding y-value:

On the overhead, plot the points and draw the line. Explain to the students that they will soon discover the second method for graphing a line from an equation.

Small-group discovery learning based on readiness. Arrange the students in small groups of three or four, based on readiness level. All groups should complete the first task before tackling the appropriate differentiated task.

Task I: All Groups

Given three equations in slope-intercept form, students will graph the lines using a T-chart. Then they will answer the following questions:

This task represented the "non-negotiables" or common ground necessary for all the students to grasp.

- What is the slope of the line?
- Where is slope found in the equation?
- Where does the line cross the y-axis?
- What is the y-value of the point when $x = 0$? (This is the y-intercept.)
- Where is the y-value found in the equation?
- Why do you think this form of the equation is called the "slope-intercept?"

LESSON SEQUENCE AND DESCRIPTION	TEACHER COMMENTARY
Task II: Differentiated *Struggling Learners* Given the points (-2, -3), (1, 1), and (3, 5), the students will plot the points and sketch the line. Then they will respond to the following: • What is the slope of the line? • Where does the line cross the y-axis? • Write the equation of the line. The students working on this particular task should repeat this process given two or three more points and/or a point and a slope. They will then create an explanation for how to graph a line starting with the equation and without finding any points using a T-chart. *Grade-Level Learners* Given an equation of a line in slope-intercept form (or several equations), the students in this group will • Identify the slope in the equation. • Identify the y-intercept in the equation. • Write the y-intercept in coordinate form $(0, y)$ and plot the point on the y-axis. • Use slope to find two additional points that will be on the line. • Sketch the line. When the students have completed these tasks, they will summarize a way to graph a line from an equation without using a T-chart. *Advanced Learners* Given the slope-intercept form of the equation of a line, $y = mx + b$, the students will answer the following questions: • Which variable represents the slope of the line? • The y-intercept is the point where the graph crosses the y-axis. What is the x-coordinate of the y-intercept? Why will this always be true? • Which variable in the slope-intercept form represents the y-coordinate of the y-intercept? Next, this group of students will complete the following tasks, given equations in slope-intercept form: • Identify the slope and the y-intercept. • Plot the y-intercept. • Use the slope to count rise and run in order to find the second and third points. • Graph the line.	The differentiated tasks moved from problems that included fewer facets to those that included more, and from problems that required a smaller leap in concept application to those that that required a larger one. Throughout the unit, I made time to work with students individually and in small groups, based on their particular needs for growth. Monitoring group and individual work time gave me insights into these needs, as did class discussions and quizzes. I found time to meet in small groups and with individuals as students worked independently and in groups.

LESSON SEQUENCE AND DESCRIPTION	TEACHER COMMENTARY
Sharing of results and discussion of various equations studied. Have the groups share what they discovered while completing their Part II tasks. Pose the following questions to students who worked in particular groups. *Struggling Learners* How can you reverse the process and find the equation of a line from a graph? *Grade-Level Learners* How can you graph a line given an equation in the slope-intercept form without using a T-chart? *Advanced Learners* How does slope-intercept form give you the slope and the y-intercept? What are the associated variables? What are the coordinates of any y-intercept?	Here, I wanted all students to be able to contribute to the discussion, but I recognized that they needed to be able to do so in ways that matched their differing levels of understanding. In addition, because they had completed different tasks prior to the discussion, I knew they would have different perspectives and ideas. Thus, I devised questions that addressed their levels of understanding and expertise.

LESSON 8   The Relationship Between the Equation   *(2 class periods)*
of a Line and the Points on a Line

LESSON SEQUENCE AND DESCRIPTION	TEACHER COMMENTARY
Review of slope-intercept form and presentation on working backwards from a graph to the equation of a line. Begin the lesson with a whole-class review of the slope-intercept form. What is it? How do we use it? Next, explain that today's lesson will focus on working backward from a graph or other information to the equation of a line. Ask: What two pieces of information do we need to write the equation of a line? Point out that we need any point on the line and the slope of the line. Show an example, such as this: Suppose the point on a line is (3, 1) and the slope is 2/3. How do we find the equation of the line? Explain the process: Slope-intercept form is $y = mx + b$. We know the slope. (It's 2/3.) In the equation, substitute the value of the slope for the variable m: $$y = 2/3\ x + b$$ What does a point have that will help us complete the equation? (An x- and y-coordinate.) Substitute from the point into x and y. Make sure the students know which is which. $$1 = (2/3)\ (3) + b$$	Again, building, building, building. . . .

LESSON SEQUENCE AND DESCRIPTION	TEACHER COMMENTARY
Now simplify and solve for *b*: $$1 = 2 + b$$ $$b = -1$$ Finally, substitute the value of *b* into the equation of the line: $$y = 2/3\, x - 1$$ Graph the line and check to see if the equation makes sense. Ask students: How will we know if it makes sense?	This was an opportunity for some logical thinking.
Application exercises in two (random) groups and discussion of results. Pose the following question and allow the students to suggest answers: What if you have two points instead of one point and the slope? Lead the students to recall that they can find the slope between two points using the slope formula. Once they have done so, divide the class into two groups. One group will use one point and the slope to find the equation of the line. The other group will use the other point and the slope to find the equation for the line. Compare answers with the whole class.	This activity allowed the students to prove for themselves that this process actually works. Again, the focus was on discovery.
Independent practice. All students should practice finding equations of lines given a point and the slope, two points, or a graph. A worksheet that the students complete independently is appropriate for this practice.	
✳ **Small-group summarization activity based on learning profile (multiple intelligences).** After the students complete their independent practice, they should break into groups based on Gardner's theory of multiple intelligences to work on one of five possible activities: *Option 1: Musical Intelligence* Prepare a rap that teaches how to find the equation of a line given two points. *Option 2: Visual/Spatial and Mathematical/Logical Intelligences* Make a flow chart that show the steps involved in finding the equation of a line using 1) two points; 2) a point and a slope; and 3) a graph of a line. *Option 3: Verbal/Linguistic Intelligence* Write a poem or short story that explains how to find the equation of a line given a graph. *Option 4: Interpersonal and Kinesthetic Intelligences* Perform a skit that demonstrates how to find the equation of a line using two points.	My goals here were to - Maximize engagement with the activities. - Promote sense making. - Promote success. - Provide variety. - Encourage group interaction.

LESSON SEQUENCE AND DESCRIPTION	TEACHER COMMENTARY
Option 5: Interpersonal Intelligence Next to each practice problem completed previously, explain the steps to finding the equation. When the students have completed their group activities, they should share their products with the whole class or with small groups representing a variety of other intelligences.	
Review. Review the process for finding the equation of a line given different information by having the first student give the first step, the second give the next step, and so on until the class has reviewed how to find the equation of a line in all three circumstance (two points, one point and the slope, a graph of the line).	

LESSON 9   **Solving Real-World Problems Using Lines**   *(1 class period)*

LESSON SEQUENCE AND DESCRIPTION	TEACHER COMMENTARY
Review of scatter plots, regression lines, slope, and appropriate graphing. Begin the lesson by asking the students what they have looked at so far during this unit (scatter plotting data, using regression lines for estimating and predicting, using slope to analyze how quickly **change** occurs, ways to graph lines).	
Presentation of related real-world problems. Tell the students that during this lesson they will be working on pulling all of this information together to look at how they can use lines to solve real-world problems. Point out that they will be working only with problems that incorporate constant **change.** Present the following example problem: Suppose the cost of building a new house depends on the number of square feet in the house. If it costs $50 per square foot to build the house, and the lot it is to be built on costs $75,000, can we write an equation of the total cost to build the house based on its square footage? Point out that the task is to write the equation that shows the total cost of the house (*c*) in terms of the number of square feet in the house (*f*). Ask the students to distinguish between the independent variable and the dependent variable. Which is which? How do they know? Make sure that they understand that *c* is dependent on *f*.	Finally, we got to the answer to that age-old question: *Why do we have to learn this?*

LESSON SEQUENCE AND DESCRIPTION	TEACHER COMMENTARY
Ask: What does the equation of a line look like? Write $y = mx + b$ on the board or an overhead. How can we make our problem look like this equation? Write $c = mf + b$. What does b represent in our equation? Lead the students to see that b represents the cost of the lot before building the house ($75,000). Given that information, what will the cost of the house be? Write $c = mf + 75,000$. What **changes** in the house? (Square footage of the house.) What is the change? ($50/square foot.) What represents the change mathematically? (Slope.) So . . . what is the slope? (It's 50.) Point out that you now have the equation that models the total cost of building the house in terms of square footage: $$c = 50f + 7,500$$ From this equation, what will it cost to build a house that is 1,500 square feet? 2,500 square feet? If the owners can afford to spend up to $225,000 on building the house, what is the largest house that they can build? Allow the students to work with partners to answer the questions, and have them explain the processes that they use to come up with their solutions.	
Real-world application problems in heterogeneous (random) groups. Divide the class into random mixed-ability groups of three or four students, and provide each group with a different application problem. When the groups have finished, give them the solution so that they can check their answers and discuss any problems or questions that they have. Rotate the problems among the groups and circulate among the groups to hear their discussions.	My goals here were to • Focus on problem solving. • Promote skill development. • Provide both self- and group assessment. • Promote metacognition.
Discussion of how to best set up and solve the problems. Close the lesson with a whole-class discussion of how to distinguish between independent and dependent variables in application problems. Invite the students to provide examples that explain their thinking.	This discussion focused on getting the students to think critically.

| LESSON 10 | Relating the Many Forms of Equations of Lines | (2–3 class periods) |

LESSON SEQUENCE AND DESCRIPTION	TEACHER COMMENTARY
Review slope, slope-intercept, and the significance of dependent and independent variables. Lead a whole-class discussion to review what slope represents, the ways to find slope, the slope-intercept form of a line, and the significance of independent and dependent variables.	Here, we referred back to some of our "big ideas" posted around the room.
Lecture on equations for a line. Prior to this lecture, distribute note-taking sheets based on student readiness. Sheets for advanced students should be very open-ended, while sheets for struggling students should include the names of the forms for equations of lines, as well as problems that have some areas already filled in.	The note-taking sheets required that all the students listen to the lecture, taking into account that some students are better at taking notes than others. I wanted all of the students to get the information down. Thus, I gave some of them a bit of help.
Move through the following steps on an overhead or the board so that the students can see as well as hear the process, and make sure that the students take notes as you move through the process.	By both speaking and showing, I addressed the needs of both auditory and visual learners.
Begin with the equation of a line in the form that the students are now familiar with:	
$$y = 2/3\ x + 7$$	
Set the equation equal to 0:	
$$0 = 2/3\ x - y + 7$$	
Explain that you do not want to work with fractions, and model how to clear the fractions from the equation:	
$$0 = 2x - 3y + 21$$	
Point out that this is the *general* form of the equation of a line in which A, B, and C are integers:	
$$Ax + By + C = 0$$	
Now, model moving the constant (C) to the other side of the equation:	
$$2x - 3y = -21$$	
Point out that this is the *standard* form of the equation of a line:	
$$Ax + By = C$$	

LESSON SEQUENCE AND DESCRIPTION	TEACHER COMMENTARY
Ask the students how they might find the slope from these two forms of the equation of a line. Write: $$m = -A\,/\,B$$ Now pose the following problem: Suppose we have a point $(2, 4)$ on a line, and the slope is 0. What does the equation of the line look like? Have the students try to figure this out based on their prior understanding that horizontal lines have a slope of 0. They may use the slope-intercept form to generate the equation if they choose. After the students have had some time to work with the previous problem, write the following on the overhead or board: $$y = 0x + b$$ $$4 = 0(2) + b$$ $$4 = b$$ $$y = 0x + 4$$ $$y = 4$$ Thus, for horizontal lines, $y = C$. Point out that for a horizontal line, the x-value never matters. Whatever x-value one chooses, the y-value will always be the same. Ask the students if they think the same is true of vertical lines and show the following on the overhead or board: 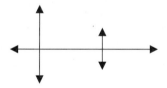	
Pose the following question: Suppose the points $(2, 1)$ and $(2, -2)$ are both on the line. What is the slope? Have the students use what they already know to arrive at this equation: $$m = 3/0$$	Time for some logical thinking . . .
Ask students what is wrong with this equation, and make sure that they understand that they cannot divide by 0. Tell them that in this case the slope is *undefined*. Explain that vertical lines have undefined slopes. Ask the students how they think they should show this in an equation. Encourage them to use the same thinking they did to figure out the equation for a horizontal line.	. . . and for some metacognitive thinking.

LESSON SEQUENCE AND DESCRIPTION	TEACHER COMMENTARY
When the students have worked with this problem for a few minutes, ask them to explain their thinking. Make sure that they understand that it does not matter what y-value is chosen because with vertical lines, the x-value will always be the same. In the problem provided, $x = 2$.	

Ask the students what equation a vertical line has. Remind them that a horizontal line has the equation $y = C$.

Quickly review the general and standard forms and tell the students that there is one more form for the equation of a line. Introduce this last form using the following process, again showing the process as you present it verbally. Begin with this line:

$$y = (1/2) x + 3$$

Ask: Is the point (2, 4) on this line? How do you know? Require the students to explain their thinking. Now ask: What is the slope of the line?

$$m = 1/2$$

Given this information, can we find the equation of the line in a way that differs from what we have already done? Show the following steps, explaining them as you go:

$$y - 4 = (1/2) (x - 2)$$

Simplify:

$$y - 4 = (1/2)x - 1$$
$$y = (1/2)x + 3$$

Point out that this is the equation of the line and that the first step is called the *point-slope* form of a line. Write it out for the students to see as follows:

$$y - y_1 = m (x - x_1)$$

Explain that (x_1, y_1) is a known point on the line and that m is the slope.

Now review all three forms of the equation of a line. What questions do the students have at this point?

Small-group processing activity based on learning profile (triarchic intelligences). In order to give students time to process this information further, put them into small groups to complete tasks based on Sternberg's triarchic intelligences.	My goals here were to • Promote evaluative thinking. • Promote group interaction. • Tie tasks to intelligence preferences. • Promote student success.

LESSON SEQUENCE AND DESCRIPTION	TEACHER COMMENTARY
Activity 1: Analytical Intelligence Compare and contrast the various forms of equations of lines. Create a flow chart, a tale, or any other product to present your ideas to the class. Be sure to consider the advantages and disadvantages of each form. *Activity 2: Practical Intelligence* Decide how and when each form of the equation of a line should be used. When is it best to use which? What are the strengths and weaknesses of each form? Find a way to present your conclusions to the class. *Activity 3: Creative Intelligence* Put each form of the equation of a line on trial. Prosecutors should try to convince the jury that a form is not needed, while the defense should defend its usefulness. Enact your trial with group members playing the various forms of the equations, the prosecuting attorneys, and the defense attorneys. The rest of the class will be the jury, and the teacher will be the judge.	
Sharing of small-group work and discussion of the need for various equations. When all groups are ready, have them share their work with the whole class. Hold the trial last. In pairs, the students should discuss whether it is necessary to have so many different forms for equations of lines. They should also share which form they like best and why.	

LESSON 11   Peer Critiques of Independent Research Projects   *(1 class period)*

LESSON SEQUENCE AND DESCRIPTION	TEACHER COMMENTARY
Independent project presentations and feedback in heterogeneous small groups. The students will present their independent research projects on **change** to small groups of their peers, who will rate presentations according to the criteria provided in Part IV of the **Guidelines for the Independent Research Project on Change** (see Sample, 5.1, page 180).	These peer feedback sessions improved everyone's work. Peer evaluation is an important piece of assessment. I encouraged students to revise their projects based on peer critique.

LESSON 12   Presentation of Independent Research Projects   *(2–4 class periods)*

LESSON SEQUENCE AND DESCRIPTION	TEACHER COMMENTARY
Presentation of independent research projects. Each student will present his or her project to the class and the teacher. Tell the students that these presentations can serve as part of the review for their unit test. Encourage the students to take notes as their classmates present.	By encouraging the students to take notes as a review for their upcoming test, I ensured that they would listen to one another by giving them a clear purpose for doing so.

| **LESSON 13** | **Unit Test Review** | *(1 class period)* |

LESSON SEQUENCE AND DESCRIPTION	TEACHER COMMENTARY
Test review with learning stations. Set up learning stations around the room that provide review problems for the major unit components: • Finding slope • Forms of equations • Scatter plotting • Regression lines and estimation • Using lines to solve real-world problems • Graphing Allow the students to move freely among the stations as they see fit, unless you know that some students need to visit particular stations. In such cases, direct students to stations that you believe they need to visit.	Use of learning stations allowed me to differentiate the review as necessary (based on need) and also provide student choice, thus increasing student engagement. Students found these stations more interesting than a traditional test review session.

| **LESSON 14** | **Unit Test** | *(1 class period)* |

LESSON SEQUENCE AND DESCRIPTION	TEACHER COMMENTARY
Test. The unit test should include problems typical of the types presented during the unit: • Given a table of data, create a scatter plot, sketch a regression line, and make estimations and predictions. • Identify independent and dependent variables. • Interpret **change** verbally in terms of what changes with respect to what else. • Find the slope using two points, graphs, and equations of lines. Interpret the slope as the rate of change. • Graph lines given initial information (points, slope, etc.). • Write the equations of lines in different forms. • Find equations of lines using two points, graphs, and one point and the slope. Finally, the students will write a paragraph stating what they learned from their project in terms of **change,** slope, and lines.	As with the quiz in Lesson 5, I wanted to address student differences through the unit assessment just as I had through the previous instruction and activities. I based portions of this test on readiness, with problems moving from • Few facets to many facets. • Less complex to more complex. • Requiring less interpretation to requiring more interpretation.

LESSON SEQUENCE AND DESCRIPTION	TEACHER COMMENTARY
Tier the test as necessary to address the students' varying readiness levels by providing integer values and more direct and concrete questions for struggling learners. While all students will be expected to reach the unit objectives, individual problems or questions for struggling students might address only one facet of what has been presented during the unit at a time, thus removing some of the complexity in the task. Advanced learners, on the other hand, should be given mixed and fractional numbers, and should be required to provide more complex written interpretation. In addition, their problems could combine different information presented during this unit. For example: Given data, scatter plot and sketch a regression line. Find the equation of the regression line in any form. What does the slope represent? What does the y-intercept represent? Make estimations and predictions.	

Teacher Reflection on the Unit

To me, the most important aspect of this unit is that it provides a context for the study of lines. Most students (and adults) do not understand *why* they should learn about lines. By clarifying that **change** and rate of change is the foundation of upper levels of math (especially Calculus), I was able to help my students understand why this learning was important. As a result, I found that most students enjoyed this unit much more than typical textbook treatment of lines.

I should note that my students often needed more explicit examples and practice as they worked on this unit. It's the teacher's prerogative to recognize when students lack the skills they need to complete the planned tasks and to meet with smaller groups of students to remedy this while the other groups continue to work on further concepts or on their independent projects. For example, I have found that students who are still struggling with the subtraction of signed numbers need to have that skill strengthened before they will have success working with the slope formula. Another common area of difficulty can be finding articles and other data to use that would be linear. Sometimes I resolved this by contriving tables of data myself.

Nanci Smith most recently taught high school math in Arizona. She can be reached at nanci_mathmaster@yahoo.com.

SAMPLE 5.1—Guidelines for the Independent Research Project on Change

Change is everywhere. You'll find it in temperatures and populations, in income levels, crime rates, pollution levels, stock prices, and in many other things. Sometimes change in one area affects another. For example, as the population changes in your hometown, the incidence of violent crime may change as well. You have already compiled a list of real-world change that you believe may be linear, and you have heard your classmates' ideas as well. You will now select an issue involving **change** to research throughout this unit.

Part I: Outline   Date due: _____

Select an issue involving change. Write a brief outline of your project including:

a. The issue being researched
b. The variables (what is changing)
c. How you expect to obtain the data needed (a minimum of _____ data points are required)
d. Your prediction about the data (what you expect to learn from the data)
e. A possible conclusion you might draw from this result

Part II: Research   Date due: _____

Locate a source (or sources) to find the information you need. Identify the sources and record all of the data points you will be using.

a. Compile and graph the data on a poster to be used in a presentation.
b. Sketch a regression line for the data.
c. Find the equation of the regression line.
d. Write a brief summary interpreting the change in your project. For example, what does the slope of the regression line represent in your study?

Part III: Conclusions   Date due: _____

Develop a list of at least ____ possible conclusions that your data support. These conclusions must be specific. For example, "There will be more than 5,000 murders in Phoenix in the year 2003" rather than "Murder rates will go up." You must be able to justify the numbers that factor into your conclusions.

SAMPLE 5.1—*(continued)*

Part IV: Peer Critique   **Date due:** _____

In small groups of three to five students, you will present your study data, graph, and conclusions. Each member of the group will critique every other member's presentation, assigning ratings on a scale of 1 (very poor) to 5 (very good) in the following categories:

a. Presenter's interest in the issue
b. Presenter's knowledge of the issue
c. Validity of data
d. Attractiveness of poster
e. Overall presentation quality

Part V: Project Presentation   **Date due:** _____

You will present your project to the entire class as you did to your small group. Choose one of your conclusions from Part III, and use your data to defend this conclusion before the class. You presentation must include the mathematics of your research and conclusions.

There's a Pattern Here, Folks!

A French I Unit on the Conjugation of –ER Verbs

Unit Developer: Cindy A. Strickland

Introduction

This three-week unit introduces students to the conjugation of regular –ER verbs in French. Throughout the unit, students use this skill to communicate information about activities they like to take part in. They also learn about some of the similarities and differences between French-speaking cultures and their own. Prerequisite skills for this unit include a comfort level with classroom spoken French, familiarity with the French sound system, and a beginner's ability to communicate in French about concrete topics such as names, greetings, weather, and dates.

The –ER category of regular verbs is the most common in the French language, and it's typically the first to be introduced in a formal study of French grammar. Although most of today's textbooks and materials emphasize a contextual approach to language acquisition (introducing grammatical structures only when these are needed for the **communication** of ideas and focusing on language *use* rather than language *analysis*), this unit incorporates both a contextual and an analytical approach to better meet the variety of learning styles present in today's classroom. When and how students begin a formal study of grammar depends to some extent on district goals and emphases and on teacher philosophy. No matter when the teacher chooses to introduce the formal conjugation process, the activities in this unit can be used and adjusted to meet the level of language sophistication that students possess.

The unit activities focus not only on how to conjugate –ER verbs, but also on the **patterns** involved in this process. Language is highly dependent on patterns, and the ability to recognize patterns will help students throughout their study of

French and other languages. This unit also gives students the chance to construct their own knowledge and understanding of how the French language works. It's designed to improve students' understanding and retention of the general rules for conjugation so that they can apply these rules later as they work with other types of verbs. Note that this unit focuses primarily on grammar, although most of the lessons do provide a cultural context for practicing the grammatical structures. A unit test assesses students' written progress with the grammatical aspects of the lessons. Performance assessments gauge student success in spoken language and in understandings related to cultural similarities and differences.

Differentiation in this unit is based primarily on student readiness for the grammatical components of instruction and primarily on student interest and learning profile for the cultural components. The unit plan also strives to ensure that whole-group activities appeal to a variety of creative, practical, and analytical learners.

Note: The sample materials provided at the end of the unit are meant to be examples only. Whenever possible, teachers can (and should!) make use of the materials that come with their text series. Pick and choose the activities in your program that fit your current objectives and that match the readiness, interests, and learning profiles of your particular students.

Teacher Reflections on Designing the Unit

Today's classroom features a great variety of student interests, learning profiles, and readiness levels. The world language classroom is no less diverse. I have noticed that regardless of the grade level I teach, some of my students have more background with French or other world languages than others. (It is not uncommon for beginners in a middle or high school class to find themselves seated next to classmates who have had several years of the language at the elementary level.) I have also noticed that some of my students pick up new languages much more quickly than their classmates. And then there are certain students who find the skills of reading and writing in a new language easier than speaking it and understanding its spoken form—and vice versa. As world language teachers, we certainly have a very complex set of student and general pedagogical needs to address!

I designed this unit to better provide for the broad range of readiness levels I see in my students. Because I crave variety (as do my students!), I always strive to present the learning activities in multiple formats and through multiple lenses. Part of the fun in a language classroom is that we constantly talk about everyday things such as personal likes and dislikes, family and friends, and school and leisure activities. As a result, I find it fairly easy to get to know my students' backgrounds and interests. And because I teach using a variety of models and strategies, I am also able to get a sense of how my students like to learn. Add to this the fact that I often have students for more than one year, and I have a very workable setting for one of the major principles of differentiated learning: Know thy students!

World/Foreign Language Standards Addressed

Communication:

- Students engage in conversations, provide and obtain information, express feelings and emotions, and exchange opinions.
- Students understand and interpret written and spoken language on a variety of topics.
- Students present information, concepts, and ideas to an audience of listeners or readers on a variety of topics.

Cultures:

- Students demonstrate an understanding of the relationship between the practices and perspectives of the culture studied.
- Students demonstrate an understanding of the relationship between the products and perspectives of the culture studied.

Connections:

- Students reinforce and further their knowledge of other disciplines through the language studied.
- Students acquire information and recognize the distinctive viewpoints that are only available through the language studied and its cultures.

Comparisons:

- Students demonstrate understanding of the nature of language through comparisons of the language studied and their own.
- Students demonstrate understanding of the concept of culture through comparisons of the cultures studied and their own.

Communities:

- Students use the language both within and beyond the school setting.
- Students show evidence of becoming lifelong learners by using the language for personal enjoyment and enrichment.

Unit Concepts and Generalizations

Patterns, Communication

- Language is made up of a variety of patterns.
- Patterns in language are observable.
- Patterns in language are predictable.

- The ability to recognize language patterns can help us understand and predict meaning in new and unfamiliar contexts.
- A language will not always follow its patterns.
- The purpose of language is to communicate.
- We can use language to communicate in both oral and written form.
- Language must be correct enough to allow for understanding between people.
- An understanding of language patterns can help us minimize language errors and maximize communication.
- There are both similarities and differences between French-speaking and other world cultures.
- Understanding similarities and differences can enhance communication and understanding between people of different cultures.

Unit Objectives

As a result of this unit, the students will *know*
- The target regular –ER verbs (beginning with either a consonant or a vowel).
- The steps in the conjugation process of regular –ER verbs.
- Subject-verb agreement endings for regular –ER verbs.
- Oral and written patterns of –ER verbs.
- Basic geographical and activity-related cultural differences between two French-speaking cultures and the local culture.

As a result of this unit, the students will *understand that*
- The conjugation of regular –ER verbs follows a pattern.
- Knowing the pattern of conjugation allows for the correct use of French verbs and improves communication in French.
- There are differences between oral and written patterns used when conjugating –ER verbs.
- Communication and understanding are enhanced when people recognize and understand cultural similarities and differences.

As a result of this unit, the students will *be able to*
- Conjugate regular –ER verbs in the present tense when speaking and writing.
- Explain patterns in verb conjugation of –ER verbs.
- Predict the conjugation of unfamiliar –ER verbs.
- Understand and participate in discussions in French about everyday activities and interests.
- Communicate in both oral and written form about everyday activities and interests in French-speaking and local cultures.

Instructional Strategies Used

- Flexible grouping
- Learning centers
- Ongoing assessment
- Tiered assessment
- Varied levels of questions
- Flexible pacing
- Metacognitive thinking
- Rubrics
- Tiered assignments
- Sternberg's triarchic intelligences

Sample Supporting Materials Provided

Unit Overview

LESSON	WHOLE-CLASS COMPONENTS	DIFFERENTIATED COMPONENTS
LESSON 1 **Introduction to Regular –ER Verbs in the Present Tense** *1 class period*	Introduction of verb vocabulary in *il/elle* form (oral and written) *15 minutes*	Some questions/prompts are adjusted for student readiness levels
	Practice in small heterogeneous groups *10–15 minutes*	
		Guided practice/written application activity based on readiness *10–15 minutes*
	Discussion relating the lesson to unit concepts *5–10 minutes*	

LESSON	WHOLE-CLASS COMPONENTS	DIFFERENTIATED COMPONENTS
LESSON 2 **Adding the Pronoun *Je*** *1–2 class periods*	Kinesthetic review of vocabulary *10 minutes*	
	Presentation of additional verb vocabulary, using the *Je* form/Drill and practice of spoken forms *30 minutes*	Some questions/prompts adjusted for student readiness levels
		Written application of verb conjugations, based on readiness *20–30 minutes*
	Cultural activity presenting related vocabulary and concepts *20–30 minutes*	
	Journal writing *5–10 minutes*	
LESSON 3 **Syntax of Affirmative and Negative Sentences** *1 class period*	Kinesthetic review activity applying syntax and verb agreement *25 minutes*	Some students receive more complex tasks based on readiness
		Correct Lesson 2 Differentiated Worksheet in readiness groups *10 minutes*
	Listening activity using verb vocabulary and syntax in heterogeneous (random) groups *10 minutes*	
	Response sharing *5 minutes*	
	Discussion of related unit concepts *5 minutes*	
LESSON 4 **Introduction to the Group Research Project** *1–2 class periods*	Listening review activity incorporating cultural similarities and differences *10–15 minutes*	
	Discussion of the group research project and the culminating product assignment *10–15 minutes*	Students are assigned to project groups based on learning profile (triarchic intelligences)
		In-class project work in learning profile groups *30–60 minutes*

LESSON	WHOLE-CLASS COMPONENTS	DIFFERENTIATED COMPONENTS
LESSON 5 **Using All Subject Pronouns** *3–4 class periods*	Oral vocabulary review activity in heterogeneous (random or self-selected) groups *15–20 minutes*	
		Reading and deductive thinking activity based on readiness *30–40 minutes*
	Cue-and-response conjugation drills *10–15 minutes*	This may also be done in readiness groups
		Work time for research projects *1–2 class periods*
	Video narration activity using –ER verb vocabulary *30 minutes*	This may also be done in readiness groups
LESSON 6 **Review of –ER Verb Conjugation** *1 class period*		Individual greetings and responses based on readiness and interest *5–10 minutes*
	Spoken and written verb conjugation review game in random heterogeneous groups *45 minutes*	
LESSON 7 **Using –ER Verbs to Communicate** *2–3 class periods*		Small-group oral performance assessment based on readiness *2–3 class periods*
LESSON 8 **Review for Unit Quiz** *1 class period*	Competitive review game between heterogeneous teams *50 minutes*	Cues are varied based on the readiness of individuals "at bat"

LESSON	WHOLE-CLASS COMPONENTS	DIFFERENTIATED COMPONENTS
LESSON 9 **Differentiated Unit Quiz on –ER Verb Conjugation** *1 class period*		Quiz based on readiness *50 minutes*
LESSON 10 **Cultural Similarities and Differences** *1–2 class periods*	Presentation and discussion of group research project culminating products *1–2 class periods* Feedback questionnaire on differentiated learning experience *10 minutes*	

Unit Description and Teacher Commentary

LESSON 1	**Introduction to Regular –ER Verbs in the Present Tense**	*(1 class period)*

LESSON SEQUENCE AND DESCRIPTION	TEACHER COMMENTARY
Introduction of verb vocabulary in *il/elle* form (oral and written). Show the class a picture of Marie Curie and display an overhead that shows common activities representing various regular –ER verbs. Point to each activity pictured as you say the following: Marie chante. Marie parle. Marie skie. Marie dîne. Marie téléphone. Marie écoute. Marie arrive.	This listening exercise introduced students to spoken –ER verbs in context with related vocabulary. I chose a picture of Marie Curie because of the cultural link and because I knew several of my students were interested in science. You could also "hook" students by using a picture of a familiar pop culture icon. You might also use a picture that depicts all the activities you're describing to present a more unified context for the discussion.

LESSON SEQUENCE AND DESCRIPTION	TEACHER COMMENTARY
Ask the students to repeat the same sentences chorally as you point to the corresponding activities. Continue to drill the students in groups (certain rows or tables) and individually.	As you speak, be careful to use only the third person singular verb form and to use names rather than pronouns as the subjects of your sentences. However, if your students are already familiar with subject pronouns, then by all means, use them!
For students who are ready, point to several pictures in a row and ask the students to provide the sentences one after another or to combine the appropriate verbs into one sentence.	Based on my general knowledge of the students and their ability to repeat the sentences on their own, I added complexity to the task for some.
Practice in small heterogeneous groups. Challenge each row or table of students to work together to practice all the sentences represented by the pictures on the overhead. When all students in a group can recite all of the sentences, they should call the teacher over for a quick check of their progress.	Here, I allowed students to work together to give them further practice and the opportunity to listen to and learn from one another.
When the students are ready to move on, show the same transparency, this time writing sentences underneath them. Ask: What do the sentences have in common? How did we get "Marie téléphone" from "téléphoner"?	Students used inductive reasoning to come up with (discover) their own ideas, and I was ready to accept all reasonable answers. This activity especially appeals to the analytical learner.
Guided practice/written application activities based on readiness. Using the above activities as a basis of assessment, divide the students into two groups based on their demonstrated grasp of –ER verbs.	Here I applied the principle of flexible pacing. I did not want to hold some students back when they were ready to move on, and I did not want to rush other students toward work that they were not yet ready for.
Group 1: Students Needing Guided Practice Repeat the choral conjugation activity, this time showing a picture of Pierre Curie.	The first activity provided further repetition for those students who needed it, allowing them to practice using verbs we had already worked with in a way that was familiar.
Group 2: Students Ready for Application Activities Have these students begin independent work on the ROUGE version of the **Lesson 1 Differentiated Worksheet.** This tiered worksheet comes in three different, color-coded versions, (collected in Sample 6.1, beginning on page 206) to provide activities on three readiness levels.	I allowed these students to skip the guided practice and move on to application.

LESSON SEQUENCE AND DESCRIPTION	TEACHER COMMENTARY
BLEU: Below Expectation Level This version requires students to work only with those verbs that have already been introduced and practiced in class. *BLANC: On Expectation Level* This version requires students to work with many of the same verbs, but in verb phrases rather than as stand-alones. It also includes a number of unfamiliar –ER verbs. *ROUGE: Above Expectation Level* This version requires students to work with both familiar and unfamiliar –ER verbs and to complete a creative thinking task in which they invent their own French verb to use in a sentence and to translate. When Group 1's guided practice is complete, assign those students to either the BLEU or BLANC version of the worksheet, based on readiness. Students working on the ROUGE version should continue their work.	Because my student groupings change frequently (and I want them to), I "color code" the *work* rather than the students, and I often change the colors for the different levels. Thus, my students do not think of themselves as always "blue" or "green." Here, I used my knowledge of the students' language and thinking skills to assign them to the appropriate worksheet. All the worksheets asked the students to think about the rule they were applying (metacognition). I often play music from a variety of Francophone cultures during independent work time. This exposes students to yet another opportunity to internalize pronunciation and even grammatical **patterns.** Many students find this soothing as well. When more advanced students finished their worksheets, I allowed them to work on other homework from class or to visit learning centers in the room. I set up a "French Culture" center featuring games, puzzles, magazines, and other items for students to peruse as well as a collection of anchor activities (see Sample 6.2, **Suggested Anchor Activities,** page 209). All students have the opportunity to visit these centers at various times throughout the year.
Discussion relating the lesson to unit concepts. Wrap up with a whole-class discussion and allow as many students as possible to share their ideas. Ask: What did you notice about the work we did with –ER verbs today? What **patterns** did you see? How does this relate to our own language? Introduce the unit generalizations concerning patterns and communication and post them in the room for all to see. Ask: How do these relate to what we did today?	In addition to bringing closure to our activities, this discussion required the students to synthesize their understanding of the lesson and to explain the **pattern** that they had worked with. It also gave me the chance to introduce the big ideas supporting this unit (the unit generalizations), which I posted so that we could refer to them often. Finally, bringing all students back together for closure reminds students they all have the same overall learning goals.

| **LESSON 2** | Adding the Pronoun *Je* | *(1–2 class periods)* |

LESSON SEQUENCE AND DESCRIPTION	TEACHER COMMENTARY
Kinesthetic review of vocabulary. Have students act out the verbs that were introduced during the previous lesson. For example, use statements such as "Marie skie" and "Marie écoute la musique rap."	This "hook" activity got the students actively involved in reviewing the verbs that they learned during Lesson 1. I added complexity to the exercise by including more cognate vocabulary. An activity such as this especially appeals to my kinesthetic learners.
Presentation of additional verb vocabulary, using the *Je* form/Drill and practice of spoken forms. Once the class has listened and responded to several statements, show a picture of yourself and say, "Voici M/Mme. (your name)." Display the activity overhead from the previous lesson and point to the pictures as you say, "Je skie," etc. Have students repeat chorally after you. After sufficient choral practice, ask individual students to say the correct sentence using the pronoun *je* as you point to specific activities on the overhead. Now show the same activity overhead but with the corresponding sentences filled in. Ask: What patterns do you notice? How does this relate to what you discovered during the previous lesson? How will this help you to learn French? Continue working with more –ER verbs by showing another overhead of activities and following the same procedure.	I introduced the pronoun *Je* and its corresponding –ER conjugation in the same way that I had introduced –ER verbs during the previous lesson. Students were already familiar with the process we used, and I wanted them to come to conclusions similar to the ones they reached previously. Thus, after we practiced using the pronoun *je* with –ER verbs, I led a discussion regarding the **patterns** in the verb conjugation. During this discussion, I adjusted my questions/prompts for various readiness levels. All questions, though, led students to the patterns and to the idea that their ability to recognize and predict the pattern would help them conjugate other –ER verbs. I conducted this discussion in French, using both written cues and gestures to give additional language input and expose students to vocabulary useful in describing grammatical structures. I like my students to be able to talk about grammar in French as well as in English. The use of this vocabulary also provides additional challenge to more advanced learners.

LESSON SEQUENCE AND DESCRIPTION	TEACHER COMMENTARY
Move on to a speaking activity in which you provide the infinitive and the subject and the students create the sentences. For example, provide the infinitive "voyager" and the subject "Marie." Students should respond with "Marie voyage."	I mixed up the subjects so that students were required to respond using both proper nouns and the pronoun *je*. I gave students verbs that they had not been exposed to previously to see how well they could transfer their understanding of the conjugation **patterns** to unfamiliar words. Using sticky notes and a clipboard, I unobtrusively jotted down my observations of individual students' ability to apply the patterns so that I could assign this lesson's worksheet activities to the appropriate students.
Begin this drill chorally, and then move to rows or tables of students and on to individual students. Choose infinitives from each of the previous lesson's worksheets. Add additional –ER cognates as desired and to challenge more advanced students.	
Now, show three verbs that begin with a vowel rather than a consonant. Have students practice using these verbs in sentences with different subjects. Ask students to explain the use of the apostrophe.	Rather than telling the students the reason for the *j'*, I chose to let them think about it on their own. I encouraged those who were able to explain *en français*.
Introduce the pronouns *elle* and *il* by asking the students to explain the difference between the sentences "Je chante" and "Marie chante." Use the students' responses to introduce *elle* and *il* as pronouns that replace "Marie" and "Pierre." Display and discuss overheads that show examples of the uses of these pronouns. Ask: What do the sentences on the overheads say? How do you know?	I wanted the students to arrive at their own conclusions regarding the differences between the sentences I posed. Although I directed my question to the whole class, I designed it with my more abstract thinkers in mind. Using the additional overheads allowed students to see the pronouns in combination with verbs (again noting **patterns**), and also allowed them to see the new vocabulary written out.
Show your picture again, and use overheads showing activities. Say, "Voici M./Mme. (your name). Je m'appelle M./Mme. (your name)." Point to something that you don't do and say, for example, "Je ne skie pas" or "Je chante bien, mais je ne danse pas."	I took the students one step further by asking them to use their new grasp of verbs and pronouns to answer questions about their performance of specific activities. I listened closely for their correct usage of *je* and –ER conjugation and for their abilities to use their developing knowledge of **patterns** to make sentences negative. In this and other activities, I tried to introduce additional –ER verbs that matched the interests and activities of the particular students in my class to increase engagement and motivation to **communicate.**
Using the same overheads, point to particular activities and ask questions such as "Tu chantes bien?" Ask individual students to respond to your questions using the pronoun *je* and the correct conjugation of the –ER verb. As a hint, show an overhead that gives statements in the negative form.	

LESSON SEQUENCE AND DESCRIPTION	TEACHER COMMENTARY
Written application of verb conjugations, based on readiness. Assign the students to the appropriate version of the **Lesson 2 Differentiated Worksheet** (collected in Sample 6.3, beginning on page 211), based on their performances during this lesson and knowledge of their need for structure in an assignment. For this worksheet, I changed the color designation for various readiness levels to VERT, GRIS, and JAUNE.	I did not assume that these worksheet groups would be the same as groups I used in the previous lesson. Changing the group membership is a response to students' changing knowledge and skills—it keeps the level of challenge appropriate. Changing group designations, seating areas, number of groups, and order of giving directions to groups draws attention away from the precise composition of the group.
VERT: Below Expectation Level This version of the worksheet provides concrete practice that closely resembles what students have already done during class and provides clear examples of **patterns.**	These application activities seem to especially appeal to analytical learners.
GRIS: On Expectation Level This version provides practice with less scaffolding, a mixture of pronouns and verbs, and no reminders about vowel changes.	
JAUNE: Above Expectation Level This version provides open-ended activities with little scaffolding and requires greater independence.	
While students work independently on their worksheets, pull groups of students aside for additional practice with verbs and pronouns. Uncompleted work should be assigned as homework.	I based my small-group work with each group of students on their readiness levels and adjusted my questions to these levels while trying to push the students a little further than they had gone previously. This promotes learning by giving me a better sense of individual student needs and by allowing me to challenge individual learners appropriately.
Cultural activity presenting related vocabulary and concepts. Show pictures you have cut from contemporary French and American magazines. In French, describe what the people in these pictures are doing. Choose pictures that illustrate cultural similarities and differences between the local culture and France or another French-speaking country. Point out these differences in your narratives about the pictures, using language that is a little above students' current level of comprehension. Some examples might include	I spent a short amount of time discussing geographical and cultural differences among the various French-speaking countries. I focused on how geographical differences influence culture (for example, how geography affects the activities in which young people typically take part) because I knew students had discussed this idea

LESSON SEQUENCE AND DESCRIPTION	TEACHER COMMENTARY
• Paul skie aux Alpes. Jim skie dans le Colorado. • Pierre dîne à 20 heures. John dîne à 6 heures. • Chantal parle français, italien, et espagnol. Mary parle anglais.	in their geography classes. This was also a good place to bring up the idea of stereotypes and their complex origins. Whenever possible, I used verbs students had already learned, pointing out both similarities and differences among the countries.
Journal writing. Close this culturally-focused portion of the lesson by asking students to write three to five sentences in their journals about what they like to do for recreation. Have them speculate about whether or not students their age in France (or in another French-speaking country) would participate in the activity or activities they've identified.	Although it's controversial, I sometimes allow students to use a mixture of French and English ("franglais") in their journals when I want them to focus on communication of ideas more than grammar or vocabulary. Students could also use a dictionary to find additional "activity vocabulary."

LESSON 3   Syntax of Affirmative and Negative Sentences   *(1 class period)*

LESSON SEQUENCE AND DESCRIPTION	TEACHER COMMENTARY
Kinesthetic review activity applying syntax and verb agreement. For this activity, prepare two sets of "syntax cards"—large index cards, each bearing a single sentence part (see Sample 6.4, **Syntax Cards,** page 216). *Set 1* These cards should contain a variety of French words. As students enter the classroom, give the majority of the class a syntax card from this set. (If there are any of these cards left over, post them on the walls around the classroom.) *Set 2* For this set, use index cards in a contrasting color. Each card in Set 2 should show one of the following words: *ne, n', pas,* and *je.*	This was a way to get the students physically involved in reviewing the skills we had previously learned. I considered Gardner's theory of multiple intelligences and chose to use bodily/kinesthetic intelligence to reinforce appropriate sentence syntax. Be sure you have enough cards for everyone in the class.
Give the more advanced learners syntax cards from Set 2. Ask these students to sit in the middle of the room with their cards. They will serve as observers/checkers during the first part of the activity.	I gave Set 2 cards to my more advanced students because 1) it removed them from the first part of the activity so I could really observe my other students' abilities; and 2) they would be more appropriately challenged by the second part of the activity, which requires transformation of the sentence syntax. Having the advanced students sit out the first part of the activity sets up their role in the second part.

LESSON SEQUENCE AND DESCRIPTION	TEACHER COMMENTARY
Explain to the rest of the class that their task is to create sentences from the words on their cards by arranging themselves (each holding a syntax card) in an appropriate order. They may show their cards as they complete their sentences, *but they may not talk*. Tell the students that each sentence should be made up of exactly three cards. Point out that extra sentence parts are posted around the room should anyone need them or want to use them.	I watched closely for the students' grasp of vocabulary as well as for their abilities to create the sentences by putting the words in the correct order.
Once students have created their sentences, tell them to form a large circle so that all the sentences can be seen. If some sentences do not make sense, have students make necessary changes, again without speaking. They should do so by *moving themselves* rather than switching cards. All the sentences must make sense before the activity proceeds.	I asked students to remain silent during this activity both to focus their attention on the physical aspects of the activity and to make it fun by having them work together without talking. This can be quite a challenge for students!
Next, have the students in the middle of the room work together to make each of the sentences negative, using their cards. Again, they should not speak during this process.	I wanted my advanced students to take the activity one step further, as the concept of making the sentences negative was relatively new to them.
As closure for this portion of the lesson, have the students read aloud both the affirmative and the negative forms of their sentences.	I also pointed out the occurrence of **patterns** in sentence syntax.
Correct Lesson 2 Differentiated Worksheet in readiness groups. Provide the correct answers to the VERT (below expectation level) and GRIS (on expectation level) versions of the worksheet on the board or an overhead so that the students in these groups can correct their own homework.	I wanted students to correct their own homework so they could really attend to their own particular mistakes. I moved around the room, listening in and taking notes. (To signal my wish to observe students rather than interact with them, I wore a special scarf around my neck. Students were used to this signal, which I'd used in previous units.)
Ask the students who completed the JAUNE (above expectation level) version of the assignment to write their sentences on the board. The whole class will correct these sentences. Once students have finished correcting their work, discuss any common errors.	I decided all students should see the more advanced JAUNE sentences. In my efforts to constantly monitor and assess students, I was interested to find out which of the students seemed to "get it" even though they did not complete that particular assignment. I also monitored for specific student problems.

LESSON SEQUENCE AND DESCRIPTION	TEACHER COMMENTARY
Listening activity using verb vocabulary and syntax in heterogeneous (random) groups. Randomly divide the students into small groups of three or four. Give each group a tape recorder and a recording of several sentences that include both masculine and feminine pronouns and are both affirmative and negative. The groups should work together to reach a consensus about the pronoun in the sentences they hear and whether the sentence is in the affirmative or negative form. They should write their responses on a group response form.	This listening discrimination activity provided more exposure to correct pronunciation and reinforcement of the skills we had been working on. I decided to let students work in mixed-readiness groups because they had not done so previously and it was appropriate that students who were more advanced help those who were struggling. Whenever possible, I use the audiotape activities that accompany my textbook series.
Response sharing. When all small groups have finished the listening activity, reassemble as a large group and allow students to share their responses and discuss the strategies they used.	This provided students with another opportunity for metacognition.
Discussion of related unit concepts. Close this lesson by discussing the relationship between **communication** and **patterns**. Ask: What clues do subject pronouns give us about the patterns we hear?	I wanted students to keep the concepts of **communication** and **patterns** in mind throughout the unit.

LESSON 4   **Introduction to the Group Research Project**   *(1–2 class periods)*

LESSON SEQUENCE AND DESCRIPTION	TEACHER COMMENTARY
Listening review activity incorporating cultural similarities and differences. Provide students with a variety of pictorial resources depicting various French-speaking cultures. Encourage students to make predictions about how young people their age in these cultures might complete the following or similar sentences: Je skie . . . (where?) J'écoute . . . (to what kind of music?) Je voyage . . . (where? when?) Je dîne . . . (when? on what?)	This warm-up reviewed the grammatical construction we were working on and also reinforced the idea that young people in various cultures enjoy many of the same activities, but also do things that are unique to their geographical and/or cultural environments.
Discussion of the group research project and the culminating product assignment. Next, divide students into research groups and distribute the **Group Research Project Guidelines** (see Sample 6.5, page 217). This project requires students to devise both a visual and a written way to compare and contrast at least two French-speaking cultures with their own U.S. (or other) culture.	I divided students into research groups based on learning profile (triarchic intelligences). Much of my grouping in this skill-based unit was by readiness. In this activity, I wanted to be sure to offer students opportunities to work together based on learning profile and/or interest.

LESSON SEQUENCE AND DESCRIPTION	TEACHER COMMENTARY
Carefully go over the instructions. Stress to students that their work must be highly illustrative of similarities and differences in the cultures they select. Distribute and discuss the **Group Research Project Checklist For Success** (see Sample 6.6, page 219), which all group members should fill out and turn in with their completed projects. This will help the groups plan their project and encourage a higher quality of performance overall.	The mixed-readiness abilities naturally found in these groups helped promote better understanding of the grammatical points we were studying. I provided resources in French and in English to accommodate the various ability levels within each group. When designing my groups, I also made sure to strategically place students with particular strengths in leadership, creativity, and task commitment into each group. I especially encouraged groups to choose at least one lesser-known francophone culture to research. When the major purpose of an assignment is cultural understanding rather than grammatical accuracy, I sometimes allow students to use French and/or English. In this case, I wanted students to focus on cultural understandings, which would likely require a greater degree of French language sophistication than they had at this point in their studies. Therefore, the products students turned in were done primarily in English.
In-class project work in learning profile groups. Allow students to start sketching out a plan for completing their group research project and its culminating product. Explain that they will have class time to work together on the project.	Because my students find it difficult to get together outside of class, it's necessary for me to provide time in class for this type of activity. I also encouraged students to work on their projects when they finished an activity early or during study hall or lunch. There's a work area in the back of my classroom set aside for this purpose.

| LESSON 5 | Using All Subject Pronouns | *(3–4 class periods)* |

LESSON SEQUENCE AND DESCRIPTION	TEACHER COMMENTARY
Oral vocabulary review activity in heterogeneous (random or self-selected) groups. Break students into random or self-selected mixed-ability groups of six to eight and ask each group to sit in a circle.	This synthesis activity required students to pull from everything they had learned regarding verb conjugation, pronouns, affirmative and negative sentences, and the various patterns involved. I wanted them to change verb conjugations and pronouns as appropriate.

One student in each group begins by choosing a verb and using it in a sentence. For example, he or she may say, "Je regarde la télé."

The next student does the same, but first repeats the first student's sentence using the correct pronoun for that student and the correct form of the –ER verb: "Elle (Il) regarde la télé. Je voyage à Dallas."

The third student then does the same: "Elle regarde la télé. Il voyage à Dallas. J'écoute la radio."

Because I wanted students to be able to work together and help monitor each other, I decided on mixed-ability groups. In my classroom, students know they will be constantly shifting groups and working with a great variety of peers over the course of a unit. I make a deliberate effort to monitor who has worked together recently in order to ensure a "fruit-basket-upset" kind of flexible grouping.

The students continue adding sentences until all have had a turn. Note that students may not choose a verb that has already been used. Students should then repeat the game, this time using negative sentences and moving in the opposite direction.

As I moved among the groups, I listened for students who were struggling and stepped in to coach as necessary.

Reading and deductive thinking activity based on readiness. Students work on two different levels for this activity (see **Lesson 5 Differentiated Worksheet**, collected in Sample 6.7, beginning on page 221). Students working below and on expectation level (ROSE) work with the teacher, while those working above expectation level (NOIR) work independently in a separate group.

ROSE: Below and On Expectation Grade Level
Use the reading passage as a springboard for introducing the complete conjugation of –ER verbs. As much as possible, speak only in French, even when using such terms as *conjugate, subject, verb, affirmative,* and *negative.* Encourage the students to use this vocabulary as well.

Once students in this group have completed the work with the reading passage, present the conjugations of *chanter* and *dîner* on the board. Have the students conjugate *monter* at their desks while you do it on the board.

I based these groups on my observations during the previous lessons, and I modified the previous readiness groupings as needed. In some cases, students who appeared very advanced benefited from slowing down a bit and working with me. In other cases, I noticed that some students were moving through the material much more quickly than they had been earlier. I moved them to the more advanced (the above expectation level) group. In this way, I ensured that my groups were changing as my students' readiness levels were changing. Also, simply by using only two groups instead of three, I encouraged a different mix of students.

LESSON SEQUENCE AND DESCRIPTION	TEACHER COMMENTARY
Assign various –ER verbs to the students and have them conjugate them on their own. When finished, students should write their conjugations on the board so the rest of the group can check them for accuracy. Discuss what happens when a verb begins with a vowel. Demonstrate and practice conjugation in the negative, and point out the spelling changes in *nager* and *voyager*. *NOIR: Above Expectation Level* Be sure to distribute parts A and B of the worksheet separately. If you don't, students will be able to look ahead, which may discourage their use of deductive thinking skills. Allot 30–40 minutes for these activities. Unfinished work should be completed as homework.	All students, regardless of their ability level, benefit from the teacher's time and attention. If you have access to a high-quality language lab, after you have completed the guided activity with the ROSE group, have those students start on some listening activities while you work with the NOIR group to check their progress and understanding. Again, push them to discuss their work *en français*. Whenever possible, promote metacognition by asking them to explain their thinking and reasoning.
Cue-and-response conjugation drills. Bring the students back together as a large group for the following (or similar) oral drills. Constant cue: *Je* Cue: *Nager* Response: *Je nage.* Cue: *Téléphoner* Response: *Je téléphone.* Continue as needed. New constant cue: *Nous* Cue: *Voyager* Response: *Nous voyageons.* Cue: *Dîner* Response: *Nous dînons.* Continue as needed.	I often make use of the audio portion of my text series in planning and designing drills like these. This kind of drill gives me another chance to assess my students' progress and their level of automaticity with this grammatical form. I listened for and corrected mistakes in both pronunciation and syntax. If you have the appropriate language lab equipment, you can have some students working on simpler drills while others work on drills better suited to their advanced abilities. Remember that some students with advanced writing skills in French may have difficulty with listening and/or speaking activities and vice versa. Be sure to assign students to activities accordingly.

LESSON SEQUENCE AND DESCRIPTION	TEACHER COMMENTARY
Cue: *Je nage.* Response: *Je ne nage pas.* Cue: *Je danse.* Response: *Je ne danse pas.* Continue as needed. Cue: *Il skie.* Response: *Il ne skie pas.* Cue: *Vous parlez.* Response: *Vous ne parlez pas.* Continue as needed. Cue: *Je nage/Tu* Response: *Tu nages.* Cue: *Nous.* Response: *Nous nageons.* Cue: *Elles* Response: *Elles nagent.*	
Work time for research projects. Have students meet in their project groups to conduct research and work on their project's culminating product assignment.	Be sure that you schedule adequate time for research project work. You may wish to devote a day or two to the research project at this point or from time to time throughout the rest of the unit. I also recommend allowing students to work on their research projects whenever there's extra time in class.
Video narration activity using –ER verb vocabulary. Show a video on French-speaking young people and their favorite activities or pastimes. Stop the video from time to time to ask questions that use the verb vocabulary students have been practicing. You might also turn off the sound and ask students to narrate short segments of the video.	This may be completed as a whole class or in readiness groups. I use the materials that come with my text series whenever possible. Many include video components that deal with both cultural and grammatical topics. Sometimes I choose short clips from commercial videos, such as *The Little Mermaid, Free Willy,* or *101 Dalmatians,* and use unit vocabulary to describe characters' actions. ("Ariel nage," in *The Little Mermaid,* for example.)

| LESSON 6 | Review of –ER Verb Conjugation | *(1 class period)* |

LESSON SEQUENCE AND DESCRIPTION	TEACHER COMMENTARY
Individual greetings and responses based on readiness and interest. As the students enter the classroom, stand at the door and ask them a question in French that they must also answer in French. Vary the questions based on the students' grasp of vocabulary and verb conjugations.	I differentiated this greeting by asking some students less complex questions and others more difficult questions. In choosing my prompts, I also applied what I knew about students' interests. For above expectation level students, I encouraged elaboration of response.
Spoken and written verb conjugation review game in random heterogeneous groups. Put the students in mixed-ability groups, four students to a group.	This activity gave students another opportunity to practice –ER verb conjugation using a game (always a good "hook" for students). I guessed that some groups would move through the first activity more quickly than others, so I created the second version to accommodate their different paces.
Tell the students that they will be playing a game that will give them an opportunity to practice –ER verb conjugations. Give each group the following materials: a die, a stack of cards showing French infinitives, and a stack of cards showing illustrations of the verbs taught thus far. The groups are to complete the following tasks:	

Task 1: All Groups
Using the stack of cards showing pictures of activities, students take turns rolling the die and making sentences based on these rolls:

1 = *je*	2 = *tu*
3 = *il*	4 = *nous*
5 = *vous*	6 = *elles*

As each student takes a turn, the others in the group should act as "checkers," making sure that everyone is following the correct conjugation.

| The goal is for the group to go through the entire stack of illustrations without making any errors. When they are ready, they may do so for the teacher. Once a group has successfully completed the first task, it should move on to the second task. | Just for fun, I gave the group members a small prize when they reached this goal. |

Task 2: Groups Finished with Task 1

| Working with the stack of French infinitives (which should include verbs in addition to the ones the students worked with in Task 1), students again roll the die to determine which pronoun to use. This time, however, they *write* their responses. | The second task was a bit more difficult than the first because it asked students to work with verbs we had not used as much or at all during our previous lessons. Thus, it provided me with information on students' facility with the **patterns** of –ER verbs and offered an extra challenge for groups that mastered the first task more readily. |

LESSON SEQUENCE AND DESCRIPTION	TEACHER COMMENTARY
Make sure each group has an answer sheet, and have the group members take turns writing the correct conjugations. You may want them to switch roles every three to four minutes or so. Play should continue until all of the groups have successfully completed Task 1.	Remind students of the different conjugation patterns found in written and spoken French.

LESSON 7　　　　**Using –ER Verbs to Communicate**　　　*(2–3 class periods)*

LESSON SEQUENCE AND DESCRIPTION	TEACHER COMMENTARY
Small-group oral performance assessment based on readiness. Students work in readiness groups to prepare and perform dialogues or skits demonstrating their understanding of and facility with –ER verb conjugation (see Sample 6.8, **Differentiated Oral Performance Assessment,** beginning on page 225). *VIOLET: Speaking and Writing Below Expectation Level* This version of the assessment is a highly structured activity and requires students to use only the singular forms of –ER verbs. *ARGENTÉ: Speaking and Writing at Expectation Level* This version of the assessment has explicit instructions, but provides students more choice in the setting and structure of their skits. In addition, students must be sure to use all subject-verb combinations. *ORANGE: Speaking and Writing Above Expectation Level* This version provides less explicit instructions and requires students to reach a consensus about how to show their advanced mastery of –ER verbs. In addition, their skits must incorporate elements of humor and surprise. Rubrics for this assessment differ accordingly (see Sample 6.9, **Oral Performance Assessment Evaluation Rubrics,** beginning on page 227).	This activity gave students an opportunity to apply their understanding in a creative and group-oriented way that focused on real **communication.** I knew that I had to differentiate this assignment because my students would be coming at it from so many different levels of preparedness. I knew that the evaluation of student performance on this differentiated activity must also be differentiated. I felt that I could effectively use one rubric to evaluate the works of students in the VIOLET and ARGENTÉ groups, but that I needed a slightly different rubric to evaluate the works created by students in the ORANGE group. I also made sure that rubric descriptors included opportunities for both individual and group evaluation.

LESSON SEQUENCE AND DESCRIPTION	TEACHER COMMENTARY
All groups should practice their dialogues and skits so that they can perform them in front of the class. When each of the groups has had enough time to create and practice its skit, have a skit performance time during which the groups share their work with one another.	After each group performed its skit, the class provided feedback using a "positive–something to work on–positive" format. (For example, "You were very dramatic. You were a little hard to hear at times. Your pronunciation was great.") I also asked students questions about the skits to assess their overall comprehension and to encourage careful listening.

LESSON 8   **Review for Unit Quiz**   *(1 class period)*

LESSON SEQUENCE AND DESCRIPTION	TEACHER COMMENTARY
Competitive review game between heterogeneous teams. Students review –ER verb conjugations through a class competition between two teams. One student from each team stands at the board while you stand at the back of the room and provide a cue such as, "Voyager. Vous." The students write the correct conjugation of the verb along with the pronoun (i.e., "Vous voyagez") on the board. The first to do so correctly wins a point for his or her team. No coaching from teammates is allowed, and the teams should rotate until all students have had several turns.	This provided a quick review in preparation for the upcoming unit quiz. I mixed up the readiness levels on the teams so that one team would not be noticeably stronger than the other. In addition, I tried to consider readiness levels when I gave my cues, although I did not draw attention to this.

LESSON 9   **Differentiated Unit Quiz on –ER Verb Conjugation**   *(1 class period)*

LESSON SEQUENCE AND DESCRIPTION	TEACHER COMMENTARY
Quiz based on readiness. Administer the **Differentiated Unit Quiz** (see Sample 6.10, beginning on page 229). The quiz contains two sections, with multiple options within each that respond to a variety of intelligence preferences. Activities focus on students' abilities to understand vocabulary, conjugate –ER verbs, and explain how the unit concept of **patterns** relates to –ER verbs.	Because many of this unit's lessons had been differentiated, it did not make sense to give all students the exact same unit evaluation. I decided to create a quiz that incorporated choice so that the students could choose how to show me their understanding. Also, one activity on the quiz encouraged students to think on a higher level, and I was interested to see who would choose that particular option. If you prefer, you may assign certain sections to particular students based on your assessment of their current skill level or learning profile.

| LESSON 10 | Cultural Similarities and Differences | (1–2 class periods) |

LESSON SEQUENCE AND DESCRIPTION	TEACHER COMMENTARY
Presentation and discussion of the group research project culminating products. Have groups share their products with the rest of the class. Use the variety of products presented to illustrate the various ways we can transmit information about culture. Discuss: What is necessary for good **communication** and understanding between peoples?	
Feedback questionnaire on differentiated learning experience. When all groups have presented their products, have the students complete the **Unit Feedback Questionnaire** (see Sample 6.11, page 232).	This questionnaire gave me information about the unit itself and its interest to the students, as well as further information about the students' interests and learning profiles.

Teacher Reflection on the Unit

Overall, I was pleased with the results of my unit. Students indicated that they liked the variety of activities offered. Most felt they were appropriately challenged. This particular unit required a lot of up-front work in designing the different levels of worksheets. Of course, the skit rubric will be useful in future years, and I will be able to reuse many of the class materials, such as the syntax cards. Still, in future applications, my goal will be to concentrate more on adapting existing series materials to the different ability levels in my class. There are so many activities provided in my text series, and I seldom get to them all in a particular unit. I think that if I pay attention to the variety of materials available, I can successfully pick and choose those activities or parts of activities that are most appropriate to my students' varied interests, learning profiles, and readiness levels.

Cindy A. Strickland has taught French in Minnesota, Indiana, and Virginia. She can be reached at cindystrickland@virginia.edu.

SAMPLE 6.1—Lesson 1 Differentiated Worksheet

BLEU

–ER Verbs in the Present Tense

Fill in the blanks with the appropriate form of the verb in parentheses:

1. Marie _____ . (parler)

2. Marie _____ . (dîner)

3. Marie _____ . (téléphoner)

4. Marie _____ . (danser)

5. Marie _____ . (jouer)

6. Marie _____ . (skier)

7. Pierre _____ . (skier)

8. Pierre _____ . (jouer)

9. Pierre _____ . (danser)

10. Pierre _____ . (téléphoner)

11. Pierre _____ . (dîner)

12. Pierre _____ . (parler)

What is the rule illustrated by the examples above?

SAMPLE 6.1—*(continued)*

BLANC

–ER Verbs in the Present Tense

Fill in the blanks with the appropriate form of the verb in parentheses:

1. Marie _____ . (dîner à Burger King)

2. Pierre _____ . (téléphoner à Marie)

3. Pierre _____ . (skier aux Alpes)

4. Marie _____ . (danser la polka)

5. Marie _____ . (jouer au foot)

6. Pierre _____ . (parler français)

Use the examples above to help you complete the following:

7. Marie _____ . (visiter Paris)

8. Pierre _____ . (arriver à New York)

9. Marie _____ . (inviter le président)

10. Marie _____ . (regarder la télévision)

11. Marie _____ . (voyager en Italie)

12. Pierre _____ . (monter la montagne)

What is the rule illustrated by the examples above?

SAMPLE 6.1—*(continued)*

ROUGE

–ER Verbs in the Present Tense

Fill in the blanks with the appropriate form of the verb in parentheses:

1. Pierre _____ . (téléphoner à Marie)

2. Pierre _____ . (skier aux Alpes)

3. Marie _____ . (voyager en Afrique)

4. Marie _____ . (inviter le président)

5. Marie _____ . (jouer au foot)

6. Pierre _____ . (parler français)

7. Marie _____ . (regarder la télé)

8. Marie _____ . (danser la polka)

9. Marie _____ . (visiter Paris)

10. Pierre _____ . (arriver à New York)

11. Marie _____ . (dîner à Burger King)

12. Pierre _____ . (monter la montagne)

What is the rule illustrated by the examples above?

Make up your own French verb that follows the pattern above and write it here:

Now write a sentence using your verb:

Pierre _____ .

SAMPLE 6.2—Suggested Anchor Activities

Note to Teachers:

The following activities are suggestions for tasks students can work on in a "French Culture" learning center. The center approach provides students with activities related to their study of French that they can work on when they first enter the classroom or when they have completed their assigned work. In addition, this type of anchor activity can help with the management of differentiation by giving groups of students independent work to complete while you focus on the needs of other groups of students. You may decide to require each student to complete one or more of the tasks, according to the student's interests, learning profile, or readiness levels. Remember that all students should have opportunities to work in areas of strength, particularly when the focus is not on a specific structure, but on using structures to **communicate**.

Suggested Activities:

1. The teacher will collect and display pictures from both French and American magazines. Choose pictures that highlight cultural differences between France and other French-speaking countries and the local culture. Audiotape a narration about the pictures in which you point out these differences in your description of the pictures in French. Be sure to use language that is a little bit above the students' current level of comprehension in order to stretch the students and thus promote learning. Also, whenever possible, use verbs the students are learning in order to reinforce their vocabulary growth. Encourage students to create their own sentences about the pictures and to look for other pictures to discuss in French. They might put these into a booklet and/or record a narration.

2. Provide a variety of visuals that depict various French-speaking cultures. Provide French sentence starters (for example, "Je skie . . ." and "J'écoute . . .") that students will add on to in response to the visual cues. How do young people in French-speaking cultures behave? What do they like? How do they compare to young people in our country? The students should come up with a way to **communicate** their comparison of their country and at least two French-speaking cultures. They may do so orally (presentation, skit), visually (poster, storybook, chart), or in some other format. Remind students to use correct syntax in their products.

SAMPLE 6.2—(continued)

3. Watch a video about French-speaking young people and their favorite activities and pastimes (such videos often accompany textbook series). Have the students stop the video from time to time to create sentences based on the activities being shown in the video. They can also turn off the volume and create narration for the video. You can also do this activity with clips from feature films that have been translated into French.

4. Using software such as The Learning Company's Kid Pix or other paint or animation programs, have students design a slide show or movie of young people enjoying various pastimes in America and a French-speaking country. Have them narrate their product in written or oral form.

Additional anchor activities might include playing French games such as Mille Bornes, Scrabble, and Monopoly; listening to French music; or browsing through a box of French children's books. There are also many children's books on tape available through companies that specialize in world language materials. And don't forget about the numerous computer programs available for French. Note, however, that these activities do not have a direct link to this unit; instead, they serve as general enrichment and language extension.

SAMPLE 6.3—Lesson 2 Differentiated Worksheet

VERT

The Pronoun *Je*

Write complete sentences using the elements given.

Example:

Je/chanter	...	*Je chante.*
Marie/jouer au piano	...	*Elle joue au piano.*
Pierre/skier mal	...	*Il skie mal.*

1. Je/regarder la télé

2. Pierre/monter la montagne

3. Marie/chanter bien

4. Je/dîner à 5h00.

5. Je/travailler à Limited Too

6. Pierre/voyager au Mexique

7. Je/téléphoner au professeur

8. Marie/nager en décembre

9. Pierre/écouter la radio

10. Marie/aimer Pierre

Study the examples below:

Je/écouter la radio	...	*J'écoute la radio.*
Je/aimer le professeur	...	*J'aime le professeur.*

11. Je/écouter l'orchestre

12. Je/habiter en Virginie

SAMPLE 6.3—*(continued)*

Now rewrite sentences 1–12, making them negative.

Example:

Je chante.	…	*Je ne chante pas.*
Elle joue du piano.	…	*Elle ne joue pas du piano.*
Il skie mal.	…	*Il ne skie pas mal.*

1. _____ .

2. _____ .

3. _____ .

4. _____ .

5. _____ .

6. _____ .

7. _____ .

8. _____ .

9. _____ .

10. _____ .

***11. _____ .

***12. _____ .

***Attention!

SAMPLE 6.3—(continued)

GRIS

The Pronoun *Je*

Write complete sentences using the elements given.

Examples:

Je/chanter	...	*Je chante.*
Marie/jouer du piano	...	*Elle joue du piano.*
Je/écouter la radio	...	*J'écoute la radio.*

1. Je/regarder la télé

2. Pierre/monter la montagne

3. Je/écouter l'orchestre

4. Marie/chanter bien

5. Je/habiter à Louisville

6. Je/travailler à Limited Too

7. Pierre/voyager au Mexique

8. Je/écouter la musique

9. Marie/nager en décembre

10. Pierre/écouter la radio

11. Marie/aimer Pierre

12. Je/habiter en Virginie

SAMPLE 6.3—*(continued)*

Now rewrite sentences 1–12, making them negative.

Examples:

Je chante.   …   *Je ne chante pas.*
Elle joue du piano.   …   *Elle ne joue pas du piano.*
J'habite en France.   …   *Je n'habite pas en France.*

1. _____ .

2. _____ .

3. _____ .

4. _____ .

5. _____ .

6. _____ .

7. _____ .

8. _____ .

9. _____ .

10. _____ .

11. _____ .

12. _____ .

Attention aux voyelles!

SAMPLE 6.3—(continued)

JAUNE

The Pronoun *Je*

Write a sentence for each of the verbs presented so far. Use a mixture of subject pronouns.

1. _____ .
2. _____ .
3. _____ .
4. _____ .
5. _____ .
6. _____ .
7. _____ .
8. _____ .
9. _____ .
10. _____ .
11. _____ .
12. _____ .
13. _____ .
14. _____ .
15. _____ .

Rewrite sentences 10–15 in the negative.

10. _____ .
11. _____ .
12. _____ .
13. _____ .
14. _____ .
15. _____ .

SAMPLE 6.4—Syntax Cards

Samples for Set 1   **(On Expectation Level)**

Marie	skie	aux Alpes
Pierre	joue	du piano
Je	téléphone	à Maman
Il	dîne	à 18h
Elle	habite	à Nice
Je	nage	bien
J'	écoute	la musique

Note that all the subjects, with the exception of J', can be matched with any verb.

Set 2   **(Above Expectation Level)**

ne	pas
n'	Je

SAMPLE 6.5—Group Research Project Guidelines

Communicating Cultural Similarities and Differences

How do young people in French-speaking cultures behave? What do they like? How do their activities compare to those of young people in our country? How do the geographical and/or cultural resources available to young people in a particular country affect their leisure time activities? What implications for cross-cultural communication and understanding would investigation of these questions have?

In this project, you will work with your group members to complete one of the tasks outlined in this document. (I will give you your task assignment.) Your group will research typical activities of young people in at least two French-speaking cultures and compare them to activities you and your friends typically do here. You will also speculate on why these similarities and differences between cultures might exist and what the ramifications of your findings might be. Finally, you will come up with a visual way to communicate the results of your research, based on the guidelines of your group's assigned task. Remember, your work must be highly illustrative of similarities and differences in the cultures you select and appropriate to your task.

Be sure to make a plan for how you will equitably divide up the work that needs to be done. Consider the unique strengths of the individual members of your group when assigning tasks.

Task A: Creative Task
You work for the local county museum in your town. The museum director is a friend of the family and knows of your interest in francophone cultures. She asks you and your friends to design a temporary museum exhibit for an upcoming show designed to interest local middle and high school students in other cultures. She particularly wants students to come away from the exhibit with an understanding of both the similarities and differences between typical leisure time activities of young people from our local region and at least two French-speaking cultures.

Once you complete your research, design a museum-quality display about each culture that clearly points out similarities and differences among them. Attach a brief written explanation, in English, to be posted alongside the exhibit. It should delineate your overall findings about similarities and differences among the cultures and encourage viewers to investigate the cultures further.

Task B: Practical Task
You are a student intern at a travel agency in your town. The boss has asked you and your friends to research at least two French-speaking cultures and compare them to local culture with respect to the activities young people typically engage in. Your results will be presented to a group of local teachers who are considering working with your agency to set up a summer study program in a variety of francophone cultures. These teachers wish to know what their students might expect in terms of leisure time activities in the various countries.

SAMPLE 6.5—*(continued)*

Once you complete your research, design an informational brochure, poster, or series of PowerPoint slides about each country that clearly points out similarities and differences among these cultures. Attach a brief editorial for publication in the group's monthly newsletter in which you summarize your overall findings about similarities and differences among the cultures and make recommendations for future study.

Task C: Analytical Task

You work as a student consultant for a think tank in your town. Your work group has been assigned to a committee on creating cultural links among young people with a variety of cultural and regional backgrounds. Because your group members are studying French, you are given the task of analyzing at least two French-speaking cultures and comparing them to local culture with respect to the activities young people typically engage in. Your work will be used as a pilot for a larger comparative analysis to be completed by the larger committee. After completing your research, design a flow chart, Venn diagram, or other graphic organizer that clearly depicts the results of your analysis. This organizer may be created on the computer, if you wish. Attach a brief outline in English, based on your overall findings, delineating your recommendations to the committee.

SAMPLE 6.6—Group Research Project Checklist for Success

Each group member must fill out this evaluation to rate your project and report how successfully you worked as a group. Please make specific comments in the appropriate box. Turn all copies into the teacher, who will also rate your group's efforts.

To what extent does your project . . .	Bravo!	Assez Bien	Un Peu	Pas du Tout
. . . accurately describe the typical leisure time activities of young people in at least two French-speaking cultures and our region of the country?				
. . . clearly illustrate the related similarities and differences among the cultures?				
. . . point out how the geographical and/or cultural resources available to young people in a particular country affect their leisure time activities?				
. . . discuss implications of your findings for cross-cultural communication and understanding?				
. . . meet the specific requirements of your assigned task?				

SAMPLE 6.6—*(continued)*

To what extent did your group. . .	Bravo!	Assez Bien	Un Peu	Pas du Tout
. . . complete your task on time?				
. . . equitably divide up the work?				
. . . treat each other with respect?				

SAMPLE 6.7—Lesson 5 Differentiated Worksheet

ROSE

Subject Pronouns

Read the following passage. You do not need to understand every word.

Bonjour, mes amis. Je m'appelle Cécile et j'habite en France, à Annecy. C'est une très jolie ville, près des Alpes. Les touristes voyagent souvent à Annecy. En été, ils nagent dans le lac et en hiver, ils skient. Moi aussi, je skie beaucoup. Mon ami, Jean-Jacques me téléphone quand il fait beau parce que nous aimons faire des sports ensemble. Je monte dans la voiture et j'arrive tout de suite chez Jean-Jacques. (Il habite près de chez moi.) De temps en temps, il invite aussi sa soeur, Marie-Claire. Je n'aime pas ça, parce qu'elle chante toujours très fort dans l'auto! Pourquoi? Je ne sais pas, mais elle travaille chez le disquaire, donc elle écoute constamment de la musique. Moi, je danse bien, mais je ne chante pas du tout! Jean-Jacques, il chante très bien et il danse bien aussi. J'aime danser avec lui. Il est très sportif. Moi, je ne suis pas très sportive, mais j'aime jouer aux sports. Et vous?

1. Reread the passage and underline in green every use of the pronouns *je, il,* and *elle*.
2. Find the verb that goes with each subject. Circle each verb in blue.
3. Identify other words that you think are verbs, but that do not follow the patterns we have learned so far. Put a red box around these verbs.

NOIR

Subject Pronouns: La Partie *A*

Read the following passage. You do not need to understand every word.

Bonjour, mes amis. Je m'appelle Cécile et j'habite en France, à Annecy. C'est une très jolie ville, près des Alpes. Les touristes voyagent souvent à Annecy. En été, ils nagent dans le lac et en hiver, ils skient. Moi aussi, je skie beaucoup. Mon ami, Jean-Jacques me téléphone quand il fait beau parce que nous aimons faire des sports ensemble. Il dit «Tu skies avec moi?» Je dis «Oui, bien sûr!» Puis, je monte dans la voiture et j'arrive tout de suite chez Jean-Jacques. (Il habite près de chez moi.) De temps en temps, il invite aussi sa soer, Marie-Claire. Je n'aime pas ça parce qu'elle chante toujours très fort dans l'auto! Pourquoi? Je ne sais pas, mais elle travaille chez le disquaire, donc elle écoute constamment de la musique. Moi, je danse bien, mais je ne chante pas du tout! Jean-Jaques, il chante très bien et il danse bien aussi. J'aime danser avec lui. Il est très sportif. Moi, je ne suis pas très sportive, mais j'aime jouer aux sports. Et vous? Vous jouez aux sports chez vous? Est-ce que vous regardez les sports à la télé ? Vous habitez en Amérique ? On joue au base-ball en Amérique, n'est-ce pas? Ma mère adore le base-ball américain. (Mon père est américain et mes parents parlent anglais ensemble.) Bien sûr, ils parlent français aussi. Et vous, vous parlez une autre langue? Français? Italien? Espagnol?

1. Reread the passage and underline in green every use of the pronouns *je, il,* and *elle*.
2. Find the verb that goes with each subject. Circle each verb in blue.
3. Identify other words that you think are verbs, but that do not seem to follow the patterns we have learned so far. Put a red box around these verbs.
4. Try to identify a pattern concerning these other verbs. What conclusions can you draw about the French verb system? Compare your conclusions with other members of the group.
5. Test out this theory by studying any posters or other visuals posted around the room. Adjust your conclusions as necessary.

When you've finished, see me for **La Partie B**.

SAMPLE 6.7—(continued)

NOIR

Subject Pronouns: La Partie *B*

Study the verb conjugation chart below.

Chanter

Je chante	Nous chantons
Tu chantes	Vous chantez
Il chante	**Ils chantent**
Elle chante	**Elles chantent**

Note on Pronunciation: The verb forms in bold are pronounced exactly the same even though they are spelled differently. Be careful that when you pronounce *Ils/Elles chantent* you do not pronounce the –ent! *Chantez* is pronounced the same as *chanter*. *Chantons* rhymes with *bonbons*.

Go back to Part A and see if this pattern is identifiable within the passage. Is it?

What questions remain in your mind? Write them below:

Now study this example:

Travailler

Je ne travaille pas.	Nous ne travaillons pas.
Tu ne travailles pas.	Vous ne travaillez pas.
Elle ne travaille pas.	**Elles ne travaillent pas.**
Il ne travaille pas.	**Ils ne travaillent pas.**

Conjugate *dîner* in the negative.

Now reread the passage in Part A. Underline the pronouns *tu, nous, vous, ils,* and *elles.* Put a blue circle around their corresponding verbs that match the pattern discussed above. Put a black triangle around any verb that does not fit the pattern. On the back of this sheet, speculate about why this is.

SAMPLE 6.7—(continued)

Study this example carefully:

Nager

Je ne nage pas.	Nous ne nageons pas.
Tu ne nages pas.	Vous ne nagez pas.
Elle ne nage pas.	**Elles ne nagent pas.**
Il ne nage pas.	**Ils ne nagent pas.**

What do you notice?

Why do you think this is?

What implications does this have for the verb *voyager?*

SAMPLE 6.8—Differentiated Oral Performance Assessment

VIOLET

Work with a partner to prepare two dialogues in which you interview each other about your activities/ interests. DO NOT WRITE YOUR DIALOGUES IN ENGLISH FIRST!

Use the following format or one that is similar. Replace the underlined sections with your own phrase or phrases.

A: Je m'appelle Linda Ellerby. Et voici John Smith. Bonjour, John.
B: Bonjour, Linda.
A: John, tu joues au basket-ball, n'est-ce pas?
B: Oui, je joue assez bien.
A: Tu joues avec tes amis?
B: Non, je ne joue pas avec mes amis. Je joue avec mes frères.
A: Et tu regardes la télévision?
B: Oui. Je regarde *Smart Guy* à Nickelodeon.
A: Moi aussi. Tu ne regardes pas *Sabrina?*
B: Non, je n'aime pas Melissa Joan Hart.
A: Merci beaucoup, John.
B: De rien, Linda. Au revoir.

Switch roles, and ask questions using different verbs.

In your dialogues, you must correctly use a minimum of 10 of the –ER verbs that we have been studying. You must also ask and answer at least one question in the negative.

Each of you must write out the entire dialogue. Please underline the subject and verb in each of your sentences. Show one copy of your completed skit to the teacher before you begin rehearsing.

Please memorize your dialogue.

Evaluation: The written version of your dialogue will be evaluated on accuracy and grammatical completeness. Your oral performance will be evaluated on your overall fluency and on how well your dialogues would be understood by a native speaker of French. See the Evaluation Rubric for more information.

Remember: Your goal is successful **communication** in French!

SAMPLE 6.8—(continued)

ARGENTÉ

Work with one or two partners to prepare a skit in which you correctly use a minimum of 10 of the –ER verbs that we have been studying. Be sure to use both affirmative and negative sentences. You must use each of the singular and plural subject pronouns at least once. DO NOT WRITE YOUR SKIT IN ENGLISH FIRST!

Each group member must write out the entire skit. Please underline the subject and verb in each of your sentences. Show one copy of your completed skit to the teacher before you begin rehearsing.

Your skit must be memorized. Be sure to evenly divide the speaking responsibilities.

Evaluation: The written version of your skit will be evaluated on accuracy and grammatical completeness. Your oral performance will be evaluated on your overall fluency and on how well your skit would be understood by a native speaker of French. See the Evaluation Rubric for more information.

Remember: Your goal is successful **communication** in French!

ORANGE:

Work with one partner or two to prepare a skit in which you demonstrate your advanced mastery of –ER verbs. Come to a consensus about which grammatical elements you need to include in order to show this advanced understanding of the grammatical concepts we have covered in this unit. Have the teacher approve your list before starting to write your skit. Your skit must include the use of humor and have a surprising or interesting ending. DO NOT WRITE YOUR SKIT IN ENGLISH FIRST!

Each group member must write out the entire skit. Please underline the subject and verb in each of your sentences. Show one copy of your completed skit to the teacher before you begin rehearsing.

Your skit must be memorized. Be sure to evenly divide the speaking responsibilities.

Evaluation: The written version of your skit will be evaluated on accuracy and grammatical completeness. Your oral performance will be evaluated on your overall fluency and on how well your skit would be understood by a native speaker of French. See the Evaluation Rubric for more information.

Remember: Your goal is successful **communication** in French!

SAMPLE 6.9—Oral Performance Assessment Evaluation Rubrics

VIOLET et ARGENTÉ	Magnifique	Bien	Comme Ci, Comme Ça	Quel Désastre!
ACCURACY (group grade)	Work is grammatically accurate.	Minor errors do not impede overall understanding of your ideas.	Minor grammatical errors distort the meaning of your ideas.	Your ideas are incomprehensible due to grammatical errors.
GRAMMAR (group grade)	You include all required grammatical structures (–ER verbs, negative sentences, subject pronouns).	You include all required grammatical structures (–ER verbs, negative sentences, subject pronouns), but you do not include the required number of examples in one of the categories.	You include all required grammatical structures (–ER verbs, negative sentences, subject pronouns), but you do not include the required number of examples in more than one of the categories.	You leave out a major type of required grammatical structure (–ER verbs, negative sentences, subject pronouns).
FLUENCY (individual grade)	You have memorized your part and speak at an appropriate pace. You speak confidently and flowingly.	You have memorized your part with the exception of minor errors or omissions. Momentary hesitations do not distract the listener.	You make frequent errors due to inadequate memorization. Your speech is halting, but you complete most of your thoughts.	You did not memorize your part. You do not communicate complete thoughts.
COMPRE-HENSIBILITY (individual grade)	A native French speaker with no previous exposure to second-language learners could easily understand your presentation.	A native French speaker with limited experience dealing with second-language learners could understand your presentation.	A native French speaker with experience dealing with second-language learners could understand the overall message of your presentation, although minor details would be lost.	A native French speaker with experience dealing with second-language learners could not understand or follow your presentation.

SAMPLE 6.9—(continued)

ORANGE	Magnifique	Bien	Comme Ci, Comme Ça	Quel Désastre!
MASTERY (group grade)	Work is grammatically accurate. Your skit demonstrates a thorough mastery of the grammatical concepts covered in this unit.	Work is grammatically accurate. Minor errors do not impede overall understanding of your ideas. Your skit demonstrates an understanding of the major grammatical concepts covered in this unit.	Minor grammatical errors distort the meaning of your ideas. Your skit demonstrates a lack of mastery of one major OR several minor grammatical concepts covered in this unit.	Your ideas are incomprehensible due to major grammatical errors. Your skit demonstrates a complete lack of understanding of the grammatical concepts covered in this unit.
FLUENCY (individual grade)	You have memorized your part and speak at an appropriate pace. You speak confidently and flowingly.	You have memorized your part with the exception of minor errors or omissions. Momentary hesitations do not distract the listener.	You make frequent errors due to inadequate memorization. You speech is halting, but you complete most of your thoughts.	You did not memorize your part. You do not communicate complete thoughts.
COMPRE-HENSIBILITY (individual grade)	A native French speaker with no previous exposure to second-language learners could easily understand your presentation.	A native French speaker with limited experience dealing with second-language learners could understand your presentation.	A native French speaker with experience dealing with second-language learners could understand the overall message of your presentation, although minor details would be lost.	A native French speaker with experience dealing with second-language learners could not understand or follow your presentation.
HUMOR/ SURPRISE (group grade)	Your skit effectively uses humor to communicate. The ending of your skit surprises and delights the audience, yet is clearly related to the skit as a whole.	You use humor to communicate. You include a surprise ending to your skit, but this ending does not seem to "fit" with the overall skit.	Your attempts at humor are unsuccessful. Your "surprise ending" is unimaginative or predictable.	You do not use humor. You do not include a surprise ending.

SAMPLE 6.10—Differentiated Unit Quiz

Section 1

Choose **one** of the options below.

Option A   *(20 points)*

Use the back of this sheet to design a quick pictorial representation of at least 10 of the –ER verbs that we have studied in this unit. Label each with an appropriate sentence in French. Then write three sentences that do not describe what is happening in the picture (use the negative!).

Option B   *(20 points)*

Match the following French verbs to their English equivalent:

1. écouter	_____	a. to adore
2. adorer	_____	b. to arrive
3. aimer	_____	c. to climb
4. arriver	_____	d. to dance
5. chanter	_____	e. to eat dinner
6. dîner	_____	f. to hate
7. détester	_____	g. to invite
8. danser	_____	h. to like
9. habiter	_____	i. to listen to
10. inviter	_____	j. to live
11. jouer	_____	k. to phone
12. monter	_____	l. to play
13. nager	_____	m. to prefer
14. parler	_____	n. to sing
15. préférer	_____	o. to ski
16. regarder	_____	p. to speak
17. skier	_____	q. to swim
18. téléphoner	_____	r. to travel
19. travailler	_____	s. to watch
20. voyager	_____	t. to work

SAMPLE 6.10—*(continued)*

Section 2

Choose from the following activities. You must choose tasks that add up to exactly 30 points

Option A   *(20 points)*

Conjugate the following verbs (include the appropriate subject pronouns).

Marcher

Étudier

Conjugate in the negative:

Bavarder

Option B   *(20 points)*

Fill in the blanks with the correct form of the verb in parentheses.

1. Je _____ la télé. (regarder)

2. Pierre _____ la montagne. (monter)

3. Marie _____ bien. (chanter)

4. Nous _____ à Limited Too. (travailler)

5. Elles _____ à 17h00. (dîner)

6. Pierre _____ au Mexique. (voyager)

7. Vous _____ au professeur. (téléphoner)

8. Tu _____ en décembre? (nager)

Now, rewrite sentences 7 and 8 in the negative.

7. _____ .

8. _____ .

SAMPLE 6.10—*(continued)*

Option C
(10 points)

Group the following infinitives into families of some kind. Explain (in English) why you grouped them the way you did. Explain how your grouping arrangement relates to the unit concept of **patterns**.

écouter	adorer
aimer	arriver
chanter	dîner
détester	danser
habiter	inviter
jouer	monter
nager	parler
préférer	regarder
skier	téléphoner
travailler	voyager

Option D
(30 points)

Use the back of this sheet to design a graphical representation (chart, flow chart, graphic organizer, etc.) of the **patterns** found in –ER verb conjugation, along with examples of how this material could be used to conjugate any –ER verb, even a made-up verb like "jugaliser." Be sure you consider any exceptions to the rules we have uncovered in class, as well as how to make verbs negative. You may not use the standard conjugation format.

SAMPLE 6.11—Unit Feedback Questionnaire

Please answer the questions below. You will not be graded on this. You do not need to put your name on this form.

1. Please tell me what **you enjoyed most** during this unit (and why).

2. What did you enjoy **least** (and why)?

3. Which activity **helped you learn** about –ER verbs the most? Why do you think it worked for you?

4. Which activity worked **least well**? Why do you think it was not successful for you?

5. **How did you feel** about having different student groups and activities assigned in the class? Circle and briefly explain your answer:

   Mostly negative

   Slightly negative

   Slightly positive

   Mostly positive

6. How would you rate **the overall level of challenge** you experienced in the activities related to this unit? Circle and briefly explain your answer:

   Not at all challenging

   A little challenging

   Moderately challenging

   Too challenging

Glossary

Anchor activities—These are tasks students automatically move to when they complete assigned work. Teachers may provide a list of possible anchor options and should encourage students to suggest other ideas. Anchor activities must be important to essential student learning and never just time-fillers. In classes with flexible pacing, all students will need anchor options. Still, if a student is consistently finishing work early, it's likely that either the student is finding the work too easy or the student is working at a lesser level of craftsmanship.

Big idea—This term is sometimes used as a synonym for a **generalization**. It refers to the key understandings a student should derive from a lesson or unit.

Complex Instruction—This instructional strategy, developed by Elizabeth Cohen and others (see Sharan, 1999), calls for students to work on tasks in small, heterogeneous groups and asks each member to make a critical contribution to the success of the group as a whole. Complex Instruction tasks are high-level, open-ended, interesting to students, and require many different talents for successful completion. Reading and writing are integrated into the tasks. Teachers design these tasks to call on a variety of intellectual strengths, and they assign students to groups based on an increasing knowledge of each learner's intellectual strengths. (*Note*: Multilingual groups should always have a bilingual student who can serve as a bridge between languages. Materials required for group success are often available in the primary language of second-language learners.) Under the Complex Instruction strategy, the teacher continually moves among groups to probe student thinking, help students plan for success and quality, and make sure students are aware of the various strengths they bring to the task at hand. Used appropriately, Complex Instruction can address student readiness, interest, and learning profile needs.

Concept—A concept is the name assigned to a category of objects or ideas with common attributes. Concepts are abstract, broad, and universal. They help learners make sense of ideas and information because they help organize and distinguish entities. They help learners look at likenesses and place similar objects or ideas in the same category. Concepts are generally stated in one word (for example, *pattern, probability, habitat, poem, perspective, energy, fraction, number, justice*). Sometimes concepts require two or three words to communicate an idea (for example, *rights and responsibilities, balance of power, checks and balances, relative size, supply and demand, central tendency, point of view*).

Concept Attainment Strategy—This instructional strategy, developed by Hilda Taba (1971), guides students in discovering the key components or elements of a particular concept.

1. The teacher selects a concept that will be central to a topic or unit and determines the components or elements that define the concept. (For example, *symmetry* is a concept and is defined as correspondence in size or arrangement of parts along a plane.)

2. The teacher selects positive and negative examples of the concept. A positive example has all the components or attributes of the concept. (For example, a jacket, a cone, a square, a valentine heart, the name *Anna,* and an Oreo cookie are all positive examples of symmetry). A negative example does not have all the components or elements. (For example, most paintings, most puzzle pieces, a tree, and the numeral 4 are negative examples of symmetry.)

3. The teacher explains the process of figuring out a concept and shows students a succession of positive and negative examples through objects, pictures, and words. However, the teacher does not usually use the name of the concept at this point.

4. As students look at an example, they decide whether an example might be positive or negative by speculating on its elements. The teacher (or a student) lists the examples in a "positive" or "negative" column as directed by the students. (For example, a student might say, "I think all these things are made of wood, so I'd put 'tree' in the positive column.") If a hypothesized attribute fails to pan out in later examples, students tell the teacher to strike out the attribute in the positive column and add it to the negative column.

5. Through the process of testing attributes over successive examples, students arrive at the key components of a concept and, ultimately, write their own concept definitions.

6. The teacher gives additional examples so students can test their definitions.

7. The teacher brings closure to the activity by ensuring that all students have a common understanding of the concept and its key components.

Concept-based teaching—Concept-based teaching uses the essential concepts and key principles of a discipline as the primary way of organizing curriculum content. For example, a middle school history teacher might tell her students that history is the study of "CREEPS." The acronym stands for *C*ulture, *R*eligion, *E*conomics, *E*sthetics, *P*olitics, and *S*ocial issues. Students define each of the concepts in their own words, and these concept definitions give students a yearlong (and, in fact, lifelong) lens for viewing history. It also helps them make connections between their own lives, current events, and historical events. Principles that relate to each concept help students think more specifically about patterns in history. One key principle they might examine is, "People shape culture and culture shapes people." Students can see how this principle plays out in history and in their own lives.

Culture-based differentiation—Culture affects many facets of our lives. Because our own culture is integral to and pervasive in our lives, we may be unconscious of how it shapes us. More to the point, we are unlikely to be aware of how our culture shapes us in ways that differ from how other people's cultures shape them. It is easy to assume "our way" is everyone's way. This habit of thinking is particularly problematic for students from minority cultures in schools shaped largely by the majority culture. Culture-based differentiation emphasizes the need to 1) understand the cultures and cultural expectations of all students in the classroom; 2) develop classrooms that are sensitive and responsive to a variety of cultures; 3) ensure that all students' cultures are represented in materials and perspectives on issues; 4) ensure equity of attention, participation, and high expectations for students from all cultures; and 5) ensure learning approaches and options that span the full range of culture-influenced possibilities. Culture can affect how we relate to authority, whether we prefer contextualized or decontextualized learning, whether we are more reserved or expressive, whether we prefer working alone or with peers, whether or not we feel constrained by time, whether we stress the individual or the group, and so on. There is great variance of learning preference within each culture. The goal of culture-based differentiation is not to label or pigeonhole students, but to understand and actively address the fact that a classroom that runs counter to a student's cultural norms and needs will impede that student's learning.

Equalizer—The Equalizer is a visual guide to help teachers think about tiering tasks and products (*see* **Tiering**). As the figure here illustrates, it suggests several continua along which teachers can adjust task or product difficulty. By matching task difficulty with learner readiness, a teacher can provide appropriate challenge for a given learner at a given time. For example, if students in a math class are working with measurement, their teacher might ask them to measure the surface area of a desk. If the teacher asks students having difficulty with measurement to measure the surface area of their bedroom floors as a homework assignment, that task, on the Equalizer, would be relatively "foundational"—that is, similar to the familiar, in-class task. If, on the other hand, the teacher finds that some students have a solid grasp of the in-class task, the teacher might assign homework asking them to develop a plan for measuring the surface area of a tree. That task is much more "transformational," or unfamiliar. In this way, both groups of students can continue to advance their ability to measure surface area, but at appropriately different degrees of difficulty.

The Equalizer: A Tool for Planning Differentiated Lessons

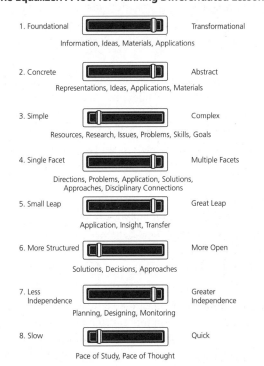

1. Foundational — Transformational
Information, Ideas, Materials, Applications

2. Concrete — Abstract
Representations, Ideas, Applications, Materials

3. Simple — Complex
Resources, Research, Issues, Problems, Skills, Goals

4. Single Facet — Multiple Facets
Directions, Problems, Application, Solutions, Approaches, Disciplinary Connections

5. Small Leap — Great Leap
Application, Insight, Transfer

6. More Structured — More Open
Solutions, Decisions, Approaches

7. Less Independence — Greater Independence
Planning, Designing, Monitoring

8. Slow — Quick
Pace of Study, Pace of Thought

Exit card—An exit card is a quick and easy method of assessing student understanding of a particular idea, skill, or topic. The teacher teaches the skill or concept that is central to the lesson and gives students a chance to work with it and discuss it. Just a few minutes before the day's lesson ends, the teacher distributes index cards to all students. Then, the teacher poses a question that probes student understanding of the topic (rather than information recall) and asks students to write their name and a response to the question on their index card. Students turn in the cards as they leave the room (or someone may collect the cards). The teacher does not grade the exit cards, but rather sorts them in categories representative of student understanding. A teacher might elect to use only two categories (students who seem to grasp the idea and those who don't) or might elect to use as many as four or five categories (students who understand little, understand some, have a basic understanding, have only a few gaps, and have a solid grasp). In this way, the exit cards become a vehicle for planning subsequent lessons aimed at helping each student continue to grow in knowledge and skill from a current point of understanding. As an alternative, teachers sometimes use a "3–2–1 format" on exit cards. In this instance, students might be asked to write the three most important ideas in the lesson, two questions they still have about the lesson, and one way they can use what they learned. Either approach can be modified to match lesson goals and learner needs.

Flexible grouping—Flexible grouping is purposeful reordering of students into working groups to ensure that all students work with a wide variety of classmates and in a wide range of contexts during a relatively short span of classroom time. Flexible grouping enables students to work with peers of both similar and dissimilar readiness levels, interests, and learning preferences, and allows the teacher to "audition" each student in a variety of arrangements. At various points in a lesson, most students have a need to work with peers at similar levels of readiness on a given topic or skill. But they also benefit from heterogeneous groupings in which the teacher takes care to ensure that each student has a significant contribution to make to the work of the group. Likewise, although most students enjoy the chance to work with peers whose interests (or learning profiles) match their own, they may be challenged and enriched by blending their interests (or learning profiles) with students of differing talents and interests (or learning profiles) to accomplish a task that draws on multiple interests (or approaches to learning). Additionally, it's important for students to work as a whole class, individually, and in small groups—and when doing so, to learn to make good choices related to working relationships. A teacher who uses flexible grouping systematically groups and regroups students as a regular feature of instructional planning.

Gender-based differentiation—It is likely that there are predominantly male learning preferences and predominantly female learning preferences. On the other hand, it is clearly the case that not *all* members of the same gender learn in the same ways. The goal of gender-based differentiation, then, is to understand the range of learning preferences that may be influenced by gender and to develop learning options that span that range, allowing students of either gender to work in ways that are most effective for them. Among the continua of learning preferences that may be gender-influenced are abstract versus concrete, still versus moving, collaboration versus competition, inductive versus deductive, and silent versus talking. Although there is great variance within each gender, *in general,* females prefer the first approach in each pair, and males the second. However, it is important to remember that there is great variance within each gender. Gender-based differentiation is one facet of learning profile differentiation.

Generalizations—Generalizations are essential understandings central to a topic or discipline. They are statements of truth about a concept. Generalizations transfer across instances, times, and cultures. Like the concepts they help explain, generalizations are broad and abstract. Unlike concepts, generalizations are written as complete sentences. An example of a generalization is "Parts of a system are interdependent." Ensuring

that students consistently work with generalizations helps them to understand what the topic is really about. It also promotes retention of information and transfer across and within topics.

Intelligence preference—According to psychologists such as Howard Gardner and Robert Sternberg, human brains are "wired" differently in different individuals. Although all normally functioning people use all parts of their brains, each of us is "wired" to be better in some areas than we are in others. Gardner (1993, 1997) suggests eight possible intelligences, which he calls *verbal/linguistic, logical/mathematical, bodily/kinesthetic, visual/spatial, musical/rhythmic, interpersonal, intrapersonal,* and *naturalist.* Sternberg (1988, 1997) suggests three intelligence preferences: *analytic* (schoolhouse intelligence), *creative* (imaginative intelligence), and *practical* (contextual, street-smart intelligence). Differentiation based on a student's intelligence preference generally suggests allowing the student to work in a preferred mode and helping the student to develop that capacity further. Sometimes teachers also ask students to extend their preferred modes of working, or they opt to use a student's preferred areas to support growth in less comfortable areas. Differentiation based on intelligence preference is one kind of learning profile differentiation.

Interest-based differentiation—As learners, we are motivated by things that interest us, and we tend to be more confident in our ability to succeed when we work with those things. Interest-based differentiation attempts to tap into the interests of a particular learner as a means of facilitating learning. Interest-based differentiation can build upon existing interests or extend interests. Further, interest-based differentiation can link student interests with required learning outcomes or can provide students the opportunity to extend their own talents and interests beyond the scope of required learning goals.

Interest centers—These are a particular kind of **learning center**. Rather than focusing on mastery of required knowledge, information, and skills (as learning centers do), interest centers allow students to explore ideas or topics of particular interest to them in greater depth and/or breadth than would be possible in the prescribed curriculum. Interest centers can focus on topics derived directly from a unit of study. They can also address topics outside the curriculum. Interest centers can be differentiated by encouraging students to participate in those centers that address their particular interests, talents, or questions.

Jigsaw—This cooperative strategy, developed by Elliot Aronson (see Aronson et al., 1978), allows students to become experts in a facet of a topic they're particularly interested in. Students first meet in small groups, sometimes called *home-base groups.* Here, they review the task they must complete and clarify goals for individuals and the group. They then divide into specialty groups, or *work groups.* Each specialty group is responsible for one facet of the overall task. Every member of the specialty group works to develop a full understanding of the assigned subtopic or subtask. After an appropriate time, students reassemble in their home-base groups. Each member of the group shares the information about his or her specialty. All group members are responsible for asking questions and learning about all facets of the topic. In effective Jigsaw arrangements, all students are both teachers and learners. Teachers may assign students to specialty groups based on assessed needs or interests, or students may select their own. Appropriately used, Jigsaw can address readiness, interest, and learning profile needs.

Learning centers—Learning centers are a collection of materials and activities designed to teach, reinforce, or extend students' knowledge, understanding, and skills. Learning centers are often associated with physical spaces in the classroom, as many teachers set up center materials and activities in a particular area of the classroom and ask students to move to that area when it is time to work "at the center." However, learning centers can also be more portable—"housed" in boxes or folders students use at designated times, then stored again when not in use. Students typically keep records of the work they do while at a learning center in order to account for

what they have accomplished during each center visit. Learning centers can be differentiated by having students visit only those centers suited to their needs (compared with having all students move to all centers), by specifying tasks and materials at a given center for particular students based on those students' learning needs, and/or by adjusting the time an individual student spends at a particular center.

Learning stations—Learning stations are areas or regions in a classroom to which students move on a specified timetable to complete particular tasks. Learning stations are similar to **learning centers** and **interest centers**, but are less fixed than those kinds of centers tend to be. Learning stations can be differentiated by having students visit only those stations suited to their needs (compared with having all students move to all stations) and/or by specifying tasks and materials at a given station for particular students based on their learning needs.

Learning style—Learning style is one facet of a student's learning profile and refers to personal and environmental factors that may affect learning. For example, some students need quiet when they work, while others prefer interaction or some noise. Some students work best while sitting up straight at a table or desk; others learn best in a more relaxed position. Differentiation based on a student's learning style is one facet of learning profile differentiation.

Metacognition—This term refers to students' thinking about their own thinking. For example, a teacher might ask students to explain how they solved a problem or to monitor their understanding of a particular concept so that they might ask for clarification. It is likely that students are more effective learners when they are aware of both the kind of thinking a particular instance calls for and the thinking processes they use to make this decision. It is important for teachers to help students develop a "vocabulary of thinking" and to monitor their own thinking processes.

Mini-workshops—This is another name for small-group instruction. When a teacher senses that some learners need additional help with a topic, understanding, or skill, the teacher might conduct a small-group teaching session on that topic to help learners make necessary progress. The teacher may open the mini-workshop to all students interested in attending, invite specific students to attend, or do both. A student who is particularly strong with a topic or skill might conduct a mini-workshop for peers, as long as the student is also effective in working with agemates and teaching what he or she knows. Mini-workshops can be particularly helpful in guiding students through complex product assignments in which some requirements are not familiar to all learners. They are also useful for helping groups of students at all skill levels know how to move to a next level of proficiency.

Negotiated criteria—This term refers to the process of developing criteria for student success based on more than one perspective. Some criteria for success may be required of most or even all learners due to the nature of a task or previously established benchmarks. However, it is helpful to a student to establish personal goals important to his or her growth. In addition, the teacher can generally set one or more criteria for success that are uniquely important for an individual learner. The "collection" of criteria for quality becomes a student's guideposts for work that meets both group and personal standards. This negotiated approach to establishing benchmarks for success is important to ensure that work is appropriately challenging for and interesting to individual students, while still supporting shared goals.

Peer critiques—This is a means of helping students provide useful feedback on peer work in progress. Typically, partners read one another's work and then provide both positive and constructive feedback by following a critique guide developed by the teacher (often with student input). The peer critique guide should adhere to criteria for success made available to students at the outset of the work in a rubric or some other format. Goals of peer critiques include helping students succeed with work, helping students work at increasingly high levels of quality, developing collegial relationships among peers, and helping students develop their ability to evaluate the quality of work.

Process log—A process log is a mechanism for helping students keep track of their thinking as they work on a product or other complex task. The goal of a process log is not so much to record concrete details such as the names of books read or the length of time spent working on a task; its main purpose is to help students think reflectively about their work (*see* **Metacognition**). What are their goals for a work session? Why have they selected those goals? How do they know whether they are on the right track with their work? What are they doing to achieve work at the highest possible level? When they get stuck, what do they do? These sorts of prompts may guide students as they write in their process logs. Typically, teachers collect and review process logs at assigned checkpoints while work is in progress and again when students turn in a finished product. The process log allows insight into the process of working *and* the product of the work.

Readiness-based differentiation—Our best understanding of how people learn is that they begin with past knowledge, understanding, and skill and extend those to new levels of complexity or sophistication. Further, we learn best when the work we do is a little too hard for us. What that means is that we have a sense of both what the task calls for and the gaps in our capacity to do what it asks of us. When these gaps are not present (in other words, when we can do a task effortlessly), we do not learn because we do not stretch what we already know. Similarly, when the gaps are too great, we cannot span them and do not learn. Learning takes place when we have to stretch a manageable amount and do so. Readiness-based differentiation attempts to design student work at varied levels of challenge so that each student has to stretch a manageable amount and is supported in doing so.

Reading buddies—This is one of a number of names used for peer reading partners. Reading buddies can take turns reading from text, read chorally (simultaneously), read antiphonally (one reader echoing the other), or read along to a tape. Teachers should guide reading buddies so that they help one another analyze and understand reading material.

Rubrics—Rubrics are tools that guide the evaluation of student work and clarify student understanding of expectations for quality work. Generally, rubrics specify several categories of significance in achieving quality (for example, quality of research, quality of expression, and work habits). In addition, a rubric describes how various levels of quality in each of the designated categories would look. The most effective rubrics help students explore *qualitative* differences in their work, rather than quantitative differences. For example, it is not necessarily an indication that a student has done better work if he or she used five resources rather than four. A more appropriate indication of quality is that the student synthesized understandings from several reliable resources.

Scaffolding—Scaffolding refers to any support system that enables students to succeed with tasks they find genuinely challenging. Goals of scaffolding include helping students be clear about the task's purpose and directions and helping students stay focused, meet the expectations for quality of work, find and use appropriate sources of information, and work effectively and efficiently. The many types of scaffolding include study guides, step-by-step directions, comprehension strategies, use of a tape recording or video to support reading or understanding, modeling, icons that help interpret print, guided lectures, and multimode teaching. When tasks are appropriately challenging (a little too difficult for the student attempting the task), all students need scaffolding in order to grow and succeed.

Skills—Skills are the actions students should be able to perform or demonstrate as the result of a lesson, a series of lessons, or a unit of study. There are many categories of skills important to student learning. Some of those categories (with examples of skills in each) are *basic skills* (reading, writing, computing), *thinking skills* (synthesizing, summarizing, creating, defending a point of view, examining evidence), *production skills* (planning, setting goals, evaluating progress, asking important questions), *skills of a discipline* (map reading in geography, recognizing tones in music, interpreting metaphorical language in language arts), and *social skills* (listening, empathizing, considering multiple perspectives on an issue, taking turns). When identifying the skills students should master in any unit, lesson, or lessons, teachers should be aware of both the categories of skills and the specific skills. Teaching those skills explicitly is at least as important as teaching information explicitly.

Think–Pair–Share (T–P–S)—This instructional strategy, developed by Frank Lyman (1992), is used to engage all learners in thinking and talking about a question or issue important to a current area of study. Typically, the teacher begins a T–P–S by posing an important thought question. Students are asked to write their ideas or think about the question, working silently until the teacher calls time (usually two to three minutes). This is the thinking phase of the process. In the second phase, pairing, students turn to a peer and exchange their thoughts about the question. In the final phase, sharing, the teacher restates the question for the class as a whole and leads the class in a discussion of the question. The Think–Pair–Share strategy increases the likelihood that all students will engage with the question, will have something to contribute to the final discussion, and will be more invested in the outcome of the discussion than they would have been if the question had simply been posed once to the entire class and answered by the first student to raise a hand.

Tiering—Tiering is a process of adjusting the degree of difficulty of a question, task, or product to match a student's current readiness level. To tier an assignment, a teacher 1) determines what students should know, understand, and be able to do as a result of the task; 2) considers the readiness range of students relative to these goals; 3) develops or selects an activity that is interesting, requires high-level thought, and causes students to work with the specified knowledge, understanding, and skill; 4) determines the complexity level of that starting-point task compared with the range of student readiness; 5) develops multiple versions of the task at different levels of difficulty, ensuring that all versions focus on the essential knowledge, understanding, and skill; and 6) assigns students to the various versions of the task at levels likely to provide attainable challenge. To guide development of multiple versions of the task, a teacher may use the continua of the Equalizer (*see* **Equalizer**), use supporting materials that range from basic to advanced, provide forms of expression that range from very familiar to very unfamiliar, and relate the task to experiences that range from very familiar to very unfamiliar.

Resources on Differentiation
and Related Topics

Armstrong, T. (1994). *Multiple intelligences in the class-room.* Alexandria, VA: Association for Supervision and Curriculum Development.

Aronson, E., Blaney, N., Stephin, C., Sikes, J., & Snapp, M. (1978). *The jigsaw classroom.* Beverly Hills, CA: Sage Publications.

Black, H., & Black, S. (1990). *Organizing thinking: Book one.* Pacific Grove, CA: Critical Thinking Press & Software.

Campbell, L., Campbell, C., & Dickinson, D. (1996). *Teaching and learning through multiple intelligences.* Needham Heights, MA: Allyn & Bacon.

Cohen, E. (1994). *Designing groupwork: Strategies for the heterogeneous classroom* (2nd ed.). New York: Teachers College Press.

Cohen, E., & Benton, J. (1988). Making groupwork work. *American Educator, 12*(3), 10–17, 45–46.

Cole, R. (Ed.). (2001). *More strategies for educating everybody's children.* Alexandria, VA: Association for Supervision and Curriculum Development.

Erickson, H. (2002). *Concept-based curriculum and instruction: Teaching beyond the facts* (2nd ed.). Thousand Oaks, CA: Corwin Press.

Gardner, H. (1993). *Multiple intelligences: The theory in practice.* New York: Basis Books.

Gardner, H. (1997). Reflections on multiple intelligences: The theory in practice. *Phi Delta Kappan, 78*(5), 200–207.

Gartin, B., Murdick, N., Imbeau, M., & Perner, D. (2003). *Differentiating instruction for students with developmental disabilities in inclusive classrooms.* Arlington, VA: Council for Exceptional Children.

Hyerle, D. (2000). *A field guide to using visual tools.* Alexandria, VA: Association for Supervision and Curriculum Development.

Jackson, A., & Davis, G. (2000). *Turning points 2000: Educating adolescents in the 21st century: A report of the Carnegie Corporation of New York.* New York: Teachers College Press.

Lyman, F. (1992). Think–Pair–Share, Thinktrix, Thinklinks, and Weird Facts: An interactive system for cooperative thinking. In N. Davidson & T. Worsham (Eds.), *Enhancing thinking through coop-erative learning* (pp. 169–181). New York: Teacher's College Press.

National Middle School Association (1995). *This we believe: Developmentally responsive middle level schools.* Columbus, OH: Author.

Nottage, C., & Morse, V. (2000). *Independent investiga-tion method: A 7-step method of student success in the research process.* Kingston, NH: Active Learning Systems.

Parks, S., & Black, H. (1992). *Organizing thinking: Book two.* Pacific Grove, CA: Critical Thinking Press & Software.

Sharan, S. (Ed.). (1999). *Handbook of cooperative learning methods* (2nd ed.). Westport, CT: Greenwood Press.

Sternberg, R. (1988). *The triarchic mind: A new theory of human intelligence.* New York: Viking Press.

Sternberg, R. (1997, March). What does it mean to be smart? *Educational Leadership, 54*(6), 20–24.

Stevenson, C. (1992). *Teaching ten to fourteen year olds.* New York: Longman.

Strachota, B. (1996). *On their side: Helping children take charge of their learning.* Greenfield, MA: Northeast Society for Children.

Taba, H. (1971). *A teacher's handbook to elementary social studies; an inductive approach* (2nd ed.). Reading, MA: Addison Wesley.

Tomlinson, C. (1995, Spring). Deciding to differentiate instruction in middle school: One school's journey. *Gifted Child Quarterly, 39*(2), 77–87.

Tomlinson, C. (1996). *Differentiating instruction for mixed-ability classrooms: An ASCD professional inquiry kit.* Alexandria, VA: Association for Supervision and Curriculum Development.

Tomlinson, C. (1998, November). For integration and differentiation choose concepts over topics. *Middle School Journal, 30*(2), 3–8.

Tomlinson, C. (1999a). *The differentiated classroom: Responding to the needs of all learners.* Alexandria, VA: Association for Supervision and Curriculum Development.

Tomlinson, C. (1999b). Leadership for differentiated classrooms. *The School Administrator, 9*(56) 6–11.

Tomlinson, C. (1999, September). Mapping a route toward differentiated instruction. *Educational Leadership, 57*(1), 12–16.

Tomlinson, C. (2000, September). Reconcilable differences: Standards-based teaching and differentiation. *Educational Leadership, 58*(1), 6–11.

Tomlinson, C. (2001). *How to differentiate instruction in mixed-ability classrooms* (2nd ed.). Alexandria, VA: Association for Supervision and Curriculum Development.

Tomlinson, C., & Allan, S. (2000). *Leadership for differentiating schools and classrooms.* Alexandria, VA: Association for Supervision and Curriculum Development.

Tomlinson, C., & Kalbfleisch, L. (1998, November). Teach me, teach my brain: A call for differentiated classrooms. *Educational Leadership, 56*(3), 52–55.

Tomlinson, C., Kaplan, S., Renzulli, J., Purcell, J., Leppien, J., & Burns, D. (2001). *The parallel curriculum: A design to develop high potential and challenge high-ability learners.* Thousand Oaks, CA: Corwin Press.

Tomlinson, C., Moon, T., & Callahan, C. (1998, January). How well are we addressing academic diversity in the middle school? *Middle School Journal, 29*(3), 3–11.

Tompkins, G. (1998). *50 literacy strategies step by step.* Upper Saddle River, NJ: Prentice Hall.

Wiggins, G. (1993). *Assessing student performance: Exploring the purpose and limits of testing.* San Francisco: Jossey-Bass Publishers.

Wiggins, G., & McTighe, J. (1998). *Understanding by design.* Alexandria, VA: Association for Supervision and Curriculum Development.

Winebrenner, S. (1992). *Teaching gifted kids in the regular classroom: Strategies and techniques every teacher can use to meet the academic needs of the gifted and talented.* Minneapolis, MN: Free Spirit Publications.

Winebrenner, S. (1996). *Teaching kids with learning difficulties in the regular classroom: Strategies and techniques every teacher can use to challenge and motivate struggling students.* Minneapolis, MN: Free Spirit Publications.

Also helpful:

Exemplars K–12 (http://www.exemplars.com) is a source for standards-based, tiered lessons with rubrics and student examples in mathematics, science, reading, writing, and research skills. Contact Exemplars, 271 Poker Hill Road, Underhill, VT, 05489.

HOTT LINX (http://hottlinx.org) is an online source for differentiated units, lessons, and instructional strategies, K–12.

Index

Note: References to figures are followed by the letter *f*. References to samples are followed by the letter *s*.

About the Authors

Carol Ann Tomlinson, Ed.D, is Professor of Educational Leadership, Foundations, and Policy at the University of Virginia and was a public school teacher for 21 years. In 1974, she was Virginia's Teacher of Year. During Carol's time in public schools, she taught in many differentiated classrooms and directed district-level programs for struggling and advanced learners. Today, as co-director of the University of Virginia Summer Institute on Academic Diversity, she works with an international community of educators committed to academically responsive classrooms.

Carol has authored several books for ASCD, including *How to Differentiate Instruction in Mixed-Ability Classrooms, The Differentiated Classroom,* and (with Susan Allan) *Leadership for Differentiating Schools and Classrooms.* She consulted on and authored facilitator's guides for ASCD video staff development sets and developed ASCD's Professional Inquiry Kit on Differentiated Instruction.

Carol can be reached at Curry School of Education, The University of Virginia, P.O. Box 400277, Charlottesville, VA, 22904, or via e-mail at cat3y@virginia.edu.

Caroline Cunningham Eidson, Ph.D, is Director of Curriculum and Instruction at Triangle Day School in Durham, North Carolina, and an educational consultant focusing on the areas of curriculum development, curriculum differentiation, and the needs of advanced learners.

In Caroline's teaching career, she has taught children in differentiated classrooms in grades K–8 in both public and private schools. Prior to moving to North Carolina, she co-founded Peabody School, a school for intellectually advanced children in Charlottesville, Virginia, and served as both a lead teacher and an administrator. She has also taught in the University of Virginia's Northern Virginia Master's Program in Gifted Education, supervising degree candidates' teaching internships.

Caroline has provided workshops and certification training at the local, state, and national levels regarding curriculum differentiation and the characteristics and needs of gifted learners. She has several publications in the field of gifted education to her credit.

Caroline can be reached at 3511 Carpenter Pond Road, Durham, NC, 27703, or via e-mail at ceidson@nc.rr.com.

Related ASCD Resources: Differentiated Instruction

Audiotapes

Building a Place to Learn: Classroom Environments and Differentiated Instruction by Carol Ann Tomlinson (#202132)

Help for Your Struggling Learners: Strategies and Materials that Support Differentiated Instruction by Char Forsten, Betty Hollas, and Jim Grant (#202214)

Using Performance Tasks and Rubrics to Support Differentiated Instruction by Carolyn Callahan, Tonya Moon, and Carol Ann Tomlinson (#297069)

CD-ROM and Multimedia

ASCD Professional Inquiry Kit: *Differentiating Instruction for Mixed-Ability Classrooms*, by Carol Ann Tomlinson (#196213)

Networks

Visit the ASCD Web site (http://www.ascd.org) and search for "networks" for information about professional educators who have formed groups around topics like "Differentiated Instruction," and "The Middle Grades." Look in the "Network Directory" for current facilitators' addresses and phone numbers.

Online Professional Development

Available on the ASCD Web site:
Online Tutorial: *Differentiating Instruction* (http://www.ascd.org/frametutorials.html)
PD Online Course: Differentiating Instruction (http://pdonline.ascd.org/pd_online/logon.cfm)

Print Products

ASCD Topic Pack: *Differentiating Instruction* (#101032) (also available online from the ASCD Web site: http://www.ascd.org)

The Differentiated Classroom: Responding to the Needs of All Learners by Carol Ann Tomlinson (#199040)

How to Differentiate Instruction in Mixed-Ability Classrooms (2nd ed.) by Carol Ann Tomlinson (#101043)

Leadership for Differentiating Schools and Classrooms by Carol Ann Tomlinson and Susan Demirsky Allan (#100216)

Videotapes

At Work in the Differentiated Classroom (3-tape series, plus facilitator's guide) (#401071)

Differentiating Instruction (2-tape series, plus facilitator's guide) (#497023)

A Visit to a Differentiated Classroom (videotape, plus online viewer's guide) (#401309)

For additional information, visit us on the World Wide Web (http://www.ascd.org), send an e-mail message to member@ascd.org, call the ASCD Service Center (1-800-933-ASCD or 703-578-9600, then press 2), send a fax to 703-575-5400, or write to Information Services, ASCD, 1703 N. Beauregard St., Alexandria, VA 22311-1714 USA.